Women
History to 1880

Uncovering the Past: Documentary Readers in American History
Series Editors: Steven Lawson and Nancy Hewitt

The books in this series introduce students in American history courses to two important dimensions of historical analysis. They enable students to engage actively in historical interpretation, and they further students' understanding of the interplay between social and political forces in historical developments.

Consisting of primary sources and an introductory essay, these readers are aimed at the major courses in the American history curriculum, as outlined further below. Each book in the series will be approximately 225–50 pages, including a 25–30 page introduction addressing key issues and questions about the subject under consideration, a discussion of sources and methodology, and a bibliography of suggested secondary readings.

Published

Paul G. E. Clemens
The Colonial Era: A Documentary Reader

Sean Patrick Adams
The Early American Republic: A Documentary Reader

Stanley Harrold
The Civil War and Reconstruction: A Documentary Reader

Steven Mintz
African American Voices: A Documentary Reader, 1619–1877

Robert P. Ingalls and David K. Johnson
The United States Since 1945: A Documentary Reader

Camilla Townsend
American Indian History: A Documentary Reader

Steven Mintz
Mexican American Voices: A Documentary Reader

Brian Ward
The 1960s: A Documentary Reader

Nancy Rosenbloom
Women in American History Since 1880: A Documentary Reader

Jeremi Suri
American Foreign Relations Since 1898: A Documentary Reader

Carol Faulkner
Women in American History to 1880: A Documentary Reader

Women in American History to 1880

A Documentary Reader

Edited by Carol Faulkner

A John Wiley & Sons, Ltd., Publication

This edition first published 2011
© 2011 Blackwell Publishing Ltd

Blackwell Publishing was acquired by John Wiley & Sons in February 2007. Blackwell's publishing program has been merged with Wiley's global Scientific, Technical, and Medical business to form Wiley-Blackwell.

Registered Office
John Wiley & Sons Ltd, The Atrium, Southern Gate, Chichester, West Sussex, PO19 8SQ, United Kingdom

Editorial Offices
350 Main Street, Malden, MA 02148-5020, USA
9600 Garsington Road, Oxford, OX4 2DQ, UK
The Atrium, Southern Gate, Chichester, West Sussex, PO19 8SQ, UK

For details of our global editorial offices, for customer services, and for information about how to apply for permission to reuse the copyright material in this book please see our website at www.wiley.com/wiley-blackwell.

The right of Carol Faulkner to be identified as the author of the editorial material in this work has been asserted in accordance with the UK Copyright, Designs and Patents Act 1988.

Library of Congress Cataloging-in-Publication Data

Women in American history to 1880 : a documentary reader / edited by Carol Faulkner.
    p.   cm. – (Uncovering the past)
  Includes bibliographical references and index.
ISBN 978-1-4443-3117-2 (hardcover : alk. paper) – ISBN 978-1-4443-3118-9 (pbk. : alk. paper)
  1. Women-United States-History-Sources.   2. United States-History-Sources.   I. Faulkner, Carol.
   HQ1410.W6473 2011
   305.40973–dc22

                                                    2010033791

A catalogue record for this book is available from the British Library.

Set in 10/12.5pt Sabon by SPi Publisher Services, Pondicherry, India
Printed and bound in Singapore by Ho Printing Singapore Pte Ltd

1   2011

Contents

List of Illustrations

Series Editors' Preface

Primary sources have become an essential component in the teaching of history to undergraduates. They engage students in the process of historical interpretation and analysis and help them understand that facts do not speak for themselves. Rather, students see how historians construct narratives that recreate the past. Most students assume that the pursuit of knowledge is a solitary endeavor; yet historians constantly interact with their peers, building upon previous research and arguing among themselves over the interpretation of documents and their larger meaning. The documentary readers in this series highlight the value of this collaborative creative process and encourage students to participate in it.

Each book in the series introduces students in American history courses to two important dimensions of historical analysis. They enable students to engage actively in historical interpretation, and they further students' understanding of the interplay among social, cultural, economic, and political forces in historical developments. In pursuit of these goals, the documents in each text embrace a broad range of sources, including such items as illustrations of material artifacts, letters and diaries, sermons, maps, photographs, song lyrics, selections from fiction and memoirs, legal statutes, court decisions, presidential orders, speeches, and political cartoons.

Each volume in the series is edited by a specialist in the field who is concerned with undergraduate teaching. The goal is not to offer a comprehensive selection of material but to provide items that reflect major themes and debates; that illustrate significant social, cultural, political, and economic dimensions of an era or subject; and that inform, intrigue, and inspire undergraduate students. The editor of each volume has written an introduction that discusses the central questions that have occupied historians in this field and the ways historians have used primary sources to answer them. In addition, each introductory essay contains an explanation of the kinds of materials available to investigate a particular subject, the methods by which scholars analyze them, and the considerations that go into interpreting them. Each source selection is introduced by a short head note that gives students the necessary information and a context for understanding the document. Also, each section of the volume includes questions to guide student reading and stimulate classroom discussion

Carol Faulkner's *Women in American History to 1880* opens with a compelling introduction that lays out key debates in the history of early American women. The volume then offers a wide array of documents to trace their diverse experiences from the 1540s through the 1870s. By dividing the book into nine chronological sections, Faulkner encourages students to explore the ways that women shaped and were shaped by major historical developments: conquest and colonization, the emergence of slavery, religious awakenings, revolution, industrialization, civil war, and reconstruction. Yet she also highlights experiences that were more distinctly female, from childbirth and domesticity to witchcraft and woman's rights. Over the course of the volume, students will be introduced to multiple and often competing perspectives. The ideas and experiences of Native American, African American, Mexican, and European American women, for instance, were shaped by their economic status, religious affiliation, residence, and education as well as their race and nationality. Men also figure prominently in this volume, describing and directing women's behaviors from their positions as explorers, government officials, priests and ministers, employers, slave owners, activists, and journalists.

The documents provided here illuminate the restrictions placed on women's lives alongside their economic and social contributions; the ideals and stereotypes that defined women's "sphere" alongside their efforts to challenge or subvert these assigned roles; the legal and cultural constraints on women's advancement alongside the disruptions caused by revolutions, wars, and religious revivals. The volume covers all regions of the United States and the multifaceted experiences of women within and across these regions. To give just one example, some European American women in the Northeast forged careers in the public sphere by campaigning to improve the lives of Native Americans and African Americans suffering under conquest and enslavement in the West and South. At the same time, many European American women opposed the efforts of their reform-minded sisters while Native American and African American women fought to make their voices heard by reformers and opponents alike.

This documentary reader moves from the first encounters among Native Americans, European Americans, and Africans through late nineteenth-century efforts to redefine the nation and its citizens following the Civil War. It introduces students not only to distinct voices and images, but also to the broad range of sources analyzed by early American historians. They include laws, contracts, petitions, reports, letters, poems, memoirs, and trial testimony as well as engravings, portraits, and political cartoons. These sources illuminate the lives of ordinary women and men as well as those who gained fame (or notoriety) through their public activities. Taken together, they inspire students to explore the representations and experiences of women across the vast landscape of early American history. *Women in American History to 1880* captures the multifaceted character of women's lives and the ways they were represented by themselves and others. It provides students with the sources to understand women's history in all of its variety and provides discussion questions and a valuable bibliography to guide students in pursuing their own research projects.

Steven F. Lawson and Nancy A. Hewitt,
Series Editors

Source Acknowledgments

Excerpt from Luys Hernández de Biedma, *The De Soto Chronicles: The Expedition of Hernando de Soto to North America 1539–1543*, Vol. 1, edited by L. A. Clayton, V. J. Knight, and E. C. Moore (University of Alabama Press, 1994), pp. 225–236. Reprinted with permission.

Letter from John Rolfe to Sir Thomas Dale, 1614. Reprinted with kind permission of Crandall Shifflett, Virtual Jamestown.

Father Chrestien Le Clercq on Micmac Women, 1691, *New Relation of Gaspesia, with the Customs and Religion of the Gaspesian Indians*, The Champlain Society, Canada. Reprinted with permission.

Excerpt from *The Pueblo Indian Revolt of 1696 and the Franciscan Missions in New Mexico* by J. Manuel Espinosa (University of Oklahoma Press), pp. 255–256 (379 words). Reprinted with permission.

"On the Death of the Rev. Mr. George Whitefield," from THE POEMS OF PHILLIS WHEATLEY, edited and with an introduction by Julian D. Mason Jr. Copyright © 1966 by the University of North Carolina Press, renewed 1989. Used by permission of the publisher. www.uncpress.unc.edu

Herbert A. Wisbey, *Pioneer Prophetess: Jemima Wilkinson, the Publick Universal Friend* (Ithaca: Cornell University Press, 1964), pp. 197–204. Copyright © 1964 by Cornell University. Used by permission of the publisher, Cornell University Press.

Extract from Carol Berkin and Leslie Horowitz (eds.), *Women's Voices, Women's Lives* (Boston: Northeastern University Press, 1998), pp. 107–108. Reprinted with permission of U. P. N. E.

David A. Hollinger and Charles Capper (eds.), *The American Intellectual Tradition*, Vol. 1 (New York: Oxford University Press, 2006), pp. 164–167. Reprinted with permission of Oxford University Press.

Elizabeth Seton, "Letters to Archbishop John Carroll, Sept. 8, 1809, Nov. 2, 1809, March 1, 1810," in Regina Bechtle and Judith Metz (eds.), *Elizabeth Bayley Seton: Collected Writings*, Vol. II: *Correspondence and Journals 1808–1820* (Hyde Park, NY: New City Press, 2002), pp. 80–82, 87–88, 107–108. Reprinted with permission of New City Press.

Marilyn Richardson (ed.), *Maria W. Stewart: America's First Black Woman Political Writer* (Bloomington: Indiana University Press, 1987), pp. 45–49. Reprinted with permission of the author and Indiana University Press.

William L. Andrews (ed.), *Sisters of the Spirit: Three Black Women's Autobiographies of the Nineteenth Century* (Bloomington: Indiana University Press, 1986), pp. 35–38. Reprinted with permission of Indiana University Press.

Stella M. Drumm (ed.), *Down the Santa Fe Trail and into Mexico: The Diary of Susan Shelby Magoffin* (Yale University Press, 1926). Reprinted with permission of Yale University Press.

Ann D. Gordon (ed.), *The Selected Papers of Elizabeth Cady Stanton & Susan B. Anthony*, Vol. II: *Against an Aristocracy of Sex, 1866–1873* (New Brunswick, NJ: Rutgers University Press, 2000), pp. 238–241, 336–353. Copyright © 2000 by Rutgers, the State University. Reprinted by permission of Rutgers University Press.

Florence Kelley to her father describing college courses, December 2, 1878. Reprinted with permission of The New York Public Library.

Frank B. Linderman, *Pretty-Shield: Medicine Woman of the Crows* (HarperCollins Publishers), pp. 248–253. Copyright © 1932 by Frank B. Linderman, renewed © 1960 by Norma Waller, Verne Linderman, and Wilda Linderman. Reprinted by permission of HarperCollins Publishers.

Introduction

The goal of *Women in American History to 1880* is to explore the diversity of women's experiences from the colonial period through Reconstruction. The documents in this collection also illuminate the simultaneous processes of constructing gender and national identity. Women viewed colonization, slavery, the American Revolution, industrialization, sectional conflict, western expansion, and emancipation from different, and often clashing, religious, ethnic, racial, and national perspectives. At the same time, women were at the center of transatlantic debates over political economy, religious truth, and empire. Politicians, businessmen, and writers used abstract images of woman as symbols for a variety of causes, but women also articulated their own political perspectives. This reader explores the way women contributed to and challenged the idealized gender roles that emerged with the young nation.

The documents are organized into nine chronological sections. The time periods covered in each section depend on the topic, and thus some focus on a broad span of time, such as Chapter 1, "Seekers, 1540–1680," while others are more narrow, such as Chapter 6, "Contested Spheres, 1835–1845." Other chapters include Chapter 2, "Colonists and Colonized, 1660–1730," Chapter 3, "Conceptions of Liberty, 1730–1780," Chapter 4, "Revolution, 1780–1810," Chapter 5, "Awakenings, 1810–1835," Chapter 7, "Partisans, 1845–1860," Chapter 8, "Civil Wars," Chapter 9, "Redefining Citizenship, 1865–1880." This organization complements the traditional chronology of American history, but many of the section titles reflect one important premise of the document collection: women have always participated in and contributed to historical change.

Within each chapter, documents address the variety of factors that shaped women's experience in early America, including but not limited to work, family, religion, and social and political activism. These categories reflect not only the daily lives of women, but also how women (and others) understood their place in society. Yet women's place was always contested. The issues – paid labor, marriage, revivalism, war – explored in these documents frequently and purposely overlap, as they did in the lives of American women. The documents also reveal both similarities and important differences in the history of Native American, African American, and European American women. These differences helped define idealized gender roles even as women attempted to subvert or transcend them.

In 1966, Barbara Welter published an influential article in the young field of women's history, which had emerged alongside the "second wave" of feminist activism. Welter examined the prevailing ideology of womanhood in the first half of the nineteenth century. The ideal or "true" woman was devout, sexually pure, and submissive to male authority; her life centered on her home and family.[1] For feminists rebelling against the confining gender ideals of the 1950s, the first half of the nineteenth century looked strikingly familiar. Welter's article prompted a flurry of scholarship on the period, and historians have since explored many aspects of nineteenth-century domesticity or "separate spheres." Recent scholarship shows that the ideological divide between the female world of the home and the male world of politics and business rarely matched the lives of even white middle-class women. Still, many women embraced these ideals, and, as writers, editors, and activists articulated a female moral authority based on the division of labor that granted women greater power over their "sphere," the home.

But nineteenth-century gender roles also served to divide women along lines of race, class, region, and religion. For example, most nineteenth-century white Americans viewed women of African descent as naturally promiscuous, and thus excluded from the important qualification of sexual purity. Such views served the economic interests of planters, who relied on African American women to reproduce the slave labor force, as well as a national economy dependent on the production and manufacture of cotton. Though abolitionists used the ideal of domesticity to point out the evils of slavery, women's rights activists protested the legal and political inequality that accompanied free women's status as wives and mothers.

Despite the way women's historians have complicated our views of the early nineteenth century, Welter's description of "true womanhood" remains

[1]   Barbara Welter, "The Cult of True Womanhood, 1820–1860," *American Quarterly*, 18(2) (Summer 1966), 152.

a compelling interpretation of women's lives. In part, the staying power of "true womanhood" has to do with the way the field itself has changed. In addition to uncovering the previously hidden history of women, scholars use gender analysis to explore how the assertion and contestation of political, economic, and cultural power shaped women's (and men's) place in society. In an influential article published in 1986, the historian Joan Scott defined gender as "a constitutive element of social relationships based on perceived differences between the sexes" and "a primary way of signifying relationships of power." Scott urged scholars to illuminate "the reciprocal nature of gender and society," particularly the ways in which "politics constructs gender and gender constructs politics."[2] Her call prompted new attention to the historical context in which gender ideals were formed, contested, and recreated. After emancipation, for example, historian Laura F. Edwards examined the *Gendered Strife and Confusion* in southern households that had previously been organized around the racial and gender hierarchy of slavery.[3] Although Scott's article revitalized women's history, opening new avenues of research and interpretation, the field remains somewhat segregated from history as a whole. Women's historians continue to have their own journals, listservs, and conferences, and historians in other fields only slowly integrate the vibrant scholarship on women and gender into their conferences, articles, and books. While college and university history departments usually offer at least one women's history course, other courses too often confine women to one or two readings or lectures.

The premise of this document collection is that women's history is essential to understanding the social, political, cultural, and economic history of the United States. In the first decades following the Revolution, Americans experienced rapid transformations in their economy, communications, transportation, political culture, and religious life. Often, they explained these changes by relying on idealized understandings of male and female roles. As a result, middle-class domesticity became central to the way Americans defined themselves as a nation. "Separate spheres" informed the structure of citizenship rights, conceptions of "free" and "unfree" labor, and the dynamic Protestant evangelicalism of the nineteenth century. The expansion of voting rights to all white men, and, after the Civil War, all men, was based in part on their status (or potential) as husbands, fathers, breadwinners, soldiers, and property owners. Yet, as women's rights

[2]   Joan Scott, "Gender: A Useful Category of Historical Analysis," *Gender and the Politics of History* (New York: Columbia University Press, 1988), 42, 46.
[3]   Laura F. Edwards, *Gendered Strife and Confusion: The Political Culture of Reconstruction* (Urbana: University of Illinois Press, 1997).

activists demonstrated, men did not and could not adequately represent the interests of women in the polity, or guarantee their economic security. Further, women's presumed moral authority in the home was undermined by their lack of political or economic power. During the religious revivalism of the Second Great Awakening, male ministers wooed their mostly female parishioners by supporting female claims of piety and purity even as they excluded women from the pulpit. But, empowered by religious faith, some women eluded ministerial control. This gendered national political culture, then, also enabled average American women – white, black, Mexican, and Indian – to fight for inclusion by pointing out the instability of gender as a determinant of citizenship. Other factors, such as race, ethnicity, religion, and class, also complicated women's relationship to a national political ideology that emphasized male equality and economic opportunity.

These nineteenth-century confrontations over women's status in the new nation took shape in the colonial period, the subject of the first three chapters. From the first exploration and settlement of the North American continent, Europeans observed the different gender arrangements of Native American societies. Such images as John White's "A chieff Ladye of the Pomeiooc" were published and circulated widely in Europe. The accompanying commentary by Thomas Hariot emphasized the nakedness of the woman and young child. During Hernando DeSoto's exploration of what is now the southeastern United States, Native Americans in the town of Mavila were able to use European assumptions about the sexual immorality of Indian women to their temporary military advantage. As European settlers defined their own gender roles in opposition to Native Americans, criticisms of Indian marital and sexual practices served as both a justification and an instrument of colonization. For example, John Rolfe viewed his future wife Pocahontas as "one whose education hath bin rude, her manners barbarous, her generation accursed, and so discrepant in all nurtriture frome my selfe." John Lawson classified Native American women as savages in part for nursing their own children. In 1696, Spanish Catholic forces captured unconverted Pueblo women to use as leverage. Some of these Pueblo women died in captivity. The relationship between colonists and Indians was also characterized by cooperation, trade, and intimacy. While intermarriage, like that between Pocahontas and John Rolfe, was rare, sexual relations were an integral element of both conflict and cooperation. As late as Pontiac's Rebellion in 1764, white female captives expressed an ardent desire to remain with their Native American conquerors. When reading these sources, however, students must use caution. Like John Lawson's description of Native American childbirth, or Father Chrestien Le Clercq's portrayal of the sexual virtue of Micmac women, most of the sources on Native American life in this period are European depictions.

Similarly, the political economy of colonial America informed the development of slavery as an institution structured in part around sexual difference. Initially, colonists preferred to import male slaves from Africa and the Caribbean, but they soon realized the utility of female slaves. By the end of the seventeenth century, colonial legislatures, including the Assembly of Virginia, passed laws defining slave status as hereditary. Significantly, slave status passed through the mother. In other words, the child of a slave mother and a free father was a slave, but the child of a free mother and a slave father was free. Virginia's Act XII and other similar laws ensured that the sexual access of slave owners to enslaved women also served a fundamental economic purpose. And, by the time of the American Revolution, the peculiar institution no longer needed to rely on imports to replenish the slave population. Though legal marriage between slaves was outlawed in most colonies, enslaved men and women, with the encouragement of their owners, had sex and reproduced. Children born of sexual relations (whether forced or consensual) between enslaved women and white men also contributed to the reproduction of American slavery. However, like other aspects of colonial life, the practice of slavery was as diverse as the individuals who populated the North American continent. In colonial Louisiana, as in parts of the Caribbean, the Code Noir governed relations between masters and slaves. As in English colonies, the child's status followed the mother, but the Code Noir also allowed marriages between slaves and encouraged owners to marry their slave mistresses. While the law could be ignored or defied, it held out the possibility of a more fluid, less racially stratified, slave society.

European women traveled to the American colonies as indentured servants, family members, and missionaries. For many of these women, migration represented a risk, but one that offered the promise of material and spiritual rewards. In reporting on the colonies of Maryland and Virginia, John Hammond reassured his female readers that indentured servants were not "put into the ground to work, but occupy such domestic employments and housewifery as in England." He held out the possibility of social advance through marriage, but also indicated that women of "loose" virtue faced harsh social and economic consequences. Indeed, some colonial women, such as Anne Bradstreet or independent businesswomen like the *feme sole* traders, established relatively comfortable if precarious lives on the frontier of the British Empire. When European women stepped outside the bounds of acceptable roles for women, they often faced brutal punishment or exile. Sister Mary Magdalene Hachard described the corporal punishment of prostitutes in colonial French New Orleans.

After Puritan Anne Hutchinson dared to question the religious authority of the Massachusetts Bay Colony's ministers, she was excommunicated.

Chapters 1 and 2 include three documents about witchcraft. In colonial New England, women were disproportionately identified and prosecuted as witches. Historian Carol Karlsen finds that 78 percent of witchcraft accusations implicated women. While some historians suggest that poor women were more likely to be accused, Karlsen argues that women who inherited property were vulnerable as "they stood in the way of the orderly transmission of property from one generation of males to another."[4] In their studies of the Salem witch trials of 1692, the most notorious witch hunt in American history, other historians have identified Puritan belief in women's spiritual weakness or ongoing warfare with Indians as factors. The cases of Elizabeth Knapp, Tituba, and Abigail Faulkner not only allow students to debate why women were the principal target of witchcraft accusations, but also to explore the place of women in colonial society.

Chapter 3, "Conceptions of Liberty, 1730–1780," also introduces the first stirrings of the American Revolution. The documents in this chapter and in Chapter 4 address two central questions in the history of women in the Revolutionary era. First, how did women contribute to Revolutionary actions and ideas? Second, what was the impact of the American Revolution on women's lives? The answers to these questions depend upon the particular women under consideration. Chapter 3 includes a fugitive slave advertisement from the *Virginia Gazette*. Though the advertisement for Violet precedes by almost 10 years Lord Dunmore's proclamation of 1775, which offered freedom to slaves who fought for the British, it raises the issue of the relationship between enslaved women (and men) and the American Revolution. Enslaved women undoubtedly absorbed some of the political and religious ideas that informed the American revolutionaries. In addition to the familiar political premise that "all men are created equal," the religious revivalism that accompanied the ministry of Englishman George Whitefield also transformed the American landscape. While he remained committed to the Calvinist (and Puritan) doctrine of predestination, Whitefield also preached that salvation was accessible to all. As the poem by Phillis Wheatley, an enslaved woman, indicates, he preached to slaves, promoting the revolutionary faith that all races were equal in the eyes of God. As a result, when the war began, slaves sought their emancipation as well. But the freedom of enslaved men and women clashed with the freedom of white colonials, especially their right to property. Women and men of African descent often sided with the British, prompting white Americans to offer their slaves liberty in exchange for loyalty.

---

[4]   Carol F. Karlsen, *The Devil in the Shape of a Woman: Witchcraft in Colonial New England* (New York: W. W. Norton, 1987, 1998), 47, 116.

European American women also differed in their views of the American Revolution. Some women, like the ladies of Edenton, North Carolina, embraced the cause, boycotting British goods in exchange for the political purity of homespun American products. News of their public statement traveled across the Atlantic, prompting British printers to mock the Edenton ladies as political neophytes. Other women, like Quaker Hannah Griffitts, were skeptical of the ideas held by revolutionaries. In her 1776 poem titled "Wrote by the same upon reading a Book entituled Common Sense," Griffitts described Tom Paine's work as a "fallacious Tale," which suppressed the voices of moderation. Griffitts urged her readers to "Hold fast yr. own, yr. charter'd Rights maintain." Her poem expressed her allegiance to the British government as well as her view of the potential danger in rebellion. In part, Quaker attitudes toward the revolutionaries grew from their religious testimony against war. Philadelphia Yearly Meeting of Friends, the largest body of Quakers in the country, advised their members to refrain from taking sides in the conflict. Nonetheless, some Quakers sympathized with their fellow colonists' desire for independence and fought in the war.

The impact of the American Revolution is more difficult to discern. The ideology of the American Revolution led northern states like Pennsylvania and Massachusetts to abolish slavery, though often very gradually. In 1781, Elizabeth Freeman successfully sued for her freedom under the new Massachusetts constitution, the beginning of the end of slavery in that state. Her portrait conveys her pride in her hard-won independence. Still, as northern states initiated the emancipation process, slavery remained alive and well. Connecticut passed a gradual emancipation act in 1784. In 1797, Connecticut resident David Bush bequeathed his female slaves to his daughters, describing his slaves Candice, Mille, and Rose as "my girls." Candice remained a slave until 1825. For Native Americans, years of warfare with the British and then the Americans decimated their communities. Mary Jemison, a European woman adopted by Seneca Indians, described how General Sullivan destroyed Seneca homes and crops. The war brought further hardship to families on the economic margins. While John Taylor's description of maternal influence on young children may have been read by elite women, the Allis family bound their 11-year-old daughter Eunice to Joseph Bennett in exchange for food, clothes, and lodging. As their marks on the document testify, both Eunice and her mother were illiterate. Finally, the Revolution had little impact on the political rights of women. In 1797, New Jersey became the only state to grant the vote to "all free inhabitants of this State of full age," only to rescind it in 1807.

The American Revolution offered new opportunities for elite women in the public sphere. In a well-known image reprinted in Chapter 4, a female "Liberty" gives water to a bald eagle, the symbol of the new nation.

Underneath her feet, she tramples representations of monarchy and tyranny. More than an allegory, this image portrayed women as central to the nation's survival. Indeed, Massachusetts native Judith Sargent Murray viewed mothers as key to the education of moral, virtuous, republican citizens. Like Declaration of Independence signer Benjamin Rush, Murray believed that American women must be well educated in order to be, to borrow historian Linda Kerber's phrase, good "Republican Mothers" and wives.[5] But Murray also asserted the innate intellectual equality of women with men, an enlightened view shared by her British counterpart Mary Wollstonecraft. Alternatively, educator Sarah Pierce envisioned unmarried women "content, in solitude" as model republicans and benefactors of slaves, the poor, and the sick. Widow Elizabeth Seton chose conversion to Catholicism and life as a nun rather than remarry. As "mother" of her order, she challenged the authority of male priests and created a female community devoted to prayer and service.

The American Revolution was a period not only of political transformation, but also of social and cultural upheaval. During the war, familial and communal means of controlling behavior broke down in the face of greater geographic mobility among young Americans. Further, young Americans rejected the guidance of their elders in their revolutionary "pursuit of happiness." By the late eighteenth century, premarital pregnancy rates had risen to new heights; between 30 and 40 percent of brides gave birth less than nine months after their marriage. But reformers soon perceived the danger of this new sexual freedom for women, especially as parents and the larger community no longer had the power to ensure that marriage followed premarital sex. Actress, author, and teacher Susanna Rowson wrote her bestselling novel *Charlotte Temple* to urge young women not to follow their hearts, but instead to seek the guidance of parents and retain their virtue. The popularity of Rowson's novel contributed to the new Victorian ideology of female purity and morality that emerged with the new nation. By the 1830s and 1840s, its strongest proponents founded a moral reform movement to protect female virtue and establish women's influence amid the upheavals of urbanization and migration.

Chapter 5, "Awakenings, 1810–1835," illuminates the rise of this new vision of womanhood. The title of this chapter refers in part to the expansion of education for women after the American Revolution. Both Sarah Pierce and Susanna Rowson founded academies for young women. Increasingly, as the *Scenes from a Seminary for Young Ladies* indicates, these schools taught subjects, like geography and history, previously reserved for men. Graduates of female seminaries emerged with the intellectual skills to engage in local and national debates over womanhood, religion, slavery, and citizenship.

[5]   Linda K. Kerber, *Women of the Republic: Intellect and Ideology in Revolutionary America* (New York: W. W. Norton, 1980, 1986), 11.

The chapter title also references the religious revivalism that swept the young nation in the first four decades of the nineteenth century. Despite its diverse spiritual manifestations, which included the founding of new denominations as well as the revitalization of mainstream Protestantism, the theology of the Second Great Awakening emphasized individual ability to overcome sin. Inspired by this message, evangelical women helped convert their families and communities. Both Mary Mathews and Catharine Beecher believed that the religious feelings of women could change American society. Beecher extended the affective ties of the middle-class home to the Cherokee. She asked her readers, "will you forget that the poor Indian loves his children too?" Similarly, Elizabeth Chandler's plea to Christian women to forgo the products of slavery presumed women's moral influence in the home. African American preacher Jarena Lee took on a non-traditional (though not uncommon) role in evangelical circles by leading revivals across the Northeast.

The religious and social privileges of domesticity rarely extended across ethnic, racial, or class lines. As the Cherokee women's petition demonstrates, marriage and motherhood did not protect all women. Excluded from the "public affairs" of the Cherokee nation, which had adopted the political, economic, and domestic institutions of Anglo-Americans, Native American women referred to the "helpless" condition of their families on the eve of Trail of Tears in 1838. Abolitionist Frederick Douglass charged that slavery separated families and deliberately destroyed the ties between husbands and wives, and parents and children. Douglass's memory of his mother highlighted the special difficulties faced by enslaved mothers as they tried to love, raise, and nurture their children. In Massachusetts, lecturer Maria Stewart deplored the alleged freedom that consigned African American girls to the status of servants regardless of their education, virtue, or sensibility.

While some women embraced the ideals of true womanhood as empowering, others viewed domesticity and its core values as restrictive. Chapter 6, "Contested Spheres, 1835–1845," explores the debate over the appropriate place of women. L.T.Y.'s letter to her sisters in the moral reform movement expresses her confidence that the combined influence and prayers of women will save prostitutes and change the behavior of "licentious" men. She portrays women as virtuous and pious, central tenets of Welter's true womanhood. Missionary Narcissa Whitman followed her religious calling to save "the hunted, despised, and unprotected Indian" in Oregon territory. But tributes to the power of female influence rarely matched the reality of women's lives. The moral reform movement failed to end prostitution. Narcissa Whitman died following an Indian attack on her home. The everyday lives of women also revealed the financial and cultural obstacles to true womanhood. Poet Lucy Larcom described her mother's economic desperation after her father's unexpected death, forcing the family to move to Lowell, and

Lucy to enter the mills at the age of 12. In urban areas like New York City, some women, like Amanda Thompson, were willing to exchange their heralded virtue for the financial possibilities of prostitution. And, as the article on "Mothers and Daughters" suggests, some young women saw their mothers not as role models but as overburdened and unhappy women.

The careers of abolitionist Angelina Grimké and Catharine Beecher best illustrate the public clash over the possibilities and limitations of the domestic ideal. Like Catharine Beecher and other evangelical women, Grimké stressed the moral obligations of women as mothers and wives. But, at the first Anti-Slavery Convention of American Women in 1837, when Grimké proclaimed that women had rights as citizens to protest slavery and racial prejudice, Beecher and mainstream ministers repudiated her. Further, the petitions of Grimké and other anti-slavery women provoked Congress to issue a gag rule, thus temporarily stifling abolitionist women's voice in national politics. Though she opposed the radical tactics of Angelina Grimké, Catharine Beecher continued to view women's moral influence as central to private and public life. Her *Treatise on Domestic Economy* instructed American women on the basic skills of caring for a home and family. She also argued that as wives, mothers, and homemakers, women were crucial to settling the frontier, expanding democracy, and building a great nation.

Faced with intense and sometimes vitriolic criticism, women used a variety of tactics to transform American politics and society. The next chapter, "Partisans, 1845–1860," documents the emergence of an organized women's rights movement. Early feminists clearly and forcefully inserted themselves into American, and even international, politics. They highlighted women's legal, social, and political inequality, or what Lucretia Mott referred to as "the relative position of woman in society." After attending the first women's rights convention in Seneca Falls, Mott placed women's rights, Indian reform, and immediate emancipation in the context of "political agitations abroad" for "larger liberty – more independence." Ernestine Rose defied social convention to espouse reforming marriage and divorce laws in order to liberate women from "the iron heel of oppression." Though middle-class women organized the women's rights movement, activists attending the 1854 Albany Women's Rights Convention described working-class women's poverty and desperation without the formal political leverage (the vote) of their brothers. Six years later, the striking shoe-stitchers in Lynn, Massachusetts, argued in vain for higher wages as "ladies," free workers, and citizens. While early women's rights activists organized conventions and presented their case in newspapers and on lecture platforms, other women became key political brokers on their own terms. Dona Gertrudis "La Tules" Barceló used her business acumen not only to profit from the War with Mexico, but to make herself indispensible to American officers in Santa Fe.

Other women expanded women's public presence in more subtle ways. Methodist women organized to save souls and confront poverty in America's worst slums. At the Five Points Mission, they employed male clergy, and directed their labor. Religious faith inspired other women to reject Victorian marriage and domesticity for alternative societies like the Oneida Community. Though John Humphrey Noyes was not interested in women's rights per se, he created a utopian community organized around spirituality and shared labor rather than gender roles. The stereograph of Oneida women emphasizes their difference from other white, middle-class American women. Rejecting the latest fashions, Oneida women embraced dress reform that allowed them to participate fully in the labor of the community.

In the 1840s and 1850s, the issue of slavery divided Americans, including American women. The anti-slavery movement continued to create new political identities for women. As the conflict over slavery turned bloody in Kansas, women's rights activist Clarina Howard Nichols urged women in the Northeast to take action as mothers, wives, and sisters. She expanded upon Beecher's conception of the home as a "free" institution to convince women to become partisans on the side of bleeding Kansas. The sectional conflict also persuaded southern white women to break out of the family circle in order to defend slavery. In a public letter to British women, Julia Gardiner Tyler argued that southern homes were models of "neatness, and order, and contentment" with "well clothed and happy domestics."

In Chapter 8, "Civil Wars," the documents explore the violent conclusion to this sectional debate over slavery. As the institution of slavery collapsed, women in the North and South seized new opportunities created by wartime exigencies. Women worked as writers, nurses, sanitary experts, laundresses, civil servants, spies, freedmen's teachers, and caretakers of the bodies and legacies of the dead. Nevertheless, historians debate the nature and lasting impact of women's new public prominence. Did the Civil War permanently alter women's status as citizens? Despite suffragists' arguments that the Civil War had "created a revolution in woman herself," historian Lyde Cullen Sizer argues, "The rule remained: women in the mid-nineteenth century had few options for public employment or for public and political power." Judith Ann Giesberg, however, sees women's war work as a necessary precondition for the grassroots and political success of later organizations like the Women's Christian Temperance Union.[6]

---

[6] Lyde Cullen Sizer, *The Political Work of Northern Women Writers and the Civil War, 1850–1872* (Chapel Hill: University of North Carolina Press, 2000), 2, 4; Judith Ann Giesberg, *Civil War Sisterhood: The U.S. Sanitary Commission and Women's Politics in Transition* (Boston: Northeastern University Press, 2000), 3, 8.

Of course, the opening shots of the Civil War had an immediate impact on enslaved women. As the Union army regained control of Confederate territory, particularly in areas like the Sea Islands of South Carolina, enslaved women and men escaped from slavery and sought freedom behind Union lines. By the time President Lincoln issued the Emancipation Proclamation on January 1, 1863, the Union Army had become an army of liberation. Yet emancipation was not a simple or easy process. Former slaves faced callous and sometimes brutal treatment in Union Army camps like Camp Nelson in Kentucky. Their former masters tried everything in their power to re-enslave African American women through threats, beatings, rape, and apprenticeship of their children. Hoping for redress and simple justice, freedwomen protested this treatment to the Union Army and the Bureau of Refugees, Freedmen, and Abandoned Lands, better known as the Freedmen's Bureau.

Inspired by patriotism, their suffering husbands and brothers, or the war's potential to end slavery, women redefined true womanhood by forming soldiers' aid societies, signing on as nurses, or organizing fundraisers and petition campaigns. Louisa May Alcott's character Tribulation Periwinkle expresses the shock and discomfort of caring for wounded soldiers at a Union Army hospital. Periwinkle overcomes her horror and transforms herself into a maternal figure, "a tidy parent," in order to do her job. With their communities devastated by the Civil War, southern white women became the principal caretakers of the Confederate dead, helping to create lasting public tributes to the "Lost Cause."

Tested in hospitals, army camps, and on the front lines, many women emerged from the war empowered to confront problems in American society and government. Chapter 9, "Redefining Citizenship, 1865–1880," explores the possibilities for women in the postwar period. The newly expanded federal government created white-collar civil service positions for women. Journalist Jeannette Gilder began her career as a clerk in the US Mint. In the Midwest, tens of thousands of temperance women crusaded against saloons as a threat to their families. These women also attacked bars as a symbol of male political and social prerogatives. In 1862, the Morrill Land Grant Act had provided funds for the establishment of state colleges devoted to "the liberal and practical education of the industrial classes," including Cornell University in Ithaca, New York, in 1865. Future resident of Hull House, Factory Inspector for Illinois, and General Secretary of the National Consumers' League, Florence Kelley, attended Cornell University from 1876 to 1882, one of the first generation of women to benefit from and attend land grant colleges.

Despite new opportunities, women's rights activists faced a national political climate staunchly resistant to enfranchising women. After the Civil War, feminists formed the American Equal Rights Association with the goal of advocating for universal suffrage. The organization splintered after four short years as activists debated the imperative of black male suffrage. Following the passage of the Fifteenth Amendment, suffragists formed the first organizations devoted to securing women's right to vote, the National Woman Suffrage Association and the American Woman Suffrage Association. As these suffragists steered their organizations toward the political mainstream, some women's rights activists continued to focus on radically divisive issues like divorce. Elizabeth Cady Stanton spoke out against the continued degradation of women in marriage after courts upheld "the husband's right of property in the wife." After the bitter fights over Reconstruction, the women's suffrage movement continued as a divided movement until 1890. And while individual states slowly enfranchised women, the Nineteenth Amendment to the Constitution was not ratified until 1920, 72 years after the first women's rights convention in Seneca Falls, New York.

By 1880, as the army, ranchers, immigrants, former slaves, suffragists, and railroad barons settled and developed western states, they permanently altered the political, environmental, and cultural landscape. In 1862, Congress had passed the Pacific Railway Act granting land to the Union Pacific and Central Pacific Railway for the construction of a transcontinental railroad. Once completed, the railroads facilitated the movement of people and goods across the United States. In 1870, the magazine *Frank Leslie's Illustrated Weekly* published a cartoon that indicated the racist fears inspired by these dramatic political and social changes. The cartoonist portrayed "Liberty" as an idealized white woman, asking "what is she to be?" Arraying other images of Liberty around her, including Irish American, Asian American, and African American women, the cartoonist hints at the uncertain racial and ethnic future of the nation. Despite the early involvement of women's rights activists in anti-slavery and Indian reform efforts, their vision for the nation was similarly exclusive. After Wyoming granted women the right to vote in 1869, women's rights activists campaigned throughout the West by railroad, horseback, and stagecoach. Elizabeth Cady Stanton complained of poor travel conditions, writing, "Women have not one word to say about railroads, stages, bridges. When we have, oh, what order and harmony will reign!"[7] Stanton's imagined order and harmony did not apply to Great Plains Indians, increasingly displaced onto reservations. As Pretty Shield remembered, the railroads had a devastating impact on the Crow Indians as whites slaughtered buffalo and appropriated Native American lands.

[7] Quoted in Lori D. Ginzberg, *Elizabeth Cady Stanton: An American Life* (New York: Hill and Wang, 2009), 144.

Stanton's belief that enfranchised women would vote to reform the railroads (or perhaps take over their management) indicates the complex interplay between ideas about gender, citizenship, and nation that had developed since the colonial period. Women's status in the colonies depended on their class, behavior, faith, race, ethnicity, and nationality. After the American Revolution, American women applauded the enlightenment values of the young nation, but they also created a visible public identity through work, education, reform, and religion. Women's rights activists fought for equality, but they also relied on arguments that women's moral influence as wives and mothers was needed in legislative halls. While these feminists argued mostly on behalf of educated white women, reformer Frances Ellen Watkins Harper used similar arguments to connect the political fates of elite and impoverished African Americans. Ten years after the end of the Civil War, she noted the "murdered people," scattered bones, and "mangled corpses," that resulted from the ongoing violent opposition to black freedom, and she called on African American women to uplift their race. In this way, references to women's morality and virtue offered both implicit criticisms of the United States and powerful appeals for full citizenship. Other women had no choice but to laugh at white Americans' claims of moral superiority. As Pretty Shield pondered the fate of her grandchildren, she speculated that they would probably wear white men's shoes. For Pretty Shield, these shoes symbolized whites' great economic, technological, and military advantages over Native Americans. Her laughter also shattered a central assumption of Victorian gender ideology: that all women had the same experiences, desires, and material and political needs.

The documents in this reader represent a wide range of primary sources in the field of women's history: laws, contracts, wills, literature, newspapers, speeches, letters, petitions, posters, and engravings. When historians reconstruct the lives of previous generations of American women, they offer interpretations of this primary evidence. This collection gives students the opportunity to analyze these documents and suggest their own interpretations. In doing so, they should ask some fundamental questions: Who wrote the document and why? Is the document an accurate depiction of women's lives? How did the author define womanhood? In what ways did the author question or challenge women's status in the nation? What did the writer(s) leave out? The documents may suggest a variety of answers to these questions. In doing so, these primary sources illuminate the changing, complex, and contested place of women in the American colonies and in the development of the United States.

Chapter 1   Seekers, 1540–1680

1 Luys Hernández de Biedma on the Destruction of Mavila, 1540

*After the Spanish Crown commissioned Hernando DeSoto to colonize
LaFlorida, a broad geographic area that included Florida, Georgia,
the Carolinas, Tennessee, Alabama, Arkansas, and Mississippi, the
conquistador and 600 men, including Biedma, arrived in the spring of 1539.
On a ruthless hunt for riches across the Southeast, DeSoto resupplied
his troops with Indian stores, enslaved Indians as guides and servants, and
destroyed Indian towns. In Alabama, the Indian leader Tascalusa
tricked DeSoto into entering the fortified town of Mavila. In Biedma's
account, Native American women played an important role in creating
this military trap, only to be enslaved as concubines after the Spanish
burned the town in October 1540. DeSoto's expedition continued for another
three years, decimating Indians through warfare and disease. The Spanish lost
half of their men, including DeSoto who died in Arkansas in 1542.*

We arrived at Mavila one day at nine in the morning. It was a small and
very strongly palisaded town and was situated on a plain. There were
some Indian houses on the outside of the palisade, but we found that the
Indians had demolished all of them to the ground in order to have the
field more clear. Some important Indians came forth to us upon seeing us
and asked the Governor, through the interpreter, whether he wished to
spend the night there on that plain or if he wished to enter within the

Women in American History to 1880: A Documentary Reader, by Carol Faulkner
© 2011 Blackwell Publishing Ltd.

town and said that in the afternoon they would give us the Indians for the burdens. It seemed to the Governor that it was better to enter in the town with them, and he commanded us all to enter in there, and so we did it.

Having entered within, we were walking with the Indians, chatting, as if we had them in peace, because only three hundred or four hundred appeared there, but there were a good five thousand Indians in the town, hidden in the houses. We did not see them, nor did the Indians appear. As they made festivity for us, they began to do their dances and songs. In order to dissemble, they had fifteen or twenty women dance in front of us. After they had danced a little while, the cacique arose and entered one of those houses. The Governor sent a message for him to come outside, and he said that he did not wish to. The Captain of the Governor's guard entered to bring him out, and he saw so many people within, and so ready for war, that he thought it a good idea to go out and leave him, and he said to the Governor that those houses were full of Indians, all with bows and arrows, ready to do some treachery.

... As we were so unprepared because we thought that we had met them in peace, we suffered so much damage that we were forced to leave, fleeing from the town, and all that the Indians brought us in our loads remained within, as they had unloaded it there. When the Indians saw us outside, they closed the gates of the town and began to beat their drums and to raise banners with a great yell, and to open our trunks and bundles and display from the top of the wall all that we had brought, since they had it in their possession.

As soon as we left the town, we mounted our horses and encircled the entire town, so that the Indians might not get away from us on any side, and the Governor decided that sixty or eighty of us should dismount. ... We entered within the town and set fire, where a quantity of Indians were burned, and all our supplied were burned, so that not one thing remained.

We fought that day until it was night, without one Indian surrendering to us, rather they fought like fierce lions. Of those who came out, we killed them all, some with the fire, others with the swords, others with the lances. Later, near nightfall, only three Indians remained, and they took those twenty women that they had brought to dance and placed them in front of themselves. The women crossed their hands, making signs to the Christians that they should take them. The Christians came to take them, and they turned aside, and the three Indians who were behind them shot arrows at the Christians. We killed two of the Indians, and one who remained alone, in order not to surrender to us, climbed a tree that was in the wall itself, and removed the cord from the bow and attached it to his neck and to a branch of the tree and hanged himself. This day the Indians killed more than twenty of our men, and two hundred and fifty of us escaped with wounds, for we had seven hundred and sixty arrows. We treated ourselves that night with the (adipose) tissue of the dead Indians themselves, since we had no other medicine, because all had burned that day. We stayed here treating ourselves twenty-seven or twenty-eight days, and thank God we all healed. We took the women and divided them among the most seriously wounded, in order that they might serve them.

connective tissue in which fat is stored

Source: Luys Hernández de Biedma, "Relation of the Island of Florida," in *The De Soto Chronicles: The Expedition of Hernando De Soto to North America 1539–1543*, Volume I (University of Alabama Press, 1994), pp. 225–236. Available at www.nps.gov/archive/deso/chronicles/index.htm (accessed August 4, 2010).

2 *A Chieff Ladye of Pomeiooc, 1590*

This image, by John White, appeared in Thomas Hariot's A Briefe and True Report of the New Found Land of Virginia (London, 1590). White and Hariot were members of Sir Walter Raleigh's first expedition to colonize Virginia in 1585. While Hariot wrote about New World people, flora, and fauna, White portrayed them in these bucolic, romanticized images. Notably, the native woman and young girl have European features. In the text, Hariot commented on the distinctive dress of the woman, a neighbor of the Roanoke Indians, including the chains made of pearls, copper, or bone, which cradled her arm. The other arm carried a vessel of "pleasant liquor." Hariot also noted that the deerskin around the woman's waist left her "almost altogither naked behinde." The girl, of seven or eight years of age, is carrying English toys, and Hariot notes that native children "are greatlye Diligted with puppetts, and babes which wear brought oute of England." These images and similar depictions of Native Americans circulated widely in Europe.

men are a threat, the native women.

adult natives – lost cause, but children are hope?

Figure 1.1   A Chief Ladye of Pomeiooc, 1590. *Used with Permission of Documenting the American South, the University of North Carolina at Chapel Hill Libraries.*

Source: From Thomas Hariot, *A Briefe and True Report of the New Found Land of Virginia* (London: 1590; republished in New York: J. Sabin, 1871). Available at http://docsouth.unc.edu/nc/hariot/hariot.html. Image available at http://docsouth. unc.edu/nc/hariot/ill10.html (accessed August 4, 2010).

3 John Rolfe, Letter to Sir Thomas Dale, 1614

John Rolfe wrote to Sir Thomas Dale, the deputy governor of the Virginia Colony, to gain approval of his marriage to Pocahontas. Though sexual relationships between Indians and European settlers were common, marriage was unusual. The English viewed the Powhatan as primitive, strange and – importantly – pagan. As a result, Rolfe listed her potential conversion to Christianity as one of the principal justifications for the marriage. Rolfe also expressed his deep and conflicted feelings for Pocahontas. Since Pocahontas never composed a similar letter, and indeed left little evidence of her life, her feelings and reasons for marrying Rolfe remain mysterious.

The coppie of the Gentle-mans letters to Sir Thomas Dale, that after married Powhatans daughter, containing the reasons moving him thereunto.

Honourable Sir, and most worthy Governor:

When your leasure shall best serve you to peruse these lines, I trust in God, the beginning will not strike you into a greater admiration, then the end will give you good content. It is a matter of no small moment, concerning my own particular, which here I impart unto you, and which toucheth mee so neerely, as the tendernesse of my salvation ... But to avoid tedious preambles, and to come neerer the matter: first suffer me with your patence, to sweepe and make cleane the way wherein I walke, from all suspicions and doubts, which may be covered therein, and faithfully to reveale unto you, what should move me hereunto.

Let therefore this my well advised protestation, which here I make betweene God and my own conscience, be a sufficient witnesse, at the dreadfull day of judgement (when the secret of all mens harts shall be opened) to condemne me herein, if my chiefest intent and purpose be not, to strive with all my power of body and minde, in the undertaking of so mightie a matter, no way led (so farre forth as mans weakenesse may permit) with the unbridled desire of carnall affection: but for the good of this plantation, for the honour of our countrie, for the glory of God, for my owne salvation, and for the converting to the true knowledge of God and Jesus Christ, an unbeleeving creature, namely Pokahuntas. To whom my hartie and best thoughts are, and have a long time bin so intagled, and inthralled in so intricate a laborinth, that I was even awearied to unwinde my selfe thereout. But almighty God, who never faileth his, that truly invocate his holy name hath opened the gate, and led me by the hand that I might plainely see and discerne the safe paths wherein to treade.

To you therefore (most noble Sir) the patron and Father of us in this countrey doe I utter the effects of this setled and long continued affection (which hath made a mightie warre in my meditations) and here I doe truely relate, to what issue this dangerous combate is come unto, wherein I have not onely examined, but throughly tried and pared my thoughts even to the quick, before I could finde any fit wholesome and apt applications to cure so daungerous an ulcer. I never failed to offer my daily and faithfull praiers to God, for his sacred and holy assistance. I forgot not to set before mine eies the frailty of mankinde, his prones to evill, his indulgencie of wicked thoughts, with many other imperfections wherein man is daily insnared, and oftentimes overthrowne, and them compared to my present estate. Nor was I ignorant of the heavie displeasure which almightie God conceived against the sonnes of Levie and Israel for marrying strange wives, nor of the inconveniences which may thereby arise, with other the like good motions which made me looke about warily and with good circumspection, into the grounds and principall agitations, which thus should provoke me to be in love with one whose education hath bin rude, her manners barbarous, her generation accursed, and so discrepant in all nurtriture frome my selfe, that oftentimes with feare and trembling, I have ended my private controversie with this: surely these are wicked instigations, hatched by him who seeketh and delighteth in mans destruction; and so with fervent praiers to be ever preserved from such diabolical assaults (as I tooke those to be) I have taken some rest.

Thus when I had thought I had obtained my peace and quietnesse, beholde another, but more gracious tentation hath made breaches into my holiest and strongest meditations; with which I have bin put to a new triall, in a straighter manner then the former: for besides the many passions and sufferings which I have daily, hourely, yea and in my sleepe indured, even awaking mee to astonishment, taxing mee with remisnesse, and carlesnesse, refusing and neglecting to performe the duetie of a good Christian, pulling me by the eare, and crying: why dost not thou indevour to make her a Christian? And these have happened to my greater wonder, even when she hath bin furthest seperated from me, which in common reason (were it not an undoubted worke of God) might breede forgetfulnesse of a farre more worthie creature. Besides, I say the holy spirit of God often demaunded of me, why I was created? If not for transitory pleasures and worldly vanities, but to labour in the Lords vineyard, there to sow and plant, to nourish and increase the fruites thereof, daily adding with the good husband in the Gospell, somewhat to the tallent, that in the end the fruites may be reaped, to the comfort of the laborer in this life, and his salvation in the world to come? And if this be, as undoubtedly this is, the service Jesus Christ requireth of his best servant: wo unto him that hath these instruments of pietie put into his hands and wilfillly despiseth to worke with them. Likewise, adding hereunto her great apparance of love to me, her desire to be taught and instructed in the knowledge of God, her capablenesse of understanding, her aptnesse and willingnesse to receive anie good impression, and also the spirituall, besides her owne incitements stirring me up hereunto.

What should I doe? Shall I be of so untoward a disposition, as to refuse to leade the blind into the right way? Shall I be so unnaturall, as not to give bread to the hungrie? or uncharitable, as not to cover the naked? Shall I despise to actuate these pious dueties of a Christian? Shall the base feares of displeasing the world, overpower and with holde mee from revealing unto man these spirituall workes of the Lord, which in my meditations and praiers, I have daily made knowne unto him? God forbid. I assuredly trust hee hath thus delt with me for my eternall felicitie, and for his glorie: and I hope so to be guided by his heavenly graice, that in the end by my faithfull paines, and christianlike labour, I shall attaine to that blessed promise, Pronounced by that holy Prophet Daniell unto the righteous that bring many unto the knowledge of God. Namely, that they shall shine like the starres forever and ever. A sweeter comfort cannot be to a true Christian, nor a greater incouragement for him to labour all the daies of his life, in the performance thereof, nor a greater gaine of consolation, to be desired at the hower of death, and in the day of judgement ...

Now if the vulgar sort, who square all mens actions by the base rule of their owne filthinesse, shall taxe or taunt me in this my godly labour: let them know, it is not any hungry appetite, to gorge my selfe with incontinency; sure (if I would, and were so sensually inclined) I might satisfie such desire, though not without a seared conscience, yet with Christians more pleasing to the eie, and lesse fearefull in the offence unlawfully committed. Nor am I in so desperate an estate, that I regard not what becommeth of mee; nor am I out of hope but one day to see my Country, nor so void of friends, nor mean in birth, but there to obtain a mach to my great content: nor have I ignorantly passed over my hopes there, or regardlesly seek to loose the love of my friends, by taking this course: I know them all, and have not rashly overslipped any.

But shal it please God thus to dispose of me (which I earnestly desire to fulfill my ends before sette down) I will heartely accept of it as a godly taxe appointed me, and I will never cease, (God assisting me) untill I have accomplished, and brought to perfection so holy a worke, in which I will daily pray God to blesse me, to mine, and her eternall happines. And thus desiring no longer to live, to enjoy the blessings of God, then this my resolution doth tend to such godly ends, as are by me before declared: not doubting of your favourable acceptance, I take my leave, beseeching Almighty God to raine downe upon you, such plenitude of his heavenly graces, as your heart can wish and desire, and so I rest,

At your command most willing to be disposed off

John Rolfe

Source: "First Hand Accounts of Virginia, 1575–1705," from the *Virtual Jamestown Project.* Available at http://etext.lib.virginia.edu/etcbin/jamestown-browse?iD= J1047 (accessed August 4, 2010).

4 *Pocahontas*, 1616

Simon Van de Passe sketched Pocahontas during her fatal journey to London. Born circa 1597, Pocahontas was the daughter of Powhatan, the paramount chief of tribes in the Virginia Tidewater region. In 1614, when she was a prisoner of war, she converted to Christianity and married John Rolfe.

Her marriage created an important alliance between the besieged Powhatan and the English settlers. Pocahontas, now known as Rebecca Rolfe, traveled with her husband to England to win support and attract new migrants for the Virginia colony. She may have had another motive for accompanying her husband: to gain more information for her father. The portrait clearly portrays her as royalty. Notably, the engraving does not identify her as Pocahontas, her childhood nickname and the name by which most English knew her. She died of pneumonia before she could make the return trip home.

Figure 1.2   Pocahontas, *Simon Van de Passe, 1616. Reproduced courtesy of the Virginia Historical Society.*

Source: Virginia Historical Society. Available at www.vahistorical.org/sva2003/pocahontas.htm (accessed August 4, 2010).

[handwritten: could be why ~~scribbled out~~ other women didn't speak out]

5 Examination of Anne Hutchinson, 1637

[handwritten: She is literate, bright and well respected and She is tried for this.]

Born in England in approximately 1591, Hutchinson migrated to Massachusetts Bay Colony in 1634. A follower of Puritan minister John Cotton, the devout Hutchinson hosted prayer meetings in her home for men and women. Hutchinson and her followers believed God's grace, rather than good works, was the true source of salvation, and she castigated Puritan ministers for deviating from this covenant of faith. Both religious and secular authorities viewed her gatherings as a challenge to their leadership. Accusing her of antinomianism, or disregard for church law, these men tried Hutchinson as both a dangerous dissenter and an insubordinate woman. After her trial, Hutchinson was excommunicated and banished; she moved to the more religiously tolerant colony of Rhode Island. In 1643, at her new home on Long Island, she was killed in an Indian raid.

Mr. Winthrop, Governor. Mrs. Hutchinson, you are called here as one of those that have troubled the peace of the commonwealth and the churches here; you are known to be a woman that hath had a great share in the promoting and divulging of those opinions that are causes of this trouble, and to be nearly joined not only in affinity and affection with some of those the court had taken notice of and passed censure upon, but you have spoken divers things as we have been informed very prejudicial to the honour of the churches and ministers thereof, and you have maintained a meeting and an assembly in your house that hath been condemned by the general assembly as a thing not tolerable nor comely in the sight of God nor fitting for your sex, and notwithstanding that was cried down you have continued the same, therefore we have thought good to send for you to understand how things are, that if you be in an erroneous way we may reduce you that so you may become a profitable member here among us, otherwise (if you be obstinate in your course that then the court may take such course that you may trouble us no further) therefore I would intreat you to express whether you do not hold the assent in practice to those opinions and factions that have been handled in court already, that is to say, whether you do not hold and assent in practice to those opinions and factions that have been handled in court already, that is to say, whether you do not justify Mr. Wheelwright's sermon and the petition.

Mrs. Hutchinson. I am called here to answer before you but I hear no things laid to my charge.

Gov. I have told you some already and more I can tell you.

Mrs. H. Name one, Sir. *[handwritten: What laws has she broken?]*

Gov. Have I not named some already?

Mrs. H. What have I said or done?

Gov. Why for your doings, this you did harbor and countenance those that are parties in this faction that you have heard of.

Mrs. H. That's a matter of conscience, Sir.

Gov. Your conscience you must keep or it must be kept for you ... Say that one brother should commit felony or treason and come to his other brother's house, if he knows him guilty and conceals him he is guilty of the same. It is his conscience to entertain him, but if his conscience comes into act in giving countenance and entertainment to him that hath broken the law he is guilty too. So if you do countenance those that are transgressors of the law you are in the same fact.

Mrs. H. What law do they transgress?

Gov. The law of God and of the state.

Mrs. H. In what particular?

Gov. Why in this among the rest, whereas the Lord doth say honour thy father and thy mother.

Mrs. H. Ey Sir in the Lord.

Gov. This honour you have broke in giving countenance to them ...

Mrs. H. ... But put the case Sir that I do fear the Lord and my parents, my not I entertain them that fear the Lord because my parents will not give me leave?

Gov. If they are the fathers of the commonwealth, and they of another religion, if you entertain them then you dishonor your parents and are justly punishable.

Mrs. H. If I entertain them, as they have dishonoured their parents I do.

Gov. No but you by countenancing them above others put honor upon them.

Mrs. H. I do acknowledge no such thing neither do I think that I ever put any dishonor upon you.

Gov. Why do you keep such a meeting at your house as you do every week upon a set day?

Mrs. H. It is lawful for me to do so, as it is all your practices and can you find a warrant for yourself and condemn me for the same thing? [I]t was in practice before I came therefore I was not the first.

Gov. For this, that you appeal to our practice you need no confutation. If your meeting had answered to the former it had not been offensive, but I will say that there was no meeting of women alone, but your meeting is of another sort for there are sometimes men among you.

Mrs. H. There was never any man with us.

Gov. Well, admit there was no man at your meeting and that you was sorry for it, there is no warrant for your doings, and by what warrant do you continue such a course?

Mrs. H. I conceive there lyes a clear rule in Titus, that the elder women should instruct the younger and then I must have a time wherein I must do it.

Gov. All this I grant you, I grant you a time for it, but what is this to the purpose that you Mrs. Hutchinson must call a company together from their callings to come to be taught of you?

Mrs. H. Will it please you to answer me this and to give me a rule for then I will willingly submit to any truth. If any come to my house to be instructed in the ways of God what rule have I to put them away?

Gov. But suppose that a hundred men came unto you to be instructed will you forbear to instruct them?

Mrs. H. As far as I conceive I cross a rule in it.

Gov. Very well and do you not so here?

Mrs. H. No Sir for my ground is they are men.

Gov. Men and women all is one for that, but suppose that a man should come and say Mrs. Hutchinson I hear that you are a woman that God hath given his grace unto and you have knowledge in the word of God I pray instruct me a little, ought you not to instruct this man?

Mrs. H. I think I may. – Do you think it not lawful for me to teach women and why do you call me to teach the court?

Gov. We do not call you to teach the court but to lay open yourself.

Mrs. H. I desire you that you would then set me down a rule by which I may put them away that come unto me and so have peace in so doing.

Gov. You must shew your rule to receive them.

Mrs. H. I have done it.

Gov. I deny it because I have brought more arguments than you have.

Mrs. H. I say, to me it is a rule.

Mr. Endicot. You say there are some rules unto you. I think there is a contradiction in your own words. What rule for your practice do you bring, only a custom in Boston.

Mrs. H. No Sir that was no rule to me but if you look upon the rule in Titus it is a rule to me. If you convince me that it is no rule I shall yield.

Gov. ... [T]his rule crosses that in the Corinthians. But you must take it in this sense that elder women must instruct the younger about their business, and to love their husbands and to make them to clash.

Mrs. H. I do not conceive but that it is meant for some publick times.

Gov. Well, have you no more to say but this?

Mrs. H. I have said sufficient for my practice.

Gov. Your course is not to be suffered for, besides that we find such a course as this to be greatly prejudicial to the state, besides the occasion that it is to seduce many honest persons that are called to those meetings and your opinions being known to be different from the word of God may seduce many simple souls that result unto you, besides that the occasion which hath come of late hath come from none but such as have frequented your meetings, so that now they are flown off from magistrates and ministers and this since they have come to you, and besides that it will not well stand with the commonwealth that families should be neglected for so many neighbors and dames and so much time spent, we see no rule of God for this, we see not that any should have authority to set up any other exercises besides what authority hath already set up and so what hurt comes of this you will be guilty of and we for suffering you.

Mrs. H. Sir I do not believe that to be so.

Gov. Well, we see how it is we must therefore put it away from you, or restrain you from maintaining this course.

Mrs. H. If you have a rule for it from God's word you may.

Gov. We are your judges, and not you ours and we must compel you to it.

Mrs. H. If it please you by authority to put it down I freely let you for I am subject to your authority.

Source: Thomas Hutchinson, *The History of the Province of Massachusetts Bay* (Boston: 1767), in Linda Kerber and Jane DeHart (eds.), *Women's America: Refocusing the Past* (New York: Oxford University Press), pp. 81–82.

6 Anne Bradstreet, "A Letter to Her Husband Absent upon Public Employment," 1650

Anne Bradstreet (c.1612–1672) and her husband Simon left England for Massachusetts in 1630, joining other Puritans, including John Winthrop, in launching a period of great migration. The Bradstreets helped found the communities of Cambridge and North Andover; Simon eventually became governor of the colony. In her poetry Anne Bradstreet reflected on a variety of public and private topics, including religious faith, monarchy, love, and childbearing. Bradstreet did not seek public recognition for her poetry, and her first book of poetry (London, 1650) was published without her knowledge. Afterward, she revised her poetry for publication, and a subsequent volume was published after her death. In this poem, one of several poems to her husband, she describes the intense emotional bond they shared, but their union was also a matter of law and custom. Her husband's travels have taken him "southward," or to the Tropic of Capricorn. Bradstreet meditates on their geographical as well as cosmic distance.

not all aspects of women's life are bad.

My head, my heart, mine eyes, my life, nay more,
My joy, my magazine, of earthly store,
If two be one, as surely thou and I,
How stayest thou there, whilst I at Ipswich lie?
So many steps, head from the heart to sever,
If but a neck, soon should we be together.
I, like the Earth this season, mourn in black,
My Sun is gone so far in's zodiac,
Whom whilst I 'joyed, nor storms, nor frost I felt,
His warmth such fridged colds did cause to melt.
My chilled limbs now numbed lie forlorn;
Return; return, sweet Sol, from Capricorn;
In this dead time, alas, what can I more
Than view those fruits which through thy heart I bore? Children
Which sweet contentment yield me for a space,
True living pictures of their father's face.
O strange effect! now thou art southward gone,
I weary grow the tedious day so long;
But when thou northward to me shalt return,
I wish my Sun may never set, but burn
Within the Cancer of my glowing breast,
The welcome house of him my dearest guest.
Where ever, ever stay, and go not thence,
Till nature's sad decree shall call thee hence;
Flesh of thy flesh, bone of thy bone,
I here, thou there, yet both but one.

a woman who is doing what she is supposed to.

Source: Anne Bradstreet, *The Tenth Muse* (1650) and from the *Manuscripts, Meditations Divine and Morall Together with Letters and Occasional Pieces* (Gainesville, Florida: Scholars' Facsimilies and Reprints, 1965). Available at http://xroads.virginia.edu/~hyper/bradstreet/bradstreet.html#dialogue (accessed August 4, 2010).

7 John Hammond, Excerpt from *Leah and Rachel, or, The Two Fruitful Sisters Virginia and Mary-land*, 1656

Before publishing this account, John Hammond lived in both Virginia and Maryland. Writing for an English audience, his goal was to dispel rumors about the colonies and encourage migration. He disputed the report that Virginia was "an unhealthy place, a nest of Rogues, whores, dissolute and rooking persons; a place of intolerable labour, bad usage, and hard Diet." Though Hammond promoted the colonies as a place of economic opportunity,

his assessment of the lives of female immigrants indicates some of the
hardships and pitfalls for women. Like their male counterparts, female
indentured servants usually signed a contract binding their labor for four to
seven years. During that time, they earned no wages and were at the mercy of
their masters. At the end of their indenture, they received their freedom and a
small amount of money.

... The labour servants are put to, is not so hard nor of such continuance as Husbandmen, nor Handcraftmen are kept at in England, I said little or nothing is done in winter time, none ever work before sun rising nor after sun set, in the summer they rest, sleep or exercise themselves five hours in the heat of the day, Saturdays afternoon is always their own, the old Holidays are observed and the Sabbath spent in good exercises.

The women are not (as is reported) put into the ground to work, but occupy such domestic employments and housewifery as in England, that is dressing victals, right up the house, milking, employed about dairies, washing, sewing, &c. and both men and women have times of recreations, as much or more than in any part of the world besides, yet some wenches that are nastily, beastly and not fit to be so employed are put into the ground, for reason tells us, they must not at charge be transported then maintained for nothing, but those that prove so awkward are rather burthensome than servants desirable or useful ...

And whereas it is rumoured that Servants have no lodging other than on boards, or by the Fire side, it is contrary to reason to believe it: First, as we are Christians; next as people living under a law, which compels as well the Master as the Servant to perform his duty; nor can true labour be either expected or exacted without sufficient clothing, diet, and lodging; all of which their Indentures (which must inviolably be observed) and the Justice of the County requires.

But if any go thither, not in a condition of a Servant, but pay his or her passage, which is some six pounds: Let them not doubt but it is money well laid out ... although they carry little else to take a Bed along with them, and then few Houses but will give them entertainment, either out of courtesy, or on reasonable terms; and I think it better for any that goes over free, and but in a mean condition, to hire himself for reasonable wages of Tobacco and Provision, the first year, provided he happen in an honest house, and where the Mistress is noted for a good Housewife, of which there are very many (notwithstanding the cry to the contrary) for by that means he will live free of disbursement, have something to help him the next year, and be carefully looked to in his sickness (if he chance to fall sick) and let him so covenant that exceptions may be made, that he work not much in the hot weather, a course we always take with our new hands (as they call them) the first year they come in.

If they are women that go after this manner, that is paying for their own passages, I advise them to sojourn in a house of honest repute, for by their good carriage, they may advance themselves in marriage, by their ill, over-throw their fortunes; and although loose persons seldom live unmarried if free; yet they match with as dissolute as themselves, and never live handsomely or are ever respected ...

Be sure to have your contract in writing and under hand and seal, for if ye go over upon promise made to do this or that, or to be free, it signifies nothing.

Source: John Hammond, *Leah and Rachel, or, The Two Fruitful Sisters Virginia and Maryland* (London, 1656), in David Brion Davis and Stephen Mintz (eds.), *The Boisterous Sea of Liberty: A Documentary History of America from Discovery through the Civil War* (New York: Oxford University Press, 1998), pp. 55–56.

[handwritten: ☆ Slaves are also in the fields, race doesn't necessarily protect you. at this time.]

8 Samuel Willard on Elizabeth Knapp, 1671–1672

Elizabeth Knapp was a young servant in the home of the Reverend Samuel Willard in Groton, Massachusetts. Willard's account of her possession by the devil offers compelling explanations for her actions. Knapp's concern with money and fine things indicates her dissatisfaction with her status as a servant. Living in the home of a prominent minister, Knapp may have worried more than usual about the state of her soul. Though Knapp implicated other women in her possession, Willard did not use these accusations to launch a witch hunt. Instead, he focused on reconciling Knapp to her status and fighting the devil. After her recovery, Knapp married and lived as a pious and respectable Puritan woman.

This poor and miserable object, about a fortnight before she was taken, we observed to carry herself in a strange and unwonted manner. Sometimes she would give sudden shrieks and, if we inquired a reason, would always put it off with some excuse, and then [she] would burst forth into immoderate and extravagant laughter ...

The next day [October 31, 1671] she was in a strange frame (as was observed by divers), sometimes weeping sometimes laughing, and many foolish and apish gestures. In the evening, going into the cellar, she shrieked suddenly and being inquired of the cause, she answered that she saw two persons in the cellar; whereupon some went down with her to search but found none – she also looking with them. At last she turned her head and looking one way steadfastly, used the expression, "What cheer, old man?" – which they that were with her took for a fancy – and so ceased. Afterwards (the same evening), the rest of the family being in bed, she was (as one lying in the room saw and she herself also afterwards related) suddenly thrown down into the midst of the floor with violence and taken with a violent fit ...

These fits continuing (though with intermission), divers (when they had opportunity), pressed upon her to declare what might be the true and real occasion of these amazing fits. She used many tergiversations [i.e., evasions] and excuses, pretending she would [declare it] to this and that young person who, coming, she put it off to another till at last on thursday night [November 2] she broke forth into a large confession in the presence of many, the substance whereof amounted to thus much: that the Devil had oftentimes appeared to her, presenting the treaty of a covenant and proffering largely to her – viz. such things as suited her youthful fancy: money, silks, fine clothes, ease from labor, to show her the whole world, etc.; that it had been three years since his first appearance, occasioned by her discontent; that at first his apparitions had been more rare, but lately more frequent; yea, those few weeks she had dwelt with us, almost constantly, [so] that she seldom went out of one room into another but he appeared to her, urging of her ... that he urged upon her constant temptations to murder her parents, her neighbors, our children, especially the youngest, tempting her to throw it into the fire on the hearth [or] into the oven; and that once he put a bill-hook into her hand to murder myself, persuading her I was asleep ...

... She then also complained against herself of many sins, disobedience to parents, neglect of attending upon ordinances, attempts to murder herself, and others. But this particular (of a covenant) she utterly disclaimed, which relation seemed fair, especially in that it was attended with bitter tears, self condemnations, good counsels given to all about her especially the youth then present, and an earnest desire of prayers ...

And in this state (coming home on Friday) [November 3] I found her, but could get nothing from her. Whenever I came in [her] presence, she fell into those fits, concerning which fits, I find this noteworthy. She knew and understood what was spoken to her but could not answer nor use any other words but the aforementioned, "money," etc., as long as the fit continued. For when she came out of it, she could give a relation of all that had been spoken to her. She was demanded a reason why she used those words in her fits and signified that the devil presented her with such things to tempt her and with sin and misery to terrify her ...

She again [after continued fits, on December 4] owned an observable passage which she also had confessed in her first declaration, but is not here inserted, viz., that the devil had often proffered her his service, but she accepted not, and once in particular to bring in chips for the fire. She refused, but when she came in she saw them lie by the fire side and was afraid. And this I remark: I, sitting by the fire, spoke to her to lay them on and she turned away in an unwonted manner. She then also declared against herself, her unprofitable life she had led and how justly God had thus permitted Satan to handle her ... But being pressed whether there were not a covenant, she earnestly professed that by God's goodness she had been prevented from doing that which she, of herself, had been ready enough to assent to and she thanked God there was no such thing ...

Friday [December 8] was a sad day with her, for she was sorely handled with fits, which some perceiving pressed that there was something yet behind not discovered by her and she, after a violent fit holding her between two and three hours, did first to one and afterwards to many, acknowledge that she had given of her blood to the devil and made a covenant with him. Whereupon I was sent for to [observe] her and understanding how things had passed, I found that there was no room for privacy. In another [room] already made by her so public, I therefore examined her concerning the matter and found her not so forward to confess as she had been to others, yet thus much I gathered from her confession ...

These things she uttered with great affection, overflowing of tears, and seeming bitterness. I asked of the reason of her weeping and bitterness. She complained of her sins and some in particular: profanation of the Sabbath, etc., but nothing of the sin of renouncing the government of God and giving herself up to the devil. I therefore (as God helped), applied it to her and asked her whether she desired not prayers with and for her. She assented with earnestness, and in prayer seemed to bewail the sin as God helped then in the aggravation of it, and afterward declared a desire to rely on the power and mercy of God in Christ ...

In this case I left her, but (not being satisfied in some things) I promised to visit her again the next day [December 9], which accordingly I did. But coming to her I found her (though her speech still remained in a case sad enough): her tears dried up and senses stupefied and (as was observed) when I could get nothing from her and therefore applied myself in counsel to her, she regarded it not, but fixed her eye steadfastly upon a place, as she was wont when the devil presented himself to her, which was a grief to her parents and brought me to a stand. In this condition I left her.

The next day [December 10], being the Sabbath, whether upon any hint given her or any advantage Satan took by it upon her, she sent for me in haste at noon. Coming to her, she immediately with tears told me that she had belied the devil in saying she had given him of her blood, etc., professed that most of the apparitions she had spoken of were but fancies, as images represented in a dream, earnestly entreated me to believe her, called God to witness to her assertions ..., and expressed a desire that all that would might hear her; that as they had heard so many lies and untruths, they might now hear the truth and engaged that in the evening she would do it.

I then repaired to her and divers more, then went. She then declared thus much. That the devil had sometimes appeared to her; that the occasion of it was her discontent, that her condition displeased her, her labor was burdensome to her. She was neither content to be at home nor abroad and had oftentime strong persuasions to practice in witchcraft, had often wished the devil would come to her at such and such times, and resolved that if he would, she would give herself up to him soul and body. But (though he had oft times appeared to her, yet) at such times he had not discovered [i.e., disclosed] himself and therefore she had been preserved from such a thing ... The next day I went to her and opened my mind to her alone and left it with her, declared (among other things) that she had used preposterous courses and therefore it was no marvel that she had been led into such contradictions and tendered her all the help I could if she would make use of me and more privately relate any weighty and serious case of conscience to me.

Thus she continued till the next Sabbath [December 17] in the afternoon, on which day in the morning, being something better than at other times, she had but little company tarried with her in the afternoon, when the devil began to make more full discovery of himself. It has been a question before, whether she might properly be called a demoniac, or person possessed of the devil. But it was then put out of question [i.e., beyond doubt]. She began (as the persons with her testify) by drawing her tongue out of her mouth most frightfully to an extraordinary length and greatness and many amazing postures of her body, and then by speaking, vocally in her, whereupon her father and another neighbor were called from the meeting, on whom (as soon as they came in) she railed, calling them "rogues," who told them nothing but a parcel of lies and deceived them and many like expressions ...

These manner of expressions filled some of the company there present with great consternation. Others put on boldness to speak to him [the devil], at which I was displeased ... I, seeing little good to be done by discourse and questioning my things in my mind concerning it, I desired the company to join in prayer unto God ...

On Tuesday following [December 19] she confessed that the devil entered into her the second night after her first taking, that when she was going to bed, he entered in (as she conceived) at her mouth and had been in her ever since and professed that if there were ever a devil in the world, there was one in her, but in what manner he spoke in her she could not tell ...

On Thursday last [January 11, 1672], in the evening, she came a season to [i.e., regained] her speech, and (as I received from them with her) again disowned a covenant with the devil, disowned that relation about the knife before mentioned, declared the occasion of her fits to be discontent, owned the temptations to murder ... expressed that she was sometimes disposed to do mischief and was as if some had laid hold of her to enforce her to it, and had double strength to her own. [She also said] that she knew not whether the devil were in her or no. If he were, she knew not when or how he entered [and] that when she was taken speechless, she fayned [i.e., felt] as if a string was tied about the roots of her tongue and reached down into her vitals and pulled her tongue down and then most when she strove to speak.

On Friday [January 12] in the evening she was taken with a passion of weeping and sighing ... I went the next morning when she strove to speak something [but] she could not, [and] was taken with her fits which held her as long as I tarried ... and thus she continues speechless to this instant, January 15, and followed with fits; concerning which state of hers I shall suspend my own judgment and willingly leave it to the censure of those that are more learned, aged, and judicious ... She is (I question not) a subject of hope and therefore all means ought to be used for her recovery. She is a monument of divine severity and the Lord grant that all that see or hear may fear and tremble. Amen.

Source: Elaine G. Breslaw (ed.), *Witches of the Atlantic World* (New York: New York University Press, 2000), pp. 235–245.

[Handwritten margin notes: "we study religion for background into." / "we don't hold one faith to look at history, we also don't look at the supernatural. not factual."]

Suggested Questions for Discussion

1   How did European explorers and settlers portray Native American women? Why?
2   Though her real motivations remain obscure, why might an Indian woman like Pocahontas marry an Englishman? What does her marriage to John Rolfe reveal about Indian–European relations?
3   What behaviors did early English settlements expect from female colonists? How did women respond?

Chapter 2   Colonists and Colonized, 1660–1730

1 Excerpts from the Code Noir, 1685

King Louis XIV's law governed slaves in Louisiana, controlled by France from 1699 to 1763 and 1800 to 1803. The edict contained important protections for slaves that were absent in the laws developed in English colonies. With the consent of their masters, slaves had the right to marry. The law also forbade owners from forcing slaves into marriage. More importantly, the Code Noir encouraged owners who impregnated their female slaves to marry and thus free them. This rule created a significant population of free people of color and a less racially stratified society. Still, the Code Noir gave slaveholders enormous power, privileging their property rights even over the interests of the Catholic Church. These masters regularly flouted many of the guidelines designed to ensure the basic rights of slaves.

Edict of the King

Concerning the enforcement of order in the French American islands from the month of March 1685 ...

IX. Free men who will have one or several children from concubinage with their slaves, as well as the masters who permitted this, will each be condemned to a fine of two thousand pounds of sugar. And if they are

Women in American History to 1880: A Documentary Reader, by Carol Faulkner
© 2011 Blackwell Publishing Ltd.

the masters of the slave by whom they have had some children, we wish that beyond the fine they be deprived of the slave and the children, and that she and they be confiscated for the profit of the [royal] hospital, without ever being manumitted. Nevertheless, we do not intend for this article to be enforced if the man ... would marry this slave in the church, which will free her and make the children free and legitimate ...

X. The marriage ceremonies prescribed by the Ordinance of Blois ... will be observed both for free persons and for slaves; nevertheless, for the slave the consent of the father and the mother is not necessary, only that of the master.

XI. We forbid priests to officiate at the marriages of slaves unless they can show the consent of their masters. We also forbid masters to make their slaves marry against their will.

XII. The children born of marriages between slaves will be slaves and will belong to the master of the female slaves, and not to those of their husbands, if the husband and the wife have different masters.

XIII. We wish that if a slave husband has married a free woman, the children, both male and girls, will follow the condition of their mother and be free like her, in spite of the servitude of their father; and that if the father is free and the mother enslaved, the children will be slaves for the same reason ...

Source: Laurent Dubois and John D. Garrigus (eds.), *Slave Revolution in the Caribbean 1789–1804* (New York: Bedford, 2006), pp. 50–51.

2 Assembly of Virginia, Act XII, 1662

This law made slavery a hereditary status, passed from enslaved women to their children. Virginia assemblymen made a deliberate financial calculation when they decreed that children follow the condition of their mother. As enslaved children increased the wealth of slaveholders, they now had an incentive for their slaves to reproduce. And, though interracial sex was illegal, the law encouraged slave owners to have sex with their female slaves (forcibly or voluntarily) to produce still more slaves. Other colonies passed similar laws, establishing slavery as an important part of the social and economic life of the American colonies. By the beginning of the nineteenth century, American slaveholders no longer needed to rely on the importation of slaves from Africa or the Caribbean; their slave population was self-reproducing.

Whereas some doubts have arisen whether children got by any Englishman upon a negro woman should be slave or free, *Be it therefore enacted and declared by this present grand assembly,* that all children borne in this country shalbe held bond or free only according to the condition of the mother, *and* that if any Christian shall commit fornication with a negro man or woman hee or shee soe offending shall pay double the [usual] fines ...

Source: Linda K. Kerber and Jane Sherron DeHart, *Women's America: Refocusing the Past* (New York: Oxford University Press, 2004), p. 67.

3 Father Chrestien Le Clercq on Micmac Women, 1691

This French missionary served on the Gaspé peninsula on the St. Lawrence River in Quebec from 1675 to 1686. After his return to France, he published New Relation of Gaspesia with the Customs and Religion of the Gaspesian Indians. *Le Clercq worked with the Micmac, who had begun to convert to Catholicism in 1610. The Micmac lived in small, male-dominated hunting and fishing camps. While their men hunted, Micmac wives managed their households. Like many European observers, Le Clercq emphasized the sexual purity of Micmac women. Even after marriage, a young husband often spent the first year hunting with his father-in-law.*

It can be said, to the praise and the glory of our Gaspesian women, that they are very modest, chaste, and continent, beyond what could be supposed; and I can say with truth that I have specially devoted myself to the mission of Gaspesia because of the natural inclination the Gaspesians have for virtue. One never hears in their wigwams any impure words, not even any of those conversations which have a double meaning. Never do they in public take any liberty – I do not say criminal alone, but even the most trifling; no kissing, no badinage between young persons of different sexes; in a word, everything is said and is done in their wigwams with much modesty and reserve.

There are among our Indian women none of those who, as in the case of the girls of some nations of this new world, take pride in prostituting themselves to the first comer, and whom their fathers and mothers themselves present to the most famous and prominent hunters and warriors. All of these shameful prostitutions are held in horror and abomination among our Gaspesians, and one sees without wonder young Indian women so chaste and modest as to serve as an example, and to teach those of their sex the love and esteem which they ought to have for modesty and chastity. I have seen one of them who, being solicited strongly to submit to the pursuit and importunities of a young warrior, whom she could not love without the loss of her honour, which was as dear to her as life, and who, wishing to escape his insolent pursuit, fled from the wigwam of her father and betook herself more than fifty leagues away, travelling with one of her companions upon the ice and in the snow, where she preferred to pass the nights in mid-winter upon some branches of fir, rather than to expose herself to committing a crime which she detested infinitely in her heart. The young Indian sought her in vain in the company of the other Indian women, who, not being able to imagine what had become of their companion, feared lest she had fallen over some precipice, or had made an attempt on her life in the displeasure and the annoyance which she felt in seeing herself persecuted by the brutality of her lover. All the Indians, however, were agreeably surprised when this girl appeared some time after in the wigwam of her father, to whom she gave an account of the matter and of the cause of her absence.

Source: Father Chrestien Le Clercq, *New Relation of Gaspesia with the Customs and Religion of the Gaspesian Indians* (Toronto, 1910), in James Axtell (ed.), *The Indian Peoples of Eastern America: A Documentary History of the Sexes* (New York: Oxford University Press, 1981), p. 84.

4   Examination of Tituba, 1692

Tituba, an Arawak Indian, was a slave in Barbados before joining the household of Samuel Parris in Salem, Massachusetts. In early 1692, Samuel's daughter Betty Parris, her cousin Abigail Williams, and friends Mercy Lewis and Ann Putnam accused Tituba and two other women of witchcraft, launching the infamous Salem witch trials, which resulted in the execution of 19 individuals. Tituba offered a full confession, escaped execution, and provided evidence against other accused witches. In the fall of 1692, as Puritan leaders grew more cautious in their prosecution of witches, Tituba recanted. She was sold to another owner and remained a slave.
'T' stands for Tituba, 'H' for John Hathorne.

The Examination of Titibe

(H) Titibe what evil spirit have you familiarity with
(T) none
(H) why do you hurt these children
(T) I do not hurt them
(H) who is it then
(T) the devil for ought I know
(H) did you never see the devil.

(T) the devil came to me and bid me serve him

(H) who have you seen

(T) 4 women sometimes hurt the children

(H) who were they?

(T) goode Osburn and Sarah good and I doe not know who the other were
Sarah good and Osburne would have me hurt the children but I would
not shee furder saith there was a tale man of Boston that shee did see

(H) when did you see them

(T) Last night at Boston

(H) what did they say to you they said hurt the children

(H) and did you hurt them

(T) no there is 4 women and one man they hurt the children and then lay all
upon me and they tell me if I will not hurt the children they will hurt me

(H) but did you not hurt them

(T) yes, but I will hurt them no more

(H) are you not sorry you did hurt them.

(T) yes.

(H) and why then doe you hurt them

(T) they say hurt children or wee will doe worse to you

(H) what have you seen a man come to me and say serve me

(H) what service

(T) hurt the children and last night there was an appearance that said Kill
the children and if I would no go on hurting the children they would do
worse to me

(H) what is this appearance you see

(T) sometimes it is like a hog and some times like a great dog this appearance shee saith shee did see 4 times

(H) what did it say to you

(T) the black dog said serve me but I said I am a fraid he said if I did not he
would doe worse to me

(H) what did you say to it

(T) I will serve you no longer then he said he would hurt me and then he
lookes like a man and threatens to hurt me shee said that this man had a
yellow bird that keept with him and he told me he had more pretty
things that he would give me if I would serve him

(H) what were these pretty things

(T) he did not show me them

(H) what else have you seen

(T) two rats, a red rat and a black rat

(H) what did they say to you

(T) they said serve me

(H) when did you see them

(T) Last night and they said serve me but shee said I would not

(H) what service

(T) shee said hurt the children

(H) did you not pinch Elizabeth Hubbard this morning

(T) the man brought her to me and made me pinch her

(H) why did you goe to thomas putnams Last night and hurt his child

(T) they pull and hall me and make goe

(H) and what would have you doe Kill her with a knif Left. fuller and others said at this time when the child saw these persons and was tormented by them that she did complain of a knif that they would have her cut her head off with a knife

(H) how did you go

(T) we ride upon stickes and are there presently

(H) doe you goe through the trees or over them

(T) we see no thing but are there presently

(H) why did you not tell your master

(T) I was a fraid they said they would cut off my head if I told

(H) would not you have hurt others if you could

(T) they said they would hurt others but they could not

(H) what attendants hath Sarah good

(T) a yellow bird and shee would have given me one

(H) what meate did she give it

(T) it did suck her between her fingers

(H) Did not you hurt mr Currins child

(T) goode good and goode Osburn told that they did hurt mr Currens child and would have had me hurt him two but I did not

(H) what hath Sarah Osburn

(T) yesterday shee had a thing with a head like a woman with 2 leggs and wings Abigail williams that lives with her uncle mr Parris said that shee did see this same creature and it turned into the shape of goode osburn

(H) what else have you seen with g osburn

(T) an other thing hairy it goes upright like a man it hath only 2 leggs

(H) did you not see Sarah good upon elisebeth Hubbar last Saturday

(T) I did see her set a wolfe upon her to afflict her the persons with this maid did say that shee did complain of a wolf

(T) shee furder said that shee saw a cat with good at another time

(H) what cloathes doth the man go in

(T) he goes in black clouthes a tal man with white hair I thinke

(H) how doth the woman go

(T) in a white whood and a black whood with a tup knot

(H) doe you see who it is that torments these children now
(T) yes it is goode good she hurts them in her own shape
(H) & who is it that hurts them now
(T) I am blind noe I cannot see

Source: Paul Boyer and Stephen Nissenbaum (eds.), *The Salem Witchcraft Papers*, Volume 3: *Verbatim Transcripts of the Legal Documents of the Salem Witchcraft Outbreak of 1692*. Available at the Electronic Text Center, University of Virginia Library, http://etext.virginia.edu/etcbin/toccer-new2?id = BoySal3.sgm&images = images/modeng&data = /texts/english/modeng/oldsalem&tag = public&part = 53& division = div2 (accessed August 5, 2010).

5 Petition of Abigail Faulkner, 1692

Abigail Faulkner faced accusations of witchcraft during the Salem witch hunt. The daughter of a prominent minister, she married a wealthy landowner. In 1687, after her husband became ill, Abigail began managing the family's land. Accused by close relatives, including two daughters and a sister-in-law, her economic independence may have made her a target. As her petition reveals, Abigail Faulkner also demonstrated her autonomy by refusing to confess (many accused witches confessed and thus avoided execution). In doing so, she denied the legitimacy of the accusation and the trial. Pregnant at the time of her conviction, Faulkner was never executed. In 1703, she petitioned to have her name cleared of all witchcraft charges.

The humblee Petition of Abigall: Falkner unto his Excellencye S'r W'm Phipps knight and Govern'r of their Majestyes Dominions in America: humbly sheweth

That your poor and humble Petitioner having been this four monthes in Salem Prison and condemned to die having had no other evidences against me but the Spectre Evidences and the Confessors w'ch Confessors have lately since I was condemned owned to my selfe and others and doe still own that they wronged me and what they had said against me was false: and that they would not that I should have been put to death for a thousand worldes for they never should have enjoyed themselves againe in this world; w'ch undoubtedly I shouled have been put to death had it not pleased the Lord I had been with child. Thankes be to the Lord I know my selfe altogether Innocent & Ignorant of the crime of witchcraft w'ch is layd to my charge: as will appeare at the great day of Judgment (May it please yo'r Excellencye) my husband about five yeares a goe was taken w'th fitts w'ch did very much impaire his memory and understanding but w'th the blessing of the Lord upon my Endeavors did recover of them againe but now through greife and sorrow they are returned to him againe as bad as Ever they were: I having six children and having little or nothing to subsist on being in a manner without a head to doe any thinge for my selfe or them and being closely confined can see no otherwayes but we shall all perish Therfore may it please your Excellencye your poor and humble petition'r doe humbly begge and Implore of yo'r Excellencye to take it into yo'r pious and Judicious consideration that some speedy Course may be taken w'th me for my releasement that I and my children perish not through meanes of my close confinement here w'ch undoubtedly we shall if the Lord does not mightily prevent and yo'r poor petitioner shall for ever pray for your health and happinesse in this life and eternall felicity in the world to come so prayes

Your poor afflicted humble sevants Petition'r

Source: Paul Boyer and Stephen Nissenbaum (eds.), *The Salem Witchcraft Papers*, Volume 1: *Verbatim Transcripts of the Legal Documents of the Salem Witchcraft Outbreak of 1692*. Available at the Electronic Text Center, University of Virginia Library, http://etext.virginia.edu/etcbin/toccer-new2?id = BoySal1.sgm&images = images/modeng&data = /texts/english/modeng/oldsalem&tag = public&part = 292 & division = div2 (accessed August 5, 2010).

6 Fray Francisco de Vargas on Taking Indian Captives, 1696

In 1680, Pueblo Indians in New Mexico successfully revolted against their Spanish rulers. Native Americans controlled the territory until 1692, when Spanish forces began efforts to reconquer and convert New Mexico. By 1694, the Spanish had subdued the Pueblos, and sent Franciscan friars to establish missions. In June 1696, Pueblo Indians made their last major attempt to repudiate Spanish rule. Warned of potential unrest by the Franciscans, Spanish authorities defeated the Indians in two months. In the midst of the fighting, Fray Vargas expresses his concern at the governor's attempts to negotiate with rebel Indians. His account also reveals how female captives served as both pawns and diplomats in relations between colonizers and Native Americans.

... As for any prospect of winning over the rebellious Indians in the mountains, there is no hope that they will submit to our holy faith. And although the governor of this kingdom, in the campaigns he has made with his soldiers and Indian allies, having punished and killed up to eighty

Indians, having captured some women and children, and having seized their food, even with all of this it is evident that the enemy is very rebellious and contumacious in their relapse to apostasy. And they are well aware of the little military strength of the Spaniards and that the rigors of winter are near at hand, at which time the Indians can make war against the Spaniards in full safety without any harm being done to them. And what is most regrettable is that the governor, seeing the wickedness that they have carried out up to now, is sending a mission of peace, as he has done with their Indian women of those taken captive, whom he sent to the mountains with some crosses to negotiate peace with them, as though the said apostates, being enemies of our holy faith, would venerate or adore the holy cross, especially when they have just completed the outrage that they committed on the priests. And I recognize that if they should come down peacefully, what minister will want to assist them, when it is seen how little progress is gained in the attempt to win their souls, and what can be expected in living with them in the future? And if the governor aspires to pacify them only by his point of honor and standing, and if this peace is only to be a pretense to cover up their wickedness, as blood-thirsty wolves in sheep's clothing, we ministers of the gospel can not profit from such evilness. And now that God our Lord has been served, with only five religious and approximately thirty Spaniards having perished, with the women captives who have remained with them, we cannot place ourselves under the risk of having all of the priestly ministers perish. For the only ones who can be administered will be those who have been proven to be loyal; these I would not fail to have assisted ...

Source: J. Manuel Espinosa (ed.), *The Pueblo Indian Revolt of 1696 and the Franciscan Missions in New Mexico* (Norman: University of Oklahoma Press, 1988), pp. 255–256.

7 John Lawson on Native American Women and Childbirth, 1709

A surveyor who traveled extensively through Native American territory, Lawson helped found the settlements of Bath and New Berne in North Carolina. Scholars consider Lawson a reliable observer, and his account is one of few sources on North Carolina Indians. Lawson emphasized Native American women's strength and reproductive capabilities, creating a stark contrast to the delicate femininity of European women. Such descriptions justified both colonialism and racial hierarchy. Though Lawson notes the benefit of some indigenous practices, he portrays Native American women as savages. Yet his description of female segregation during childbirth and menstruation raises interesting questions about his sources.

The Savage Women of *America*, have very easy Travail with their Children; sometimes they bring Twins, and are brought to bed [delivered] by themselves, when took at a Disadvantage; not but that they have Midwives amongst them, as well as Doctors, who make it their Profession (for Gain) to assist and deliver Women, and some of these Midwives are very knowing in several Medicines that *Carolina* affords, which certainly expedite, and make easy Births. Besides, they are unacquainted with those severe pains which follow the Birth in our *European* Women. Their Remedies are a great Cause of this Easiness in that State; for the *Indian* Women will run up and down the Plantation, the same day, very briskly, and without any sign of Pain or Sickness; yet they look very meager and thin. Not but that we must allow a great deal owing to the Climate, and the natural Constitution of these Women, whose Course of Nature [menstrual period] never visits them in such Quantities, as the *European* Women have. And tho' they never want Plenty of Milk, yet I never saw an *Indian* Woman with very large Breasts; neither does the youngest Wife ever fail of proving so good a Nurse, as to bring her Child up Free from the Rickets and Disasters that proceed from the Teeth, with many other Distempers which attack our infants in *England,* and other Parts of *Europe*. They let their Children suck till they are well grown, unless they prove big with Child [pregnant] sooner. They always nurse their own Children themselves, unless Sickness or Death prevents. I once saw a nurse hired to give Suck to an *Indian* Woman's Child ... After Delivery, they absent the Company of a Man for forty days. As soon as the Child is born, they wash it in cold Water at the next Stream, and then bedawb it [with "Bears Oil, and a Colour like burnt Cork"]. After which, the Husband takes care to provide a Cradle, which is soon made, consisting of a piece of flat Wood, which they hew with their Hatchets to the Likeness of a Board; it is about two Foot long, and a Foot broad; to this they brace and tie the Child down very close, having, near the middle, a Stick fasten'd about two Inches from the Board. which is for the Child's Breech to rest on, under which they put a Wad of Moss, that receives the Child's Excrements, by which means they can shift the Moss, and keep all clean and sweet. Some Nations have very flat Heads ... which is made whilst tied on this Cradle ... These Cradles are apt to make the Body flat; yet they are the most portable things that can be invented; for there is a String which goes from one corner of the board to the other, whereby the Mother slings her Child on her Back; so the Infant's Back is towards hers, and its Face looks up towards the Sky. If it rains, she throws her leather or Woollen Match-coat, over her Head, which covers the Child all over, and secures her and it from the Injuries of rainy Weather. The Savage Women quit all Company, and dress not their own Victuals, during their Purgations [menstruation].

After they have had several children, they grow strangely out of Shape in their Bodies; As for Barrenness, I never knew any of their Women, that have not Children when marry'd.

Source: John Lawson, *A New Voyage to Carolina* (London, 1709), in James Axtell (ed.), *The Indian Peoples of Eastern America: A Documentary History of the Sexes* (New York: Oxford University Press, 1981), pp. 26–27.

8 An Act Concerning Feme Sole Traders, 1718

Under English common law, married women held the legal status of feme covert, *or covered woman, meaning their husband was their legal, political, and economic representative. Since the colonial economy was heavily dependent on the sea and trade with Britain, the status of mariners' wives became a matter of public concern. Lawmakers worried that impoverished women and children might turn to public officials for relief. This Pennsylvania law enabled women to conduct business, and support their families, in their husband's absence. The language of the law also reveals that female shopkeepers were a common feature in the colonial economy.*

WHEREAS it often happens that mariners and others, whose circumstances as well as vocations oblige them to go to sea, leave their wives in a way of shopkeeping; and such of them as are industrious, and take due care to pay the merchants they gain so much credit with, as to be well supplied with shop-goods from time to time, whereby they get a competent maintenance for themselves and children, and have been enabled to discharge considerable debts, left unpaid by their husbands at their going away; but some of those husbands, having so far lost sight of their duty to their wives and tender children, that their affections are turned to those, who, in all probability, will put them upon measures, not only to waste what they may get abroad, but misapply such effects as they leave in this province: For preventing whereof, and to the end that the estates belonging to such absent husbands may be secured for the maintenance of their wives and children, and that the goods and effects which such wives acquire, or are entrusted to sell in their husband's absence, may be preserved for satisfying of those who so entrust them. *Be it enacted,* That where any mariners or others are gone, or hereafter shall go, to sea, leaving their wives at shop-keeping, or to work for their livelihood at any other trade in this province all such wives shall be deemed, adjudged and taken, and are hereby declared to be, feme-sole traders, and shall have ability and are by this act enabled, to sue and be sued, plead and be impleded at law, in any court or courts of this province, during their husbands' natural lives, without naming their husbands in such suits, pleas or actions: And when judgments are given against such wives for any debts contracted, or sums of money due from them, since their husbands left them, executions shall be awarded against the goods and chattels in the possession of such wives, or in the hands or possession of others in trust for them, and not against the goods and chattels of their husbands; unless it may appear to the court where those executions are returnable, that such wives have, out of their separate stock or profit of their trade, paid debts which were contracted by their husbands, or laid out money for the necessary support and mainten-ance of themselves and children; then, and in such case, executions shall be levied upon the estate, real and personal, of such husbands, to the value so paid or laid out, and no more.

II. *And be it further enacted,* That if any of the said absent husbands, being owners of lands, tenements, or other estate in this province, have alien[at]ed, or hereafter shall give, grant, mortgage or alienate, from his wife and chil-dren, any of his said lands, tenements or estate, without making an equivalent provision for the maintenance, in lieu thereof, every such gift, grant, mort-gage or alienation, shall be deemed, adjudged and taken to be null and void.

III. *Provided nevertheless,* That if such absent husband shall happen to suffer shipwreck, or be by sickness or other casualty disabled to maintain himself, then, and in such case, and not otherwise, it shall be lawful for such distressed husband to sell or mortgage so much of his said estate, as shall be necessary to relieve him, and bring him home again to his family, and thing herein contained to the contrary notwithstanding.

IV. But if such absent husband, having his health and liberty, stays away so long from his wife and children, without making such provision for their maintenance before or after his going away, till they are like to become chargeable to the town or place where they inhabit; or in case such husband doth live or shall live in adultery, or cohabit unlawfully with another woman, and refuses or neglects, within seven years next after his going to sea, or departing his province, to return to his wife, and cohabit with her again; then, and in every such case, the lands, tenements and estate, belonging to such husbands, shall be and are hereby made liable and subject to be seized and taken in execution, to satisfy any sums of money, which the wives of such husbands, or guardians of their children, shall necessarily expend or lay out for their support and maintenance; which execution shall be founded upon process of attachment against such estate, wherein the absent husband shall be made defendant; any law or usage to the contrary in any wise notwithstanding.

Source: *Laws of the Commonwealth of Pennsylvania* (Philadelphia: John Bioren, 1810), Vol. 1, pp. 99–100, in Carol Berkin and Leslie Horowitz (eds.), *Women's Voices, Women's Lives* (Boston: Northeastern University Press, 1998), pp. 98–100.

9 Letters of Sister Mary Magdalene Hachard, 1728

In 1727, 12 French nuns, members of the Ursulines, arrived in New Orleans. Their aim was to instruct and convert Indians, but instead they found themselves ministering not only to Native Americans but also to enslaved women and girls. African American women became some of their most enthusiastic converts, forming a vibrant Afro-Catholic church in the city. Sister Mary Magdalene Hachard's letters offer a glimpse (as well as judgment) of the lives of diverse women in colonial French New Orleans, including Native Americans, slaves, prostitutes, slave owners, and nuns.

New Orleans, January 1, 1728

... All our Community is in perfect health. We have at present nine boarders, and as many more are coming after the festival of the Epiphany. We instruct a number of day scholars.

They are working hard on our house. Mr. Perier, our Commandant, always interested in everything that can afford us pleasure, promises to lodge us there within this year. The engineer came to show us the plan. We desire nothing so much as to see ourselves in this house, in order to be also occupied at the hospital to attend the sick, for we learn every day that it is the greatest pity in the world to see the bad arrangement there, and that the greater part of the patients die for lack of help. The intention of M. the Commandant and of the inhabitants of this city is that we should also take care of the girls and women of evil life; this is not yet determined on our side; but we have been given to understand that it would do a great good to the colony; and for that they propose to build for us a special apartment at the end of our enclosure to shut up all these people.

We keep also a school to instruct the negro and Indian girls and women; they come every day from one o'clock in the afternoon to half-past two. You see, my dear father, that we are not useless in this country, I assure you that all our moments are counted and that we have not a single one to ourselves. We have lately taken charge of a little orphan girl who was serving in a house where she did not have a very good example. It is further the intention of Rv. Father de Beaubois that we should take charge, through charity, of some little orphan girls; and he tells us, in order to engage us to do it, that he and Mr. Perier charge themselves with all the orphan boys.

We are determined not to spare ourselves in anything that will be for the greater glory of God. I am sometimes employed with the day-scholars. I cannot express the pleasure which I find in instructing these little souls and in teaching them to know and love God. I pray the Lord that He may grant me the grace to succeed. In a few years, we shall need some more girls from France, supposing that it may not be possible to provide for all; when we shall have absolute need for them, we will ask for them ...

New Orleans, April 24, 1728
... The women, while ignorant about things concerning their salvation, are not so about vanity. The luxury which prevails in this city is the reason that nobody can here be distinguished. All is of equal magnificence. The generality are obliged to live with their families on *sagamité*, which is a sort of pap, and are dressed in stuffs of damask full of ribbons, notwhithstanding the dearness, for these stuffs usually cost in this country three times more than in France. Women here, as elsewhere, paint white and red, (*portent du blanc et du rouge*) to hide the wrinkles of their faces, on which they also wear beauty spots. In fine, the demon possesses here a great empire, but that does not take away our hope of destroying it, God desiring, as often before, to display His strength in our weakness. The more the enemy is powerful, the more are we encouraged to fight him. What causes us great pleasure, is the docility of the children, whom we can direct as we wish. The negresses are also easy to be instructed when they know how to speak French. But it is not the same with the savages, who are baptized only with fear and trembling, because of the inclination which they seem to have to sin; above all, the women who under a modest air hide beastly passions ...

During Holy Week, this Rev. Father gave a retreat to us and to our boarders. Several ladies of the city repaired here assiduously. There were sometimes as many as two hundred at the exhortations and converences. We had the Tenebrae Lessons in Music and a Miserere every day, accompanied by instruments ... All this has a good enough effect and helps much to draw the public. Some come by a commencement of devotion, others through curiosity. There always follows a sermon at the end, for our Rev. Father is a man of admirable zeal; it seems as if he has undertaken to convert everybody and feels certain that he will do so, but I assure you, my dear father, that he has yet to labor much in order to succeed. For not only debauchery, but dishonesty and all other vices reign here more than elsewhere. As for the girls of evil life, though they are watched closely and punished severely by putting them on a wooden horse and having them whipped by all the soldiers of the regiment that guards our city, there is more than enough to fill a refuge ...

Our little community is increasing from day to day. We have twenty boarders, of whom eight have to-day made their First Communion; there lady boarders, and three orphans whom we take through charity. We have also seven slave boarders to teach and prepare for Baptism and First Communion. Besides we have a large number of day-scholars and negresses and savages who come two hours a day to be instructed.

The custom here is to marry girls at the age of twelve or fourteen years. Before our arrival many had been married without even knowing how many gods there are. Judge of the rest. But since we came here, none are married unless they have attended our instructions. We are accustomed to see black people. Not long since, there were given to us two colored boarders, one six years old and the other seventeen, in order to instruct them in our religion; and they will remain to serve us. If it were fashion here that negresses would wear beauty spots on the face, it would be necessary to give them white ones, which would produce a rather comical effect. You see, my dear father, that there is wherewith to exercise our zeal. I cannot express to you the pleasure which we find in instructing all these young people ...

When we tell them the most ordinary things, they are for them as oracles which come out of our mouth. We have the consolation of finding in them much docility and an ardent desire to be instructed. All would like to be religious, but this is not to the liking of Rev. Father de Beaubois, our very worthy Superior. He finds it more expedient that they should become Christian mothers, in order to establish religion in this country by their good example ...

Source: Mother Therese Wolfe, *The Ursulines in New Orleans and Our Lady of Prompt Succor: A Record of Two Centuries, 1727–1925* (New York: P. J. Kennedy, 1925), pp. 198–200, 226, 229–231.

Suggested Questions for Discussion

1 How did different religious faiths and European powers create or limit opportunities for female colonists?
2 How did the development of slavery and the experience of enslaved women
   differ across regions?
3 What do witchcraft accusations reveal about women's status in the colonies?

Chapter 3   Conceptions of Liberty, 1730–1780

1 John Taylor, Excerpt from *The Value of a Child*, 1753

John Taylor, of Norwich, England, was a professor of divinity at Warrington Academy. His advice to his daughter on the birth of his grandson was published in Philadelphia by Benjamin Franklin & David Hall in 1753. Following John Locke's influential Some Thoughts Concerning Education *(1693), Taylor and other eighteenth-century prescriptive writers emphasized reason over physical discipline. Taylor stressed the important role of mothers in creating virtuous, self-governing, and intelligent citizens, anticipating later appeals for the education of women to raise good republican citizens for the new nation.*

Dear Daughter,

It is my most sincere Desire, and highest Ambition, that the Increase of my Family may be to the Spread of Wisdom, Virtue and Piety in the World. And as God has graciously made you the Mother of a lovely Boy, I would gladly make you sensible, how much it is incumbent upon you, to whom nature has committed the first and most flexible Years of Life, to bring him up, and as many more as God may give you, to this best and noblest Purpose.

Women in American History to 1880: A Documentary Reader, by Carol Faulkner
© 2011 Blackwell Publishing Ltd.

Of all Creatures in the Earth it seemeth proper to Man alone to reflect upon himself, to compute the Value of his own Being, and to consider what is agreeable to the Dignity of it. This, not only shews the Extent of our Capacities; but moreover, is necessary to the right Conduct of Life. For, if Men were duly sensible of their own Worth, could they so commonly and so carelessly abandon themselves to sensual Pursuits; to act as if they were nothing but a perishing Body; when, in Fact, they are Spirits, created for all the Glories of Intelligence, and all the Happiness of Immortality?

But this Way of thinking ought particularly to be applied to our CHILDREN; whom Providence designedly puts into our Hands altogether helpless and ignorant; to shew us from the very first our great Duty as Parents; namely, that we ought to employ our Understandings, and use the best Industry, for the Preservation and Welfare of our Offspring. ...

But Nature never puts us into any wrong Tract. We mistake her sweet and gentle Language, and, thro' Inconsiderateness, push the Inclinations she gives quite beyond the Bounds of Truth and Right. We are naturally delighted with our Young, that we may carefully guard and nurse their tender Age, and cheerfully perform the various Attendance they require. But it is a common, tho' most deplorable Case, for People to pervert this lovely Principle to the utter Ruin of their Children; whist they consider them only as Objects of Delight, and under that Mistake fancy they have nothing to do but to cocker and indulge what so much pleaseth them, and in which they are not willing to see any Irregularity that needs Correction, or the Restraint of a wholesome Discipline. A father, it is true, may fall into this Error; but here the Mother's Weakness is commonly the greater ... And the good Conduct of the wisest Father may easily, and to him insensibly, be defeated by a Mother's excessive Fondness. Against which even a competent Measure of good Sense and Virtue may not be a sufficient Guard, without a particular Attention, and serious Reflection upon the Nature and Worth of a Child.

Reason is the grand Measure of our Being and Actions. Here lieth our highest Excellence, our truest Riches, and most solid Happiness. In the just Exercise of *this* a Man is a God to himself and others; neglecting *this*, we are only Brutes in a different Shape ...

Now, a little Creature endowed with this noble Principle, and in whom it may grow to a high Degree of Perfection, ought to be regarded as a Being of Importance; as containing in it something divine, and much superior to any of the Works of Art or Nature, which we view with our Eyes, either in the Heavens, or in the Earth. It must be vastly more than only an Object of

Fancy and Amusement. It demands even our Reverence; and certainly ought to be treated with a particular Address.

Especially considering that the forming the tender Mind depends very much upon our Conduct. By humouring and indulging, caressing and admiring a Child at any Rate; by being loth to gaul the Neck with the Yoke of Discipline; by tincturing the Palate with a Taste of soft and effeminate Pleasures, we cruelly abandon the lovely Creature to all the Weaknesses of its Constitution; lead it out of the Way of Truth and Life, and expose it to be inslaved and devoured by ravenous Appetites. Which is something far worse than crafting Pearls upon a Dunghill; it is to extinguish a Mind; to murder an Angel; to destroy an Intelligence, of all Natures in the Universe the most excellent. But if we carefully guard and tutor the young Soul, that he be not commonly dealt with in a ludicrous, trifling Way, but accustomed to the early Exercise of Reason; if nothing absurd in his Actions is suffered to pass, without bringing it to the Test of good Sense; if we teach him to attend to the essential Differences of Things, which appear very evident even to Children; if he be inured betimes to Self-denial and Patience, and is made to know, that he recommends himself only by what is good, virtuous and ingenious; this is to do him Justice ...

The bringing up of Children should not be regarded as a Thing of Course, but as a matter of the most serious Attention and Care. I have myself experienced the Advantages of a good Education; and have seen the dismal Consequences of Neglect and unreasonable Indulgence. Fixe it in your Heart, that the Happiness of your beloved Offspring, both temporal, and eternal, depends upon your wise and early Tutorage.

Let the following Rules be well observed. In Care, Reproof, Correction, Encouragement, Husband and Wife should act in perfect Concert. Teach your Child Submission to yourself, or you will be able to teach him nothing besides. Remove all bad Examples from his Sight. Understand yourselves what you would have your Children understand; be yourselves what you would have them be; and do yourselves, what you would have them practice. Parents are the original Models upon which we form our tempers and Behaviour. Gradually infuse into the empty Mind the dearest and most affecting Notions of God; his Omnipresence, Almighty Power, his Goodness and over-ruling Providence, his Regards to pious Men, his hearing and answering of Prayer. Whet these Things upon the tender Spirit, and fix them by Scripture Instances ... Shew him the Vanity of the World, the Frailty of the Body, the Dignity and infinite Worth of the Mind. Often inculate, that he is made, not to live here below, but in the glorious and external World above; and that he is here only to have his Virtue tried and exercised, that he may be fit to live in Heaven ... Let him be well established in Liberty (Liberty to use and improve his Understanding) and the Rights of Conscience, but for others as well as himself. Address his Understanding; encourage his Enquiries, and use him betimes to think and reason. Represent Vice in the most odious, Virtue in the most amiable Colours ... Suffer him not to be a Man, but as Years and Understanding allow. Boys are by no Means fit to govern themselves, or to direct others. Inure him to Diligence and close Application (properly intermixed with Play and Diversion) when he is strong enough to apply to Learning; and let him want no Advantage of increasing in Knowledge and Wisdom you can procure, or he can improve. And rest persuaded that your sincere and pious Endeavours will not be in vain. The Nature of Things, and the Promise of God, insure Success ...

Source: John Taylor, *The Value of a Child; Or, Motives to the Good Education of Children* (Philadelphia: B. Franklin and D. Hall, 1753), pp. 3–11, 24–29.

2 William Smith on the Relations between Indians and Their Captives during Pontiac's War, 1764

During the Seven Years War, also known as the French and Indian War, many Native American tribes in the Great Lakes, Illinois, and Ohio regions allied with the French. After British victory, these tribes, including Pontiac's people, the Ottawa, rebelled against English rule. William Smith's account of Colonel Henry Bouquet's victory over Native Americans indicates the importance of captives in relations between whites and Indians. Though some former captives published accounts of their captivity that furthered European assumptions about Indian savagery, others preferred to remain with their Indian captors.

... They delivered up their beloved captives with the utmost reluctance; shed torrents of tears over them, recommending them to the care and protection of the commanding officer. Their regard to them continued all the time they remained in camp. They visited them from day to day; and brought them what corn, skins, horses and other matters, they had bestowed on them, while in their families; accompanied with other presents, and all the marks of the most sincere and tender affection.

Nay, they did not stop there, but, when the army marched, some of the Indians sollicited [sic] and obtained leave to accompany their former captives all the way to Fort-Pitt, and employed themselves in hunting and bringing provisions for them on the road. A young Mingo carried this still further, and gave an instance of love which would make a figure even in romance. A young woman of Virginia was among the captives, to whom he had form'd so strong an attachment, as to call her his wife. Against all remonstrances of the imminent danger to which he exposed himself by approaching the frontiers, he persisted in following her, at the risk of being killed by the surviving relations of many unfortunate persons, who had been captivated or scalped by those of his nation ...

Among the children who had been carried off young, and had long lived with the Indians, it is not to be expected that any marks of joy would appear on being restored to their parents or relatives. Having been accustomed to look upon the Indians as the only connexions they had, having been tenderly treated by them, and speaking their language, it is no wonder that they considered their new state in the light of captivity, and parted from the savages with tears.

But it must not be denied that there were even some grown persons who shewed an unwillingness to return. The Shawanese were obliged to bind several of their prisoners and force them along to the camp; and some women, who had been delivered up, afterwards found means to escape and run back to the Indian towns. Some, who could not make their escape, clung to their savage acquaintance at parting, and continued many days in bitter lamentations, even refusing sustenance.

Source: William Smith, *An Historical Account of an Expedition Against the Ohio Indians, in the Year 1764* (1765), in Virgil J. Vogel, *This Country Was Ours: A Documentary History of the American Indian* (New York: Harper & Row, 1972), pp. 54–55.

3 Fugitive Slave Ad for Violet, 1766

Prior to the American Revolution, the institution of slavery existed in both northern and southern colonies. Unlike their southern counterparts, slaveholders in the north usually owned only a few slaves, which was more suited to their small farms and city dwellings. As a result, slaves and masters often lived and worked together. Published in the Virginia Gazette *on May 2, 1766, Philip Kearny's advertisement for Violet offers clues to their conflicted economic and personal relationship. But this advertisement also reveals Violet's rebellion against her status as a slave and the means by which she sought freedom.*

Five Pounds Reward. RUN away from the subscriber, some time in October 1762, a Mulatto woman named VIOLET, about 30 years of age, of a middle stature, was born at Princetown, in the province of New Jersey, very active, and pretends to be a free woman; she has since been seen in company with one James Lock, somewhere upon the Susquehanna, and by information was afterwards, in the year 1764, taken up, and committed to the gaol of Frederick town in Maryland, on suspicion of her being runaway, from whence she is said to have made her escape; she then acknowledged that she had belonged to the subscriber, but being imposed upon by being sold a slave for life, run away, which is only an invention of her's, for she was born a slave, and as such was sold to the subscriber by the executors of her former master, one Edward Bonnell, late of Freehold in the county of Monmouth, and province aforesaid, deceased, for the sum of 90£ proc. money. She is now supposed to be somewhere in Maryland, Virginia, or North Carolina, she is cunning and artful, and very probably may have changed her name, and will make her escape, if taken, unless great care is taken to secure her. Whoever shall take her up, and secure her in any gaol or prison in Maryland, Virginia, North Carolina, or elsewhere, so that she can be brought home, or sold there, shall have the above reward paid to them by the Printer hereof,
PHILIP KEARNY. PERTH AMBOY, in New Jersey, March 16, 1766

Source: Matthew Mason and Rita G. Koman, "Complicating Slavery: Teaching with Runaway Slave Advertisements from Northern Colonies," *OAH Magazine of History*, 17(3) (April 2003), 34.

4 Phillis Wheatley, "On the Death of the Rev. Mr. George Whitefield," 1770

Born in Senegambia, Phillis was sold into slavery in 1761. Her masters, John and Susanna Wheatley of Boston, taught her to read and write. This poem, a tribute to British evangelical George Whitefield, made her famous. Since her owners knew Whitefield's patron, Lady Huntingdon, Phillis may have heard Whitefield preach in Boston prior to his death. A popular revivalist, Whitefield was notable for preaching to black and white, slave and free. Two years after she published this poem, Phillis Wheatley appeared before a committee of 18 distinguished white men, charged with determining if Wheatley – a slave and an African – really authored her poems. They decided in her favor.

AN ELEGIAC POEM, On the DEATH of that celebrated divine, and eminent servant of JESUS CHRIST, the late Reverend, and pious GEORGE WHITEFIELD, Chaplain to the Right Honourable the Countess of Huntingdon, &c. &c. Who made his Exit from this transitory State, to dwell in the celestial Realms of Bliss, on LORD's Day 30th of September, 1770, when he was seiz'd with a Fit of the Asthma, at NEWBURYPORT, near BOSTON, in NEW ENGLAND. In which is a Condolatory Address to His truly noble Benefactress the worthy and pious Lady HUNTINGDON, – and the Orphan-Children in GEORGIA; who, with many Thousands, are left, by the Death of this great Man, to Lament the Loss of a Father, Friend and Benefactor.

By PHILLIS, a Servant Girl of 17 Years of Age, Belonging to Mr. J. WHEATLEY, of Boston: – And has been but 9 Years in this Country from Africa.

> Hail, happy Saint, on thy immortal throne!
> To thee complaints of grievance are unknown;
> We hear no more the music of thy tongue,
> Thy wonted auditories cease to throng.
> Thy lessons in unequal'd accents flow'd!
> While emulation in each bosom glow'd;
> Thou didst, in strains of eloquence refin'd,
> Inflame the soul, and captivate the mind.
> Unhappy we, the setting Sun deplore!
> Which once was splendid, but it shines no more;
> He leaves this earth for Heav'n's unmeasur'd height,
> And worlds unknown, receive him from our sight;
> There WHITEFIELD wings, with rapid course his way,
> And sails to Zion, through vast seas of day.
>
> When his AMERICANS were burden'd sore,
> When streets were crimson'd with their guiltless gore!
> Unrival'd friendship in his breast now strove:
> The fruit thereof was charity and love.

Towards *America* – couldst thou do more
Than leave thy native home, the *British* shore,
To cross the great Atlantic's wat'ry road,
To see *America's* distress'd abode?
Thy prayers, great Saint, and thy incessant cries,
Have pierc'd the bosom of thy native skies!
Thou moon hast seen, and ye bright stars of light
Have witness been of his requests by night!
He pray'd that grace in every heart might dwell:
He long'd to see *America* excell;
He charg'd its youth to let the grace divine
Arise, and in their future actions shine;
He offer'd THAT he did himself receive,
A greater gift not GOD himself can give:
He urg'd the need of HIM to every one;
It was no less than GOD's co-equal SON!
Take HIM ye wretched for your only good;
Take HIM ye starving souls to be your food.
Ye thirsty, come to his life giving stream:
Take HIM "my dear AMERICANS," he said,
Be your complaints in his kind bosom laid:
Take HIM ye *Africans*, he longs for you;
Impartial SAVIOUR, is his title due;
If you will chuse to walk in grace's road,
You shall be sons, and kings, and priests to GOD.

Great COUNTESS! we *Americans* revere
Thy name, and thus condole thy grief sincere:
We mourn with thee, that TOMB obscurely plac'd,
In which thy Chaplain undisturb'd doth rest.
New-England sure, doth feel the ORPHAN's smart;
Reveals the true sensations of his heart:
Since this fair Sun, withdraws his golden rays,
No more to brighten these distressful days!
His lonely *Tabernacle*, sees no more
A WHITEFIELD landing on the *British* shore:
Then let us view him in yon azure skies:
Let every mind with this lov'd object rise.
No more can he exert his lab'ring breath,
Seiz'd by the cruel messenger of death.
What can his dear AMERICA return?

> But drop a tear upon his happy urn,
> Thou tomb, shalt safe retain thy sacred trust,
> Till life divine re-animate his dust.

Sold by EZEKIAL RUSSELL, in Queen-Street, and JOHN BOYLES, in Marlborough-Street.

Source: "An Elegaic, On the death of that celebrated Divine, and eminent servant of Jesus Christ, the late Reverend, and pious George Whitefield," from *The Poems of Phillis Wheatley*, edited and with an introduction by Julian D. Mason Jr. (University of North Carolina Press, 1989), 132–135.

5 Edenton Ladies' Agreement, 1774

In this document, published in the Morning Chronicle and London Advertiser, *51 women in Edenton, North Carolina, stated their loyalty to the republican cause. In a time when women rarely asserted a public interest in politics, female patriots across the colonies boycotted British tea and other goods. The women of Edenton were unusual in publishing their names and articulating a broader commitment to the goals of the provincial congress. Such actions paved the way for later boycotts by anti-slavery women in Britain and the United States.*

The provincial deputies of North Carolina having resolved not to drink any more tea nor wear any more British cloth, etc., many ladies of this province have determined to give a memorable proof of their patriotism, and have accordingly entered into the following honorable and spirited association. I send it to you to show your fair countrywomen how zealously and faithfully American ladies follow the laudable example of their husbands, and what opposition your *matchless* ministers may expect to receive from a people, thus firmly united against them:

Edenton, North Carolina, October 25 (1774).

As we cannot be indifferent on any occasion that appears nearly to affect the peace and happiness of our country, and as it has been thought necessary, for the public good, to enter into several particular resolves by a meeting of members deputed from the whole province, it is a duty which we owe, not only to our near and dear connections, who have concurred in them, but to ourselves, who are essentially interested in their welfare, to do everything, as far as lies in our power, to testify our sincere adherence to the same; and we do therefore accordingly subscribe this paper as a witness of our fixed intention and solemn determination to do so:

Abagail Charlton,	Sarah Beasley,	Sarah Valentine,
Elizabeth Creacy,	Grace Clayton,	Mary Bonner,
Anne Johnstone,	Mary Jones,	Mary Ramsey,
Mary Woolard,	Mary Creacy,	Lydia Bennett,
Jean Blair,	Anne Hall,	Tresia Cunningham,
Frances Hall,	Sarah Littlejohn,	Anne Haughton,
Mary Creacy,	Sarah Hoskins,	Elizabeth Roberts,
Mary Blount,	M. Payne,	Ruth Benbury,
Margaret Cathcart,	Elizabeth Cricket,	Penelope Barker,
Jane Wellwood,	Lydia Bonner,	Mary Littledle,
Penelope Dawson,	Anne Horniblow,	Elizabeth Johnstone,
Susanna Vail,	Marion Wells,	Elizabeth Green,
Elizabeth Vail,	Sarah Mathews,	Sarah Howe,
Elizabeth Vail,	Elizabeth Roberts,	Mary Hunter,
J. Johnstone,	Rebecca Bondfield,	Anne Anderson,
Elizabeth Patterson,	Sarah Howcott,	Elizabeth Bearsley,
Margaret Pearson,	Elizabeth P. Ormond,	Elizabeth Roberts.

Source: Document 4: Edenton Ladies' Agreement, 27 October 1774, *Morning Chronicle and London Advertiser*, 16 January 1775, in Kathryn Kish Sklar and Gregory Duffy, *How Did the Ladies' Association of Philadelphia Shape New Forms of Women's Activism during the American Revolution, 1780–1781?* (Binghamton, NY: State University of New York at Binghamton, 2001).

6 *A Society of Patriotic Ladies,* 1775

In response to the Edenton Ladies' Agreement, the British firm of R. Sayer and J. Bennett published this satirical image, which imagined the North Carolina women as unattractive, promiscuous political novices as well as negligent mothers. The print circulated in both Great Britain and the American colonies. The women's agreement in this image reads "We the Ladys of Edenton do hereby solemnly Engage not to Conform to that Pernicious Custom of Drinking Tea, or that we the aforesaid Ladys will not promote the wear of any Manufacture from England untill such time that all Acts which tend to Enslave this our Native Country shall be Repealed." Revolutionaries relied on the metaphor of slavery. By placing an enslaved woman in the picture, the author may have offered a criticism of American hypocrisy.

Figure 3.1   A Society of Patriotic Ladies, 1775. *Reproduced courtesy of the Library of Congress.*

Source: "A society of patriotic ladies, at Edenton in North Carolina." London: Printed for R. Sayer & J. Bennett, 1775 March 25. Library of Congress, Prints and Photographs Division. Available at www.loc.gov/pictures/item/96511606/ (accessed August 5, 2010).

7 Hannah Griffitts, "Upon Reading a book Entituled [*sic*] Common Sense," 1776

Philadelphian Hannah Griffitts (1727–1817) was the cousin of Milcah Martha Moore, who preserved the prose and poetry of Griffitts and other Quaker women in her commonplace book. In this poem, Griffitts responds to

Tom Paine's Common Sense, *which urged Americans to declare their*
independence from England. Published in January 1776, the pamphlet
sold approximately 100 000 copies by the end of the year. Though it inspired
patriots, it outraged and frightened Hannah Griffitts, who, like other
loyalists, felt allegiance toward the king and the "charter'd" rights of British
citizens. Griffitts and other Quaker pacifists also opposed Paine's extreme
rhetoric. Her poem expressed the reaction of many neutral Quakers, who
feared the impact of independence and war on their families, their city, and
their country.

The Vizard drop'd, see Subtilty prevail,
Thro' ev'ry Page of this fallacious Tale,
Sylvania let it not unanswer'd pass,
But heed the well guess'd Snake beneath the Grass,
A deeper Wound at Freedom, ne'er was made,
Than by this Oliverian is display'd.
Orders confounded, – Dignities thrown down,
Charters degraded equal with the Crown,
The impartial Press, most partially maintain'd
Freedom infring'd, & Conscience is restrain'd,
The moderate Man is held to publick View,
"The Friend of Tyranny & Foe to you,"
Deny'd the common Right to represent
Forbid to give his Reasons for Dissent,
Whilst base Informers – (own'd a pubkick Pest)
Are round the Land encourag'd & caress'd
Our Representatives, – the Peoples Choice
Are held contemptuous by this daring Voice
Persons are seiz'd & Posts monopoliz'd
And all our Form of Government despis'd, –
– Then from this "Specimen of Rule" bewar,
Behold the Serpent & avoid his Snare.
'Tis not in Names, our present Danger lyes
Sixty as well as one can tyrannize,
Ah! Then awake Sylvania & beware,
The fatal Danger of this subtle Snare,
Hold fast yr. own, yr. charter'd Rights maintain
Nor let them weave the Snare into the Chain,
And whilst firm Union stands the British Foes,
Let not the native Hand yr. Date of Freedom close. –

Source: Catherine La Courreye Blecki and Karin A. Wulf (eds.), *Milcah Martha Moore's Book: A Commonplace Book from Revolutionary America* (University Park: Pennsylvania State University Press, 1997), pp. 255–256.

Suggested Questions for Discussion

1   How did different American women define liberty?
2   What religious and political ideas shaped American women's expectations of independence?
3   Examine the cartoon of the Edenton women. How did opponents of the Revolution use women to symbolize the social and political disorder to come?

Chapter 4 Revolution, 1780–1810

1 Jemima Wilkinson, Excerpts from *The Universal Friend's Advice, to Those of the Same Religious Society*, 1784

Born a Quaker, Wilkinson (1752–1819) was disowned for her attendance at the enthusiastic revivals of eighteenth-century evangelical preachers. Following an illness in 1776, Wilkinson reinvented herself as the Public Universal Friend, speaking throughout New England during the American Revolution. Attracting a number of followers, she blended Quaker tenets, radical evangelical belief in free will, her personal dynamism, and a distinctive gender-neutral appearance (she wore long robes). In 1790, Wilkinson and her followers settled in the frontier of western New York. Aside from the Society of Friends, most mainstream denominations excluded women from the ministry. Following the revivalism of the mid-eighteenth century, as newer denominations, like the Methodists and Baptists, gained adherents, female preachers became a more common feature in American religious life. Unlike Wilkinson, however, most of these female preachers did not challenge male religious leadership.

RECOMMENDED TO BE READ IN THEIR PUBLIC MEETINGS FOR DIVINE WORSHIP.

ADVISETH all, who desire to be *one* with the *Friend* in spirit, and to be wise unto salvation, that they be punctual in attending meetings, as many as conveniently can ...

Do good to all as opportunity offers, especially to the *household of faith* ...

Women in American History to 1880: A Documentary Reader, by Carol Faulkner
© 2011 Blackwell Publishing Ltd.

Obey and practice the divine counsel you have heard, or may hear from time to time; living every day as if it were the *last*; remembering you are always in the presence of the HIGH and LOFTY ONE who inhabiteth eternity, whose name is HOLY; and, without holiness, no one can see the LORD in peace, therefore, be ye holy in all your conversation, and labor to keep yourselves unspotted from the world, and possess your vessels in sanctification and honor, knowing, that ye ought to be temples for the HOLY SPIRIT to dwell in, and, if your vessels are unclean, that which is holy cannot dwell in you: And know ye not your ownselves, that if CHRIST dwells not, yea, and reigns not in you, ye are in a reprobate state, or out of favor with GOD and his HOLY ONE; therefore, ye are to shun the very appearance of evil in all things, as foolish talking, and vain jesting, with all unprofitable conversation, which is not convenient, but flee from bad company as from a serpent. Be not drunk with wine, or any other spirituous liquors, wherein is excess; but be filled with the HOLY SPIRIT, building one another up in the most holy faith, praying in the HOLY GHOST ...

Use plainness of speech and apparel, and let your adorning, not be outward, but inward, even that of a meek and quiet spirit, which, in the sight of GOD is of great price. Thus saith the Psalmist – It is most like the King's daughter, all glorious within; her clothing is of wrought gold ...

Above all, give all diligence to make your calling and election sure, and work out your salvation with fear and trembling, redeeming your time, because the days are evil. Forget the things that are behind, and press forward towards the mark and the prize of the high calling of GOD in CHRIST JESUS; that ye may be found without spot or rebuike before the LORD; that ye may be delivered from the bondage of corruption, and brought into the glorious liberty of the Sons of GOD, where the Morning Stars sing together, and all the Sons of GOD shout for joy; having oil in your vessels with your lamps, like the wise virgins, trimmed and burning; having on your wedding garments, that when the HOLY ONE ceaseth to intercede for a dying world, you may also appear with him in glory, not having on your righteousness, but the righteousness of GOD in CHRIST JESUS.

You, who are PARENTS, or intrusted with the tuition of children, consider your calling, and the charge committed unto you, and be careful to bring them up in the nurture and admonition of the LORD, and educate them in a just and reverend regard thereunto: And whilst you are careful to provide for the support of their bodies, do not neglect the welfare of their souls, seeing, the earliest impression, in general, lasts the longest. As it is written, "Train up a child in the way that he should go, and when he is old, he will not, easily, depart from it;" and let example teach as loud as your precepts.

CHILDREN, obey your parents in all things, in the LORD, for it is right and acceptable in the sight of GOD. Honor your fathers and mothers, and the way to honor father and mother is not to give them flattering titles, or vain compliments, but to obey the counsel of the LORD, and them, in the LORD. Thus saith the wisdom of the LORD, by the mouth of the wise king Solomon, My son, forget not my law, but let thine heart keep my commandments, for length of days, long life, and peace, shall they add to thee … My son, hear the instruction of thy father, and forsake not the law of thy mother, for they shall be an ornament of grace unto thy head, and chains about thy neck …

AND *all of you,* who have been, or may be so divinely favored, as to be, mouth for the HOLY ONE, I entreat you, in the bonds of love, that when you are moved upon to speak in public, that ye speak as the *Oracles of GOD,* and as the HOLY SPIRIT giveth utterance, not withholding more than it meet, which tendeth to poverty; neither add to his words, lest he reprove thee, and thou be found a liar: But do all with a single eye to the glory of GOD, that GOD and the LAMB may be glorified by you and through you; for he that winneth souls is wise, and the wise shall shine as the brightness of the firmament, and they that turn many be righteousness, as stars for ever and ever.

THE *time is fulfilled* – the *kingdom of* GOD *is at hand. Repent ye,* and *believe the GOSPEL,* that the kingdom of GOD may begin within you.

HE hath shewed thee, O *Man!* What is good: and what doth the LORD require of thee, but to
DO JUSTLY,
LOVE MERCY, and
WALK HUMBLY WITH THY GOD!
AMEN.

Source: Herbert A. Wisbey, *Pioneer Prophetess: Jemima Wilkinson, the Publick Universal Friend* (Ithaca: Cornell University Press, 1964), pp. 197–204.

2 Indenture of Eunice Allis, 1789

Though slavery had overtaken indentured servitude as the principal source of labor in the South, indentured servitude remained an important part of the northern economy even after the American Revolution. With the consent of their parents, young men and women bound themselves to an employer in order to learn a trade or to ease economic strain on their families. The indenture does not specify Eunice's job, but she probably worked as a domestic servant in the household of farmer Joseph Bennett. The legal document clearly spells out her obligations to him as well as Bennett's duties to this 11-year-old girl.

This indenture witnesseth that Eunice Allis Daughter of Benjamin Allis all of Lebanon in Columbia County and State of New York hat [*sic*] put herself, by and with the consent of her Parents and by those present doth put herself Apprentice to Joseph Bennett of Lebanon aforesaid yeoman to be taught by him from the Day of this Date for and during the term of Seven years, six months and twenty one days next issuing of these presents, which renders her the age of eighteen years. During all which time she the said Apprentice her said master shall faithfully serve, his secrets keep, his lawful commands obey. She shall do him no damage, nor see it done by others without telling him or giving him notice of the same, she shall not waste his goods, nor lend them unlawfully to others, she shall not commit fornication, nor contract Matrimony during said time, nor haunt bad houses, but in all things behave herself as a faithful apprentice ought to do during said time. And the said Joseph Bennett shall in the utmost of his [indeavor] to teach her as aforesaid and honoure or cause to be procured for the said apprentice sufficient meat, drink, apperal, washing and lodging fitting for an apprentice during said term and give her suitable learning. And at the expiration of said term will decently cloth her after the Manner of the Church to which she belongs. And for the true performance of all and every of the said covenants and agreements each of the said parties bind themselves to the other by those present. In witness thereof they have hereunto interchanged their hands and seals this tenth day of January in the year of our Lord one thousand seven hundred and eighty nine.

In the presence of Amos Hammon [and] Isaac Crouch

> Benjamin Allis [signature]
> Mary Allis her mark
> Joseph Bennett [signature]
> Eunice Allis her mark

Source: Carol Berkin and Leslie Horowitz (eds.), *Women's Voices, Women's Lives* (Boston: Northeastern University Press, 1998), pp. 107–108.

3 Judith Sargent Murray, "On the Equality of the Sexes," 1790

Born in Gloucester, Massachusetts, Judith Sargent Murray (1751–1820) was a patriot, writer, and, in the words of historian Mary Beth Norton, the "chief theorist of republican womanhood."[1] Following the American

---

[1] Mary Beth Norton, *Liberty's Daughters: The Revolutionary Experience of American Women, 1750–1800* (New York: Harper Collins, 1980), 238.

Revolution, she and others promoted female education as essential to the
survival of the republic. Drawing on Enlightenment ideas, Murray argued that
custom and habit limited women's opportunity for intellectual advancement.
Rather than detracting from their domestic duties, she proposed that female
education was essential to good marriages. Building upon Murray's assertion
of female capability and equality, Declaration of Independence signer
Benjamin Rush suggested that educated women were essential to raising good
(male) citizens. Female academies, including schools run by Sarah Pierce and
Susanna Rowson, appeared around the country.

Is it upon mature consideration we adopt the idea, that nature is thus partial in her distribution? Is it indeed a fact, that she hath yielded to one half of the human species to unquestionable a mental superiority? I know that to both sexes elevated understandings, and the reverse, are common. But, suffer me to ask, in what the minds of females are so notoriously deficient, or unequal. May not the intellectual powers be ranged under these four heads – imagination, reason, memory and judgment. The province of imagination hath long since been surrendered up to us, and we have been crowned undoubted sovereigns of the regions of fancy. Invention is perhaps the most arduous effort of the mind; this branch of imagination hath been particularly ceded to us, and we have been time out of mind invested with that creative faculty. Observe the variety of fashions (here I bar the contemptuous smile) which distinguish and adorn the female world; how continually they are changing, insomuch that they almost render the wise man's assertion problematical, and we are ready to say, *there is something new under the sun.* Now, what a playfulness, what an exuberance of fancy, what strength of inventive imagination, doth this continual variation discover? Again, it hath been observed, that if the turpitude of the conduct of our sex, hath been ever so enormous, so extremely ready are we, that the very first thought presents us with an apology, so plausible, as to produce our actions even in an amiable light. Another instance of our creative powers, is our talent for slander; how ingenious are we at inventive scandal? ... Perhaps it will be asked if I furnish these facts as instances of excellency in our sex. Certainly not; but as proofs of a creative faculty, of a lively imagination. Assuredly great activity of mind is thereby discovered, and was this activity properly directed, what beneficial effects would follow. Is the needle and kitchen sufficient to employ the operations of a soul thus organized? ... We can only reason from what we know, and if an opportunity of acquiring knowledge hath been denied us, the inferiority of our sex, cannot fairly be deduced from thence ... "But our judgment is not so strong – we do not distinguish so well." – Yet it may be questioned, from what doth this superiority, in this determining faculty of the soul, proceed. May we not trace its source in the difference of education, and continued advantages? ... How is the one exalted, and the other depressed, by the contrary modes of education which are adopted! The one is taught to aspire, the other is early confined and limited. As their years increase, the sister must be wholly domesticated, while the brother is led by the hand through all the flowery paths of science. Grant that their minds are by nature equal, yet who shall wonder at the *apparent* superiority, if indeed custom becomes *second nature*; nay if it taketh place of nature, and that it doth the experience of each day will envince. At length arrived at womanhood, the uncultivated fair one feels a void, which the employments allotted her are by no means capable of filling ... Meantime she herself is most unhappy; she feels the want of a cultivated mind ... Now, was she permitted the same instructors as her brother, (with an eye however to their particular departments) for the enjoyment of a rational mind an ample field would be opened ... an unhappy Hymen would then be as rare, as is now the reverse.

Will it be urged that those acquirements would supersede our domestick duties. I answer that every requisite in female economy is easily attained; and, with truth I can add, that when once attained, they require no further *mental attention*. Nay, while we are pursuing the needle, or the superintendency of the family, I repeat, that our minds are at full liberty for reflection; that imagination may exert itself in full vigor; and that if a just foundation is early laid, our ideas will then be worthy of rational beings ... Should it still be vociferated, "Your domestik employments are sufficient" – I would calmly ask, is it reasonable, that a candidate for immortality, for the joys of heaven, an intelligent being, who is to spend an eternity in contemplating the works of deity, should at present be so degraded, as to be allowed no other ideas, than those which are suggested by the mechanism of a pudding, or the sewing the seams of a garment? Pity that all such censurers of female improvement do not go one step further, and deny their future existence; to be consistent they surely ought.

Yes, ye lordly, ye haughty sex, our souls are by nature *equal* to yours ... I dare confidently believe, that from the commencement of time to the present day, there hath been as many females, as males, who, by the *mere force of natural powers*, have merited the crown of applause; who, thus unassisted, have seized the wreath of fame. I know there are who assert, that as the animal powers of one sex are superiour, of course their mental faculties also must be stronger; thus attributing strength of mind to the transient organization of this earth born tenement ... Were we to grant that animal strength proved any thing, taking into consideration the accustomed impartiality of nature, we should be induced to imagine, that she had invested the female mind with superiour strength as an equivalent for the bodily powers of man. But waving this however palpable advantage, for *equality only*, we wish to contend.

I am aware that there are many passages in the sacred oracles which seem to give the advantage to the other sex; but I consider all these as wholly metaphorical. Thus David was a man after God's own heart, yet see him enervated by his licentious passions! Behold him following Uriah to the death, and shew me wherein could consist the immaculate Being's complacency ... the superiority of man, as exhibited in scripture, being also emblematical, all arguments deduced from thence, of course fall to the ground. The exquisite delicacy of the female mind proclaimeth the exactness of its texture, while its nice sense of honour announceth its innate, its native grandeur ... And if we are allowed an equality of requirement, let serious studies equally employ our minds, and we will bid our souls arise to equal strength. We will meet upon even ground, the despot man; we will rush with alacrity to the combat, and, crowned by success, we shall then answer the exalted expectations, which are formed ... If we meet an equal, a sensible friend, we will reward him with the hand of amity, and through life we will be assiduous to promote his happiness; but from every deep laid scheme for our ruin, retiring into ourselves, amid the flowery paths of science, we will indulge in all the refined and sentimental pleasures of contemplation. And should it still be urged, that studies thus insisted upon would interfere with our more peculiar department, I must further reply, that *early hours*, and close application, will do wonders ... But in one respect, O ye arbiters of our fate! We confess that the superiority is indubitably yours; you are by nature formed for our protectors; we pretend not to vie with you in bodily strength; upon this point we will never contend for victory. Shield us then, we beseech you, from external evils, and in return we will transact *your* domestick affairs. Yes, *your*, for are you not equally interested in those matters with ourselves? Is not the elegancy of neatness as agreeable to your sight as to ours; is not the well favoured viand equally delightful to your taste; and doth not your sense of hearing suffer as much, from the discordant founds [*sic*] prevalent in an ill-regulated family, produced by the voices of children and many *et ceteras?*

CONSTANTIA

Source: David A. Hollinger and Charles Capper (eds.), *The American Intellectual Tradition*, Vol. 1 (New York: Oxford University Press, 2006), pp. 164–167.

4 Sarah Pierce, Verses, 1792

Sarah Pierce (1767–1852) founded the Litchfield, Connecticut, Female Academy, and her students included famous sisters Catharine Beecher and Harriet Beecher Stowe. Pierce never married, and this poem, written for her close friend Abigail Smith, offers an alternative vision of female life beyond marriage and motherhood. In the early years of the nation, Pierce and other male and female writers suggested that egalitarian friendships fulfilled republican political ideals in ways that traditional marriage did not. While Abigail Smith eventually married, her older brother, who recorded this poem in his diary, did not.

On rising ground we'll rear a little dome;
　　Plain, neat, and elegant, it shall appear;
No slaves shall there lament their native home,
　　Or, silent, drop the unavailing tear.

Content and cheerfulness shall dwell within,
　　And each domestic serve thro' love alone;
Coy Happiness we'll strive, for once, to win,
　　With meek Religion there to build her throne.

And oft our friends shall bless the lonely vale,
　　And, social, pass the wintry eves away;
Or, when soft Summer swells the fragrant gale,
　　Delighted mark new beauties as they stray.

Pleased with the scene, by Fancy's pencil drawn,
　　The various landscape rushes on my view;
The cultivated farm, the flowery lawn,
　　That sucks the fragrance of the honied dew.

The fertile "meadows trim with daisies pied";
　　The garden, breathing Flora's best perfumes;
And stored with herbs, whose worth, by Matrons tried,
　　Dispels disease, and gives health's roseate blooms.

Here vines, with purple clusters bending low,
　　And various fruit-trees loaded branches bear;
There roots of every kind profusely grow,
　　Bespeaking plenty thro' the circling year.

See yonder hillock, where our golden corn
    Waves it's bright head to every passing breeze;
Yon fruitful fields our sportive flocks adorn,
    Our cows at rest beneath the neighboring trees.

As misty clouds from silent streams arise,
    Yon distant Town attracts the gazer's view;
Yon mount, whose lofty summit meets the skies,
    Shelters the Village on the plain below.

Behind our lot, a Wood defies the storm,
    Like those where Druids wont, in days of yore,
When Superstition wore Religion's form,
    With mystic rites their unknown Gods adore.

Within this grove we'll oft retire to muse,
    Where Contemplation builds her silent seat;
Her soothing influence she will ne'er refuse
    To those who wander in this blest retreat.

A river solemn murmurs thro' the shades,
    The whispering pines, in echoes soft, reply,
Then, hoarse o'er rocks, it seeks the distant glades,
    Forming a rain-bow in the moistened sky –

Nor leaves us here – but thro' the Village winds,
    Where simply elegance, in neat array,
Might teach even pomp that, not to wealth confined,
    Genius & taste might to a cottage stray.

In front, a level grass-plot smooth & green,
    Where neighboring children, pass sweet hours at play,
And Fairies oft, (if Fairies e'er have been,)
    Will featly foot the moonlight hours away.

Our plenteous store we'll freely give to all;
    Want ne'er shall pass, in sorrow, from our door;
With joy we'll seat the beggar in our hall,
    And learn the tale of woe that sunk his store.

But chiefly those who pine, by sickness prest;
    Whose merit, known to few, unheeded lies;
How sweet, to banish sorrow from the breast,
    And bid fair hope shine sparkling in the eyes.

Thus, humbly blest, when youthful years are flown,
    (Proud to be good, not wishing to be great,)
And swift-wing'd Time proclaimed our moments run,
    Resign'd to heaven, we'll cheerful bow to fate.

Placed in one grave, beneath a plain, smooth, stone, –
    Where oft the tear unfeign'd shall dew the face,
The sick, the poor, shall long our fate bemoan,
    But wealth & grandeur never mark the place.

This simple Epitaph the stone adorns, –
    Which calls, from artless eyes, the frequent tear –
Matrons & maids shall often stoop to learn,
    And all the Village think it passing rare.

The Epitaph
Beneath this stone two female friends interr'd,
    Who past their lives content, in solitutde;
They wish'd no ill, yet oft, thro' ignorance, err'd;
    Reader! depart, reflect, and be as good.

Source: Sarah Pierce, *"Verses, Written in the Winter of 1792, & Addressed to Abigail Smith Jr."* Available at Early American Women Writers, University of Connecticut, www.eaww.uconn.edu/writings/poem_pierce.html (accessed August 10, 2010).

5 Susanna Rowson, Excerpt from *Charlotte Temple*, 1794

The political ideals and social turmoil of the American Revolution encouraged young men and women to cast aside parental guidance and pursue romantic love and personal happiness. Yet this period of sexual freedom held more dangers for young women. Premarital pregnancy rates rose, but parents and community elders no longer had the authority to force young couples to marry. This bestselling seduction novel, written by Susanna Rowson, the principal of the Young Ladies' Academy in Boston, warned readers that following their hearts endangered their reputations. The title character dies at the end of the novel, unable to recover her lost virtue. Rowson's novel contributed to the rise of Victorian sexual mores emphasizing female sexual purity.

In affairs of love, a young heart is never in more danger than when attempted by a handsome young soldier. A man of an indifferent appearance, will, when arrayed in a military habit, shew to advantage; but when beauty of person, elegance of manner, and an easy method of paying compliments, are united to the scarlet coat, smart cockade, and military sash, ah! well-a-day for the poor girl who gazes on him: she is in imminent danger; but if she listens to him with pleasure, 'tis all over with her, and from that moment she has neither eyes nor ears for any other object.

Now, my dear sober matron, (if a sober matron should deign to turn over these pages, before she trusts them to the eye of a darling daughter,) let me intreat you not to put on a grave face, and throw down the book in a passion and declare 'tis enough to turn the heads of half the girls in England; I do solemnly protest, my dear madam, I mean no more by what I have here advanced, than to ridicule those romantic girls, who foolishly imagine a red coat and silver epaulet constitute the fine gentleman; and should that fine gentleman make half a dozen fine speeches to them, they will imagine themselves so much in love as to fancy it a meritorious action to jump out of a two pair of stairs window, abandon their friends, and trust entirely to the honour of a man, who perhaps hardly knows the meaning of the word, and if he does, will be too much the modern man of refinement, to practise it in their favour.

Gracious heaven! when I think on the miseries that must rend the heart of a doating parent, when he sees the darling of his age at first seduced from his protection, and afterwards abandoned, by the very wretch whose promises of love decoyed her from the paternal roof – when he sees her poor and wretched, her bosom torn between remorse for her crime and love for her vile betrayer – when fancy paints to me the good old man stooping to raise the weeping penitent, while every tear from her eye is numbered by drops from his bleeding heart, my bosom glows with honest indignation, and I wish for power to extirpate those monsters of seduction from the earth.

Oh my dear girls – for to such only am I writing – listen not to the voice of love, unless sanctioned by paternal approbation: be assured, it is now past the days of romance: no woman can be run away with contrary to her own inclination: then kneel down each morning, and request kind heaven to keep you free from temptation, or, should it please to suffer you to be tried, pray for fortitude to resist the impulse of inclination when it runs counter to the precepts of religion and virtue.

Source: Susanna Rowson, *Charlotte: A Tale of Truth* (Philadelphia: D. Humphreys, 1794). Available by subscription at http://asp6new.alexanderstreet.com/was2/was2.object.details.aspx?dorpid=1000684306

6 *Liberty*, 1796

In this popular print, as in other similar images, the artist portrayed the concept of liberty as a woman. Philadelphia engraver Edward Savage also chose a specific female image, the goddess of youth, or Hebe, the daughter of Zeus and

Hera, in Greek mythology. The goddess offers a cup to the bald eagle, the symbol of the young nation. Other patriotic items include the American flag and a liberty cap. Crushed representations of the British monarchy, including a scepter and royal medal and garter, appear beneath Liberty's feet. Such images suggested an important place for women in the future of the new nation even as their political and legal status remained unchanged.

Figure 4.1 Liberty, 1796. *Reproduced courtesy of the Library of Congress.*

Source: Liberty. In the form of the goddess of youth, giving support to the bald eagle / painted & engrav'd by E. Savage. Philadelphia: Pubd. by E. Savage, 1796 June 11. Library of Congress, Prints and Photographs Division. Available at www.loc.gov/pictures/item/2003689261/ (accessed August 10, 2010).

7 Excerpt from the Will of David Bush, Connecticut Slave Owner, 1797

Following the American Revolution, northern states implemented plans to end slavery. In 1784, Connecticut passed its gradual emancipation act, stating that any enslaved child born after March 1, 1784 would be free at the age of 25. This law did not free any slaves born prior to this date. David Bush, a wealthy landowner in Greenwich, Connecticut, included slaves among his property at his death. He left his wife personal items as well as the traditional widow's thirds. He also bequeathed specific slaves to his wife and daughters. In 1825, Bush's heirs manumitted Candice. In 1848, Connecticut finally freed all remaining slaves in the state.

IN THE NAME OF GOD, AMEN.

I, David Bush, of Greenwich in Fairfield County and State of Connecticut, although weak in body yet of a sound disposing mind and memory, do make and publish this my last will and testament in the following manner:

I order my debts and funeral charges to be paid out of my personal estate, excepting the part thereof that I shall in this will otherwise dispose of.

I give and bequeath unto my well beloved wife, Sarah Bush, and to her heirs and assigns forever:–

All my household furniture (clocks excepted), all the bedding and furniture thereof, curtains, sheets, pillow cases, bedsteds, all the crockery in the house, working utensils and all other moveable property in the house, also my negro girls, Patience and Phillis, also my young pied oxen with a yoke and chain compleat for use and my best cart with a good ax and hoe, two horse such as she shall shoes [choose] with three cows, also my swine and half my sheep, also during the time my said wife shall continue my widow, I will that my negro man, Cull, shall live with her as her slave which I give her the improvement of as aforesaid, also I give and bequeath to my said wife the use and improvement of the one third part of all the residue of my estate, both real and personal, she remaining my widow, but if she should marry, my will is that she shall thereafter have only the one half of the said third part during her natural life and from this last provision I exclude my mills and any part in my dwelling house or other buildings on or about the landing adjacent or near to my said dwelling house ...

I give, devise, and bequeath unto my daughters, Mary, Sally, Elizabeth, Fanny, Charlotte, and Grace and to their heirs and assigns forever (excepting a lot being in said Greenwich – one tract or parsel of land hereafter excepted) the following tracts or parsels of land ...

It is my will that the above property shall be divided between said daughters. Mary, Sally and Elizabeth shall have? hundred pounds New York money each more than Fanny, Charlotte, and Grace. It is my will that what I have given to my daughters Sally and Elizabeth is not to be to them their heirs and assigns forever, only the use and improvement thereof, and at their decease to be to their heirs forever at the time they shall respectively decease, and it is my will if it shall be thought best by my executors hereafter named to sell the lands above devised to my said daughters Sally and Elizabeth that they sell said lands and that my said daughters Sally and Elizabeth shall have the interest thereof during their lives and at the time they shall respectively decease, the principal shall be divided to each of them. Also, I give and devise to my said daughter Fanny, her heirs and assigns my black girl, Candice, to my daughter, Charlotte, my black girl, Mille, to my daughter, Grace, my black girl, Rose ...

(signed)

David Bush

Witnesses:

Bezaliel Brown

John Truslow

William Marshal

Source: "Enslaved Africans in the Colony of Connecticut," *Citizens ALL: African Americans in Connecticut 1700–1850*, Gilder Lehrman Center for the Study of Slavery, Resistance, and Abolition, Yale University. Available at http://cmi2.yale.edu/citizens_ all/stories/module1/documents/david_bush_will.html (accessed August 10, 2010).

8 Elizabeth Seton, Letters to Archbishop John Carroll, 1809–1810

Despite opposition from her family and friends, New Yorker Elizabeth Ann Bayley Seton (1774–1821), a widow with five children, converted from the Episcopal Church to Roman Catholicism in 1805. She then moved to Baltimore, where she taught school and formed a religious order that later became the Sisters of Charity. In 1809, she and the other sisters moved to property in rural Emmitsburg, Maryland. Her letters to Archbishop John Carroll reveal the tension between being "Mother" to her order and being subservient to the male leadership who owned the land, appointed supervising priests, such as Father Dubourg, and otherwise directed her religious and educational labors.

8th September 1809
My Father in God
   – Our Superior [William Dubourg] has written us the welcome news that
we may expect our father [Pierre] Babade here in a short time but mentioned
that he did not know if you would give him permission to hear the Sisters. –
how many times since have I begged our Lord to direct me what to do – on
the one hand I know it may displease you if I say any more on the subject,
and on the other side my dear girls are continually begging me "O dear
Mother do write to the Bishop [John Carroll] he is a Father to us and will
not deny your request" but I have put them off until the last few days my
Cecilia [Seton, her sister-in-law] is again sick and blistered and her pains are
being accompanied by a particular depression of spirits the only consolation
I can give her is the promise of writing you to beg in her name and the names
of four other Sisters who desire the comfort and feel the necessity as she
does of unfolding our souls to him that you will allow them the privilege
which will insure their contentment and Peace – for my part I assure you
that if it is not granted to me you will leave a Soul so dear to you in a cloud
of uneasiness which can be dissipated in no other way. It would seem as if
our Lord has inspired this confidence in my Soul and in those of many
others round me for my severe and most painful trial, circumstanced as I am
– is ever blessed adorable will be done, but as he permits us to desire and
express that desire to you as our Father you will not be displeased with me
for again troubling you on a subject on which you seemed already to have
made known your intentions...
   Committing the success of our requests to our dear Virgin Mother
I am and always must be your faithful Affectionate child and servant
MEASeton
   May I beg *as the penitent at your feet* that this may not be communicated
to any one – if Mr. Dubois should know this request was made his feelings
would be hurt and it would answer no purpose.

2d November 1809
My dear Reverend Father
   Two days after your departure I received a letter inclosed for you from
Leghorn which Mr. [John] Dubois has forwarded and I hope you have
received. Since you left us Mr. [William] Dubourg has been here some
days, and I am not without hope that he will again resume his charge as
Superior – You know there are many reasons why I wish it, and if it cannot
be for any length of time at least until the Rev. Mr. [John] Davids situation
is decided for you know if he should go with Mr. [Benedict] Flaget we shall
have three changes in one year – besides the temporal management could

not be done by him and it is very difficult to divide it (under one circumstance) from the spiritual, also since it is our first Superior I have offended
to him I ought to be permitted to make the reparation, if it may be allowed
– Yet if it is the will of our Lord it should not be so, I must do my best to
make all go right – the truth is I have been made a Mother before being
initiated – and that must excuse all – to you I attempt no justification –
you know all – being a convert, and very much left to my own devotion,
how gratefully attached must I be to the one who has shewn an unceasing
care for my Soul and done every thing to enlighten it, and discover to it the
full consolation of our holy Faith. In my place my dear Father you would
have experienced my trial, but you would at once have offered it up to
God – I am late in seeing the necessity of this measure, but not too late I
hope since it is never too late with our good Lord and he can dispose every
heart to accommodation – you will see how good a child I am going to be
– quite a little child, and perhaps you will have often to give me the food
of little children yet, but I will do my best as I have promised you in every
case. that I am sure of your prayers for my advancement is one of my
greatest comforts...

25th January 1810
dear and Most honoured Father
    St. Joseph's House is almost ready, in a very short time we expect to be
settled in it – you know our rules have hitherto been very imperfectly
observed but now the moment approaches when *order must be the
foundation of all the good we can hope to do*, and as so much depends
on the Mother of the Community I beg you to take her first in hand for I
must candidly tell you she is all in the wrong – *not from discontent with
the place* I am in since the very corner of the world is the same to me if I
may but serve our Lord, *nor with the intention of our institution* for I
long to be in the fullest exercise of it – but circumstances have all so
combined as to create in my mind a confusion and want of confidence in
my Superiors which is indescribable. if my own happiness was only in
question I should say how good is the cross for me this is my opportunity
to ground myself in patience and perseverance, and *my reluctance to
speak* on a subject which I know will give you uneasiness is so great
that I would certainly be silent – but as the good our Almighty God may
intend to do by means of this community may be very much impeded by
the present state of things it is absolutely necessary You as the head of it and
to whom of course the Spirit of discernment for its good is given should be
made acquainted with it before the evil is irreparable. Sincerely I promised
you and really *I have endeavored to do every thing in my power* to bend

myself to meet the last appointed Superior in every way but after continual reflection on the *necessity of absolute conformity with him,* and *constant prayer* to our Lord to help me, yet the *heart is closed* and when the pen should freely give him the necessary detail and information he requires it stops, and *he remains now as uninformed in the essential points* as if he had nothing to do with us, *an unconquerable reluctance and diffidence takes place of those dispositions* which ought to influence every action and with every desire to serve God and these excellent beings who surround me I remain motionless and inactive. it is for you my most revered Father to decide if this is temptation or what it is – Mr. [Samuel] Cooper who is on a visit to Baltimore knows many particulars I cannot write which his interest in our community has made him unavoidably observe and which I beg him to make known to you – if you think proper to make known the contents of this to the holy Mr. [Charles] Nagot you will do so, but if after consideration of every circumstance you still think things must remain as they are what-ever you dictate I will abide by through every difficulty, continuing at all times and in every situation

Your most Affectionate Daughter in Christ *MEASeton*

Source: Regina Bechtle and Judith Metz (eds.), *Elizabeth Bayley Seton: Collected Writings,* Volume II: *Correspondence and Journals 1808–1820* (Hyde Park, NY: New City Press, 2002), pp. 80–82, 87–88, 107–108.

9 Portrait of Elizabeth Freeman, 1811

Elizabeth Freeman, also known as Mumbet, an enslaved Massachusetts woman, successfully sued for her freedom in 1781. Her lawyer, Theodore Sedgwick, argued that slavery was illegal under the new Massachusetts state constitution, which declared "all men are born free and equal." Her case, Brom & Bett v. John Ashley, Esq., helped undermine the institution of slavery in Massachusetts. After winning her freedom, Elizabeth Freeman became a servant in the Sedgwick household. Sedgwick's daughter, the author Catharine Maria Sedgwick, discussed Freeman's biography in an article titled "Slavery in New England." Theodore Sedgwick's daughter- in-law, Susan Anne Livingston Sedgwick, painted this portrait, which shows Freeman wearing typical period clothing and a necklace given to her by Catharine Maria Sedgwick. Elizabeth Freeman died in 1829, when she was approximately 85 years old.

Figure 4.2   *Portrait of Elizabeth "Mumbet" Freeman (c.1742–1829), 1811 (w/c on ivory) by Susan Anne Livingston Ridley Sedgwick (fl.1811); MHS175741.* © *Massachusetts Historical Society, Boston, MA, USA/The Bridgeman Art Library.*

Source: Miniature portrait of Elizabeth Freeman (Mumbet) by Susan Anne Livingston Ridley Sedgwick, 1811. 7.5 cm × 5.5 cm; in gilded wood frame (visible in large digital image): 13 cm × 9.7 cm. From the collections of the Massachusetts Historical Society. Available at www.masshist.org/database/onview_full.cfm?queryID=25 and www. bridgemanart.com/image/Sedgwick-Susan-Anne-Livingston-Ridley-fl-1811/Portrait-of-Elizabeth-Mumbet-Freeman-c-1742-1829-1811-w-c-on-ivory/831ed5fced7e4861bbe5 fc5b0c9281c0?key=mhs&filter= CBPOIHV& thumb=x150&num=15&page=49 (both accessed August 10, 2010).

10 Mary Jemison on her Experiences during the American Revolution, 1824

In 1758, during the French and Indian War, a group of Shawnee and French murdered the parents of white teenager Mary Jemison and took her captive. After her capture, Jemison was adopted by two Seneca women. From that time, she identified as a Seneca. Mary Jemison married a Delaware Indian, and, after his death, married a Seneca Indian named Hiokatoo. In 1823, one year before she died, she told her life story to James Everett Seaver, who published her narrative. In this excerpt, she describes her experiences during the Revolution, when General John Sullivan attacked the Seneca, driving some of them to the British army at Fort Niagara.

At length, in the fall of 1779, intelligence was received that a large and powerful army of the rebels, under the command of General Sullivan, was making rapid progress towards our settlement, burning and destroying the huts and corn-fields; killing the cattle, hogs and horses, and cutting down the fruit trees belonging to the Indians throughout the country.

Our Indians immediately became alarmed, and suffered every thing but death from fear that they should be taken by surprize, and totally destroyed at a single blow. But in order to prevent so great a catastrophe, they sent out a few spies who were to keep themselves at a short distance in front of the invading army, in order to watch its operations, and give information of its advances and success.

Sullivan arrived at Canandaigua Lake, and had finished his work of destruction there, and it was ascertained that he was about to march to our flats when our Indians resolved to give him battle on the way, and prevent, if possible, the distresses to which they knew we should be subjected, if he should succeed in reaching our town. Accordingly, they sent all their women and children into the woods a little west of Little Beard's Town, in order that we might make a good retreat if it should be necessary, and then, well armed, set out to face the conquering enemy . . .

At that time I had three children who went with me on foot, one who rode horse back, and one whom I carried on my back.

Our corn was good that year; a part of which we had gathered and secured for winter.

In one or two days after the skirmish at Connissius lake, Sullivan and his army arrived at Genesee river, where they destroyed every article of the food kind that they could lay their hands on. A part of our corn they burnt, and threw the remainder into the river. They burnt our houses, killed what few cattle and horses they could find, destroyed our fruit trees, and left nothing but bare soil and timber. But the Indians had eloped and were not to be found ...

The weather by this time had become cold and stormy; and as we were destitute of houses and food too, I immediately resolved to take my children and look out for myself without delay. With this intention I took two of my little ones on my back, bade the other three follow, and the same night arrived on the Gardow flats, where I have ever since resided.

Source: James E. Seaver, *Life of Mary Jemison: DEH-HE-WÄ-MIS* (New York: Miller, Orton & Mulligan, 1856), pp. 54, 58–59.

11   William A. Whitehead on New Jersey's Early Female Voters, 1858

Historian William Whitehead wrote this history of New Jersey's experiment with female suffrage at a time when newly organized women's rights activists demanded the right to vote. Despite its birth in revolutionaries' calls for "no taxation without representation," Whitehead viewed women's suffrage as fundamentally flawed, a violation of proper etiquette as well as idealized gender roles. Since the New Jersey constitution only enfranchised male and female property owners, the number of women who could vote was limited. Female voters also had to travel long distances and brave unruly polling places to exercise their right. As Whitehead indicates, partisan accusations of voter fraud eventually caused the legislature to repeal the statute enfranchising women. New Jersey disenfranchised its free black population at the same time.

In 1790, however, a revision of the election law then in force was proposed, and upon the committee of the Legislature to whom the subject was referred was Mr. Joseph Cooper, of West Jersey, a prominent member of the Society of Friends. As the regulations of that society authorized females to vote in matters relating thereto, Mr. Cooper claimed for them the like privilege in matters connected with the State, and to support his views, quoted the provisions of the Constitution as sanctioning such a course. It was therefore to satisfy him that the committee consented to report a bill in which the expression, "he or she," applied to the voter, was introduced into the section specifying the necessary qualifications; thus giving a legislative endorsement of the alleged meaning of the Constitution. Still, no cases of females voting by virtue of this more definite provision are on record, and we are warranted in believing that the women of New Jersey then, as now, were not apt to overstep the bounds of decorum, or intrude where their characteristic modesty and self-respect might be wounded.

This law and its supplements were repealed in 1797, and it is some proof that the peculiar provision under review had not been availed of to any extent, if at all (as its evil consequences would otherwise have become apparent), that we find similar phraseology introduced into the new act. The right of suffrage was conferred upon "all free inhabitants of this State of full age," etc., thus adopting the language of the Constitution with the addition of the word "free," and "no person shall be entitled to vote in any other township or precinct than that in which he or she doth actually reside," etc., and in two other places is the possible difference in the sex of the voters recognized.

The first occasion on which females voted, of which any precise information has been obtained, was at an election held this year (1797) at Elizabethtown, Essex County, for members of the Legislature. The candidates between whom the greatest rivalry existed, were John Condit and William Crane, the heads of what were known a year or two later as the "Federal Republican" and "Federal Aristocratic" parties, the former the candidate of Newark and the northern portions of the county, and the latter the candidate of Elizabethtown and the adjoining country, for the Council. Under the impression that the candidates would poll nearly the same number of votes, the Elizabethtown leaders thought that by a bold *coup d'etat* they might secure the success of Mr. Crane. At a late hour of the day, and, as I have been informed, just before the close of the poll, a number of females were brought up, and under the provisions of the existing laws, allowed to vote; but the manœuvre was unsuccessful, the majority for Mr. Condit, in the county, being ninety-three, notwithstanding. These proceedings were made the topic of two or three brief articles in the *Newark Sentinel*, in one of which the fact that "no less than seventy-five women were polled at the late election in a neighboring borough," was used as a pretended argument for the admission of females to office, and to service in the diplomatic corps; while another ironically asserts that "too much credit can not be given to the Federal leaders of Elizabethtown for the heroic virtue displayed in advancing in a body to the poll to support their favorite candidates."

So discreditable was this occurrence thought, that although another closely contested election took place the following year, we do not find any other than male votes deposited then, in Essex County, or elsewhere, until the Presidential election of 1800, between Mr. Adams and Mr. Jefferson, at which females voted very generally throughout the State; and such continued to be the practice until the passage of the act positively excluding them from the polls. At first the law had been so construed as to admit single women only, but as the practice extended, the construction of the privilege became broader and was made to include females eighteen years old, married or single; and even women of color. At a contested election in Hunterdon County, in 1802, the votes of two or three such, actually electing a member of the Legislature. It is remarkable that these proceedings did not sooner bring about a repeal of the laws which were thought to sanction them; but that event did not occur until 1807, and it is noticeable that, as the practice originated in Essex County, so the flagrant abuses which resulted from it reached their maximum in that county, and brought about its prohibition.

Source: Elizabeth Cady Stanton, Susan B. Anthony, and Matilda Joslyn Gage (eds.), *The History of Woman Suffrage*, Vol. 1: *1848–1861* (New York, NY: Fowler and Wells, Publishers, 1881), pp. 447–448. Available by subscription at http://asp6new. alexanderstreet.com/was2/was2.object.details.aspx?dorpid=100686358

Suggested Questions for Discussion

1   What was the impact of the American Revolution on the lives of white, black, and Native women?
2   In different ways, both images in this chapter represent liberty. What possibilities do these images suggest for white and black women after the American Revolution?
3   Teachers and writers like Sarah Pierce and Judith Sargent Murray helped shape a new ideal of American womanhood. In their view, what were women's moral, intellectual, and political obligations to the new nation?

1) White Women adv. → education, personal liberties
natives = lives destroyed
black- some got better (freedom) while some got worse

2.) Both had more oppurtunity for freedom, or that freedom was coming their way

3.) Women needed education. How are they supposed to raise men, when their education was lacking?

Chapter 5   Awakenings, 1810–1835

1 *Scenes from a Seminary for Young Ladies, c.1810–1820*

In the early years of the republic, the number of schools for young women expanded. This watercolor on silk fabric (shown on next page) depicts two scenes from an unidentified female academy. In the left image, a woman plays the piano, a traditional talent that young women might have learned before the American Revolution. The image on the right shows how female education changed, including typically "male" subjects like geography, math, and science. As historian Mary Kelley argues, women's greater access to education allowed them "to envision themselves as historical actors who had claim to rights and obligations of citizenship."[1] Educated women embarked on careers as teachers, writers, and activists, determined to engage in national conversations about gender, race, religion, and politics.

---

2 Frederick Douglass Describes His Mother, 1845

In this excerpt from his Narrative of the Life of Frederick Douglass, *Douglass recalls what little he knew of his enslaved mother. The property of a large plantation owner in Maryland, Douglass escaped and became one of the*

---

[1] Mary Kelley, *Learning to Stand and Speak: Women, Education, and Public Life in America's Republic* (Chapel Hill: University of North Carolina Press, 2006), 17.

Women in American History to 1880: A Documentary Reader, by Carol Faulkner © 2011 Blackwell Publishing Ltd.

Figure 5.1   Scenes from a Seminary for Young Ladies (*detail*), *c.1810–1820. Reproduced courtesy of Saint Louis Art Museum, Museum Purchase and funds given by the Decorative Arts Society.*

Source: Miniature Panorama: *Scenes from a Seminary for Young Ladies* (detail), *c.*1810–1820. Watercolor and ink on silk, 7 1/16 × 96 5/8 in. (17.9 × 245.4 cm). Saint Louis Art Museum, Museum Purchase and funds given by the Decorative Arts Society 89: 1976.

anti-slavery movement's most powerful speakers and writers. At this point in his career, Douglass was affiliated with William Lloyd Garrison's American Anti-Slavery Society. Garrisonian abolitionists relied on moral arguments to expose the evils of slavery. Douglass simultaneously criticizes slave owners' callous disregard for enslaved families and illuminates his mother's extraordinary effort to see her son.

My mother was named Harriet Bailey. She was the daughter of Isaac and Betsey Bailey, both colored, and quite dark. My mother was of a darker complexion than either my grandmother or grandfather.

My father was a white man. He was admitted to be such by all I ever heard speak of my parentage. The opinion was also whispered that my master was my father; but of the correctness of this opinion, I know nothing; the means of knowing was withheld from me. My mother and I were separated when I was but an infant – before I knew her as my mother. It is a common custom, in the part of Maryland from which I ran away, to part children from their mothers at a very early age. Frequently, before the child has reached its twelfth month, its mother is taken from it, and hired out on some farm a considerable distance off, and the child is placed under the care of an old woman, too old for field labor. For what this separation is done, I do not know, unless it be to hinder the development of the child's affection toward its mother, and to blunt and destroy the natural affection of the mother for the child. This is the inevitable result.

I never saw my mother, to know her as such, more than four or five times in my life; and each of these times was very short in duration, and at night. She was hired by a Mr. Stewart, who lived about twelve miles from my home. She made her journeys to see me in the night, travelling the whole distance on foot, after the performance of her day's work. She was a field hand, and a whipping is the penalty of not being in the field at sunrise, unless a slave has special permission from his or her master to the contrary – a permission which they seldom get, and one that gives to him that gives it the proud name of being a kind master. I do not recollect of ever seeing my mother by the light of day. She was with me in the night. She would lie down with me, and get me to sleep, but long before I waked she was gone. Very little communication ever took place between us. Death soon ended what little we could have while she lived, and with it her hardships and suffering. She died when I was about seven years old, on one of my master's farms, near Lee's Mill. I was not allowed to be present during her illness, at her death, or burial. She was gone long before I knew any thing about it. Never having enjoyed, to any considerable extent, her soothing presence, her tender and watchful care, I received the tidings of her death with much the same emotions I should have probably felt at the death of a stranger.

Called thus suddenly away, she left me without the slightest intimation of who my father was. The whisper that my master was my father, may or may not be true; and, true or false, it is of but little consequence to my purpose whilst the fact remains, in all its glaring odiousness, that slaveholders have ordained, and by law established, that the children of slave women shall in all cases follow the condition of their mothers; and this is done too obviously to administer to their own lusts, and make a gratification of their wicked desires profitable as well as pleasurable; for by this cunning arrangement, the slaveholder, in cases not a few, sustains to his slaves the double relation of master and father ...

Source: *Narrative of the Life of Frederick Douglass: An American Slave* (The Anti Slavery Office, 1845), in David W. Blight (ed.), *Narrative of the Life of Frederick Douglass* (New York: Bedford Books, 1993), pp. 39–41.

3 Catharine Beecher, "Circular Addressed to Benevolent Ladies of the U. States," 1829

After his election in 1828, President Andrew Jackson supported the efforts of Georgia legislators and settlers to appropriate Cherokee land. His policies aroused opposition from many benevolent white northerners. In 1829, Jeremiah Evarts, of the American Board of Commissioners of Foreign Missions, a Congregationalist organization with a long history of involvement with the Cherokee, published a series of articles against Indian removal in the National Intelligencer. *He also asked Catharine Beecher, daughter of the famous evangelical minister Lyman Beecher and principal of the Hartford Female Seminary, to mobilize women against Cherokee removal. Her circular launched the first petition drive among women. Building on their work in charitable and missionary societies, hundreds of women signed anti-removal petitions.*

The present crisis in the affairs of the Indian nations in the United States demands the immediate and interested attention of all who make any claims to benevolence or humanity. The calamities now hanging over them threaten not only these relies [relics] of an interesting race, but, if there is a Being who avenges the wrongs of the oppressed, are causes of alarm to our whole country.

The following are facts of the case: – This continent was once possessed only by the Indians, and earliest accounts represent them as a race numerous, warlind powerful. When our forefathers sought refuge from oppression on these shores, this people supplied their necessities, and ministered to their comfort; and though some of them, when they saw the white man continually encroaching upon their land, fought bravely for their existence and their country, yet often, too, the Indian has shed his blood to protect and sustain our infant nation.

As we have risen in greatness and glory, the Indian nations have faded away. Their proud and powerful tribes have gone; their noble sachems and mighty warriors are heard of no more; and it is said the Indian often comes to the borders of his limited retreat to gaze on the beautiful country no longer his own, and to cry with bitterness at the remembrance of past greatness and power.

Ever since the existence of this nation, our general government, pursuing the course alike of policy and benevolence, have acknowledged these people as free and independent nations, and has protected them in the quiet possession of their lands. In repeated treaties with the Indians, the United States, by the hands of the most distinguished statesmen, after purchasing the greater part of their best lands, have *promised* them *"to continue the guarantee of the remainder of their country* FOR EVER." And so strictly has government guarded the Indian's right to his lands, that even to go on to their boundaries to survey the land, subjects to heavy fines and imprisonment.

Our government also, with parental care, has persuaded the Indians to forsake their savage life, and to adopt the habits and pursuits of civilized nations, while the charities of Christians and the labors of missionaries have sent to them the blessings of the gospel to purify and enlighten. The laws and regular forms of a civilized government are instituted; their simple and beautiful language, by the remarkable ingenuity of one of their race, has become a written language with its own peculiar alphabet, and, by the printing press, is sending forth among these people the principles of knowledge, and liberty, and religion. Their fields are beginning to smile with the labours of the husbandman; their villages are busy with the toils of the mechanic and the artisan; schools are rising in their hamlets, and the temple of the living God is seen among their forests ...

Nor are we to think of these people only as naked and wandering savages. The various grades of intellect and refinement exist among them as among us; and those who visit their chieftains and families of the higher class, speak with wonder and admiration of their dignified propriety, nobleness of appearance, and refined characteristics as often exhibited in both sexes. Among them are men fitted by native talents to shine among the statesmen of any land, and who have received no inferior degree of cultivation. Among them, also, are those who, by honest industry, have assembled around them most of the comforts and many of the elegancies of life.

But the lands of this people are *claimed* to be embraced within the limits of some of our southern states, and as they are fertile and valuable they are demanded by the whites as their own possessions, and efforts are making to dispossess the Indians of their native soil. And such is the singular state of concurring circumstances, that it has become almost a certainty that these people are to have their lands torn from them, and to be driven into western wilds and to final annihilation, unless the feelings of a humane and Christian nation shall be aroused to prevent the unhallowed sacrifice ...

It appears, then, that measures are fast ripening, which, if put in execution, are to exterminate the Indians. If they remain where they are, and the laws of the different states are permitted to be extended over them, and their lands divided among the whites, intoxication, quarrels, and unrestrained oppressions, will soon change them to vagabonds, and ensure their final extinction. Should they be driven to the west, a fate no less cruel awaits them there, where they lose even the last sad hope of reposing from their oppressions in the sepulchres of their fathers, and beneath their native soil.

But why should this deed of infamy and shame be perpetrated before the nations of the earth, and in the face of high Heaven? Are the people who claim the Indian's country in need of land? They have more than they can possibly occupy for a hundred years to come. Has not our government power to prevent this deed? If our government has not power to fulfil its treaties, it would be a most humiliating fact thus to be exposed before the nations of the earth. But our president is empowered by the constitution to issue his proclamation forbidding any such encroachments as are threatened; and if this is disregarded, he has power, by his sole authority, to command *the whole military force of our nation* to protect and sustain the Indian in his rights ...

It cannot but seem a matter of grief and astonishment that such facts exist in this country – in a nation blessed with wealth, and power, and laws, and religion, and whose possessions reach from ocean to ocean. But humiliating as is the reflection, *the Indians must perish*, unless their destruction can be averted by a most decided and energetic expression of the wishes and feelings of a Christian nation, addressed to the congress now assembling, and which is soon to decide their doom.

Have not then the females of this country some duties devolving upon them in relation to this helpless race? – They are protected from the blinding influence of party spirit, and the asperities of political violence. They have nothing to do with any struggle for power, nor any right to dictate the decisions of those that rule over them. – But they may *feel* for the distressed; they may stretch out the supplicating hand for them, and by their prayers strive to avert the calamities that are impending over them. It may be, that female petitioners can lawfully be heard, even by the highest rulers of our land. Why may we not approach and supplicate that we and our dearest friends may be saved from the awful curses denounced on all who oppress the poor and needy, by Him whose anger is to be dreaded more than the wrath of man; who can "blast us with the breath of his nostrils," and scatter our hopes like chaff before the storm. It may be this will be *forbidden*; yet still we remember the Jewish princess who, being sent to supplicate for a nation's life, was thus reproved for hesitating even when *death* stared her in the way: "If thou altogether hold thy peace at this time, then shall deliverance arise from another place; but thou and thy father's house shall be destroyed. And who knoweth whether thou art come to the kingdom for such a cause as this?"

To woman it is given to administer the sweet charities of life, and to *sway the empire of affection*; and to her it may also be said, "Who knoweth whether thou art come to the kingdom for such a cause as this?"

In the days of chivalry, at the female voice, thousands of lances would have been laid in rest to protect the helpless and oppressed. But these are days of literature, refinement, charity, and religion; and may we not appeal to nobler champions than chivalry could boast? Will the liberal and refined, those who are delighted with the charms of eloquence and poetry; those who love the legends of romance, and the records of antiquity; those who celebrate and admire the stern virtues of Roman warriors and patriots; will these permit such a race to be swept from the earth? – a nation who have emerged from the deepest shades of antiquity; whose story, and whose wild and interesting traits are becoming the theme of the poet and novelist; who command a native eloquence unequalled for pathos and sublimity; whose stern fortitude, and unbending courage, exceed the Roman renown? Will the naturalist, who laments the extinction of the mammoth race of the forest, allow this singular and interesting species of the *human* race to cease from the earth? Will those who boast of liberty, and feel their breasts throb at the name of freedom and their country, will they permit the free and noble Indian to be driven from his native land, or to crouch and perish under the scourge of oppression? And those whose hearts thrill at the magic sound of *home*, and turn with delightful remembrance to the woods and valleys of their childhood and youth, will they allow this helpless race to be forced for ever from such blessed scenes, and to look back upon them with hopeless regret and despair?

You who gather the youthful group around your fireside, and rejoice in their future hopes and joys, will you forget that the poor Indian loves his children too, and would as bitterly mourn over all their blasted hopes? And, while surrounded by such treasured blessings, ponder with dread and awe these fearful words of Him, who thus forbids the violence, and records the malediction of those, who either as individuals, or as nations, shall oppress the needy and helpless.

"Thou shalt not vex the stranger not oppress him, for ye were strangers in the land. If thou afflict them, and they cry at all unto me, I will surely hear their cry: and my wrath shall wax hot, and I will kill you with the sword, and your wives shall be widows, and your children fatherless."

P.S. Should the facts alluded to in the preceding be doubted, they can be fully substantiated by consulting the communications signed "William Penn," and the statements made and signed by many of the most distinguished philanthropists of our country, which are to be found in the recent numbers of our public prints.

This communication was written and sent abroad solely by the female hand. Let every woman who peruses it, exert that influence in society which falls within her lawful province, and endeavour by every suitable expedient to interest the feelings of her friends, relatives, and acquaintances, in behalf of this people, that are ready to perish. *A few weeks* must decide this interesting and important question, and after that time sympathy and regret will all be in vain.

Source: "Circular Addressed to Benevolent Ladies of the U. States," 1 December 1829. Printed in *Christian Advocate and Journal*, 25 December 1829, pp. 65–66 (American Periodical Series, 1800–1850, Microfilm, Reel 1749), in Kathryn Kish Sklar, *How Did the Removal of the Cherokee Nation from Georgia Shape Women's Activism in the North, 1917–1838?* Available by subscription at http://asp6new. alexanderstreet.com.was2/was2.object.details.aspx?dorpid=1000686547

4 Cherokee Women's Petition against Removal, 1831

In 1830, President Jackson signed the Indian Removal Act, giving him the power to negotiate a removal treaty with the Cherokee. As members of one of the "civilized" tribes, Cherokee women had lost much of their traditional influence over tribal affairs. In this letter, published in the Cherokee Phoenix, *women explained their intervention by referring to the "present difficulties." Though the US Supreme Court ruled in favor of the Cherokee and their allies in Worcester v. Georgia in 1832, Jackson ignored the decision. In 1835, the federal government and one faction of the Cherokee negotiated the Treaty of New Echota, providing for the removal of Cherokee from Georgia to west of the Mississippi.*

To the Committee and Council,

We the females, residing in Salequoree and Pine Log, believing that the present difficulties and embarrassments under which this nation is placed demands a full expression of the mind of every individual, on the subject of emigrating to Arkansas, would take upon ourselves to address you. Although it is not common for our sex to take part in public measures, we nevertheless feel justified in expressing our sentiments on any subject where our interest is as much at stake as any other part of the community.

We believe the present plan of the General Government to effect our removal West of the Mississippi, and thus obtain our lands for the use of the State of Georgia, to be highly oppressive, cruel and unjust. And we sincerely hope there is no consideration which can induce our citizens to forsake the land of our fathers of which they have been in possession from time immemorial, and thus compel us, against our will, to undergo the toils and difficulties of removing with our helpless families hundreds of miles to unhealthy and unproductive country. We hope therefore the Committee and Council will take into deep consideration our deplorable situation, and do everything in their power to avert such a state of things. And we trust by a prudent course their transactions with the General Government will enlist in our behalf the sympathies of the good people of the United States.

Source: Theda Purdue and Michael Greene (eds.), *The Cherokee Removal* (New York: Bedford, 1995), p. 126.

5 Mrs. Mary Mathews to Mrs. Lydia Finney, 1831

From September 1830 to June 1831, in the midst of the evangelical ferment known as the Second Great Awakening, the fiery minister Charles Grandison Finney led a series of revivals in Rochester, New York. Mrs. Mary Mathews, wife of the wealthy Selah Mathews, was one of his earliest and most important converts. As her letter shows, women were key figures in promoting evangelical Christianity. Dedicated to purging the world of sin, Mary Mathews and other evangelical women joined missionary, moral reform, anti-slavery, and temperance associations. They also founded maternal associations, orphan asylums, and homes for "friendless" and "virtuous" women.

Rochester August 1, 1831:

My dear Mrs. Finney.

You may rest assured that it affords me no small degree of pleasure that the time has arrived when I have the prospect at least of a hidden hour to devote to you. You can easily believe that my time has been occupied when I tell you that since the receipt of your letter I have been night and day watching by the sick bed of my husband. He is now I trust convalescing but is unable to sit up thru the day. He has never at any time been what physicians would call alarmingly ill – but wives and physicians feel differently.

I was really rejoiced to hear from you my dear Mrs. Finney – and should have written long since if I could have ascertained where you were. You speak of your last visit here. I did feel really grieved that you would stay so long in the village without ever calling upon me and in spite of myself found I had some unsanctified feelings about it. I really supposed I had laid you under a sort of obligation to stay with me whenever you came to Rochester – whether your inclination would have you to do it or not. However it is all over and I had almost forgotten it. And next time you come you shall go where you choose and I will try to feel right about it.

Now I will endeavor to answer some of your questions and tell you all about Rochester. To commence with Mrs. Bissell, her health is pretty good. She seems cheerful but very solemn. Then our mother and sister have been to visit her and Mrs. Hillo of Auburn – and after all her violent grief and nervous feeling seemed just as usual and I hope Mrs. Bissell will be troubled no longer with her bursts of grief. Mrs. Bissell lives and acts like a Christian and seems perfectly submissive to the will of her Heavenly Father. Mrs. Ely has left Rochester. Mrs. Ely has returned – says her health is tolerable.

My sister was confined on the 4th of July. Her health is now nearly restored. She has a daughter which she <u>honors</u> with the name of Mary Matthews. Mrs. Atkinson gave birth to a son about a week previous. She is still in very feeble health. Mrs [illegible] wishes to be specially remembered to you and says she is still hoping and expecting the conversion of her husband but the fact is she does think he has her conviction – altho he does not prefer our Christian duty – and I fear she has let him know it. Horace Bissell "would to be a Christian" yet – but God is not willing he thinks. You enquire about the state of religious feeling here ... I will state facts. Our new ministers were installed on Wednesday and Thursday and the meetings have been continued until to day and I think they number 10 or 12 conversions. I have been unable to attend but twice we have a tolerable congregation. ... There has been but little excitement – least I think from what I can learn it has worked up many of our church and the 2d church. ... I cannot give you as particular account of the state of things as I wish I could as I have been too long occupied to the house – but I think I can say with truth that there is much more feeling just now than there has been during the summer. Some most blasphemous handbills have been issued. A Theatre bill made out performance at the brick theater in which Mr. [illegible] was to perform the Tragedy of "Man made God" and act off Mr. Finney and ... say truly blasphemous things ... When will the church of God be as faithful to the Heavenly Father as Satan's followers are to him!

You enquire about the Maternal Societies. There have now been found in the other churches – and I believe the one in our church is still in existence ... There has been a great deal of sickness here during the summer – especially among children – and mothers have been mainly occupied at home.

There have been several marriages here among our acquaintances. I have called upon Mrs. Gardner – and she really has improved wonderfully in refinement of manner and seems to feel very much for the conversion of her husband ... She can't prevail upon her husband to attend evening meetings but she goes without him when her health will allow of it. She says she will go to church when she chooses, notwithstanding her matrimonial vow of obedience ...

I presume you are anxious to hear what sort of a minister we have got at last and I will tell you. He is a man of a lovely spirit – very easy and accessible in his manners and quite sensible and agreeable ... His preaching is good – but he lacks energy. I can't actually judge fairly of him as he has been in miserable health and does not seem so much waked up as I wish our minister to feel. I only wish he had sit [sic] at Mr. Finney's feet a short time. I think he would be just about right. He approves of all the new measures ... Your husband's spiritual children want revival preaching and are unsatisfied with any church falls short of it. Do not imagine that there is any dissatisfaction – far from it – we love Mr. Lyons very much and his wife too – and we have only to pray for him to make him right.

I do not wish to love my minister as I did Mr. Finney for I believe it was a species of idolatry. I think the Lord has shown me my sin ... and begin to feel that after all he is a man. Do give my love to him when you write – and say to him that I hope he does not forget his children in Rochester. You enquire whether we are growing in grace. I think I can say that my husband is a growing consistent Christian. I am half way between sleeping and waking but begin to think it is now high time to wake out of "sleep." Do remember us in your prayers ...

Source: Mrs. Mary Mathews to Mrs. Lydia Finney, August 12, 1831, Charles
Grandison Finney Papers, Oberlin College Library.

6 Maria Stewart, Lecture Delivered at Franklin Hall, 1832

*Maria Stewart (1803–1879) was the first African American woman to speak
publicly to mixed audiences of men and women. An active participant in
Boston's radical, interracial anti-slavery movement, Stewart combined her
evangelical fervor with a political commitment to ending slavery and racial
prejudice. Her personal experiences as a former indentured servant, a widow,
and a self-supporting woman informed this speech on the economic and
educational impact of racial prejudice on African American girls. She decried
the segregated labor market that consigned black women to a life of domestic
service. Facing condemnation from black male leaders because of her sex, she
left Boston and became a teacher.*

Why sit ye here and die? If we say we will go to a foreign land, the famine
and the pestilence are there, and there we shall die. If we sit here, we shall
die. Come let us plead our cause before the whites: if they save us alive, we
shall live – and if they kill us, we shall but die.

Methinks I heard a spiritual interrogation – 'Who shall go forward, and
take off the reproach that is cast upon the people of color? Shall it be a
woman?' And my heart made this reply – 'If it is they will, be it even so,
Lord Jesus!'

I have heard much respecting the horrors of slavery; but may Heaven
forbid that the generality of my color throughout these United States
should experience any more of its horrors than to be a servant of servants,
or hewers of wood and drawers of water [Joshua 9:23]! Tell us no more
of southern slavery; for with few exceptions, though I may be very erroneous in my opinion, yet I consider our condition but little better than
that. Yet, after all, methinks there are no chains so galling as those that
bind the soul, and exclude it from the vast field of useful and scientific
knowledge. O, had I received the advantages of an early education, my
ideas would, ere now, have expanded far and wide; but, alas! I possess
nothing but moral capability – no teachings but the teachings of the
Holy Spirit.

I have asked several individuals of my sex, who transact business for
themselves, if providing our girls were to give them the most satisfactory
references, they would not be willing to grant them an equal opportunity
with others? Their reply has been – for their own part, they had no

objection; but as it was not the custom, were they to take them into their employ, they would be in danger of losing the public patronage.

And such is the powerful force of prejudice. Let our girls possess whatever amiable qualities of soul they may; let their characters be fair and spotless as innocence itself; let their natural taste and ingenuity be what they may; it is impossible for scarce an individual of them to rise above the condition of servants. Ah! why is this cruel and unfeeling distinction? Is it merely because God has made our complexion to vary? If it be, O shame to soft, relenting humanity! "Tell it not in Gath! publish it not in the streets of Askelon!" [2 Samuel 1:20]. Yet, after all, methinks were the American free people of color to turn their attention more assiduously to moral worth and intellectual improvement, this would be the result: prejudice would gradually diminish, and the whites would be compelled to say, unloose those fetters! . . .

I do not consider it derogatory, my friends, for persons to live out to service. There are many whose inclination leads them to aspire no higher; and I would highly commend the performance of almost anything for an honest livelihood; but where constitutional strength is wanting, labor of this kind, in its mildest form, is painful. And doubtless many are the prayers that have ascended to Heaven from Afric's daughters for strength to perform their work. Oh, many are the tears that have been shed for the want of that strength! Most of our color have dragged out a miserable existence of servitude from the cradle to the grave. And what literary acquirement can be made, or useful knowledge derived, from either maps, books, or charts, by those who continually drudge from Monday morning until Sunday noon? O, ye fairer sisters, whose hands are never soiled, whose nerves and muscles are never strained, go learn by experience! Had we had the opportunity that you have had, to improve our moral and mental faculties, what would have hindered our intellects from being as bright, our manners from being as dignified as yours? Had it been our lot to have been nursed in the lap of affluence and ease, and to have basked beneath the smiles and sunshine of fortune, should we not have naturally supposed that we were never made to toil? And why are not our forms as delicate, and our constitutions as slender, as yours? Is not the workmanship as curious and complete? Have pity upon us, have pity upon us, O ye who have hearts to feel for other's woes; for the hand of God has touched us. Owing to the disadvantages under which we labor, there are many flowers among us that are

> . . . born to bloom unseen
> And waste their fragrance on the desert air.

My beloved brethren, as Christ has died in vain for those who will not accept his offered mercy, so will it be vain for the advocates of freedom to spend their breath on our behalf, unless with united hearts and souls you make some mighty efforts to raise your sons and daughters from the horrible state of servitude and degradation in which they are placed. It is upon you that woman depends; she can do but little besides using her influence; and it is for her sake and yours that I have come forward and made myself a hissing and a reproach among the people [Jeremiah 29:18]; for I am also one of the wretched and miserable daughters of the descendants of fallen Africa. Do you ask, why are you wretched and miserable? I reply, look at many of the most worthy and most interesting of us doomed to spend our lives in gentlemen's kitchens. Look at our young men, smart, active and energetic, with souls filled with ambitious fire; if they look forward, alas! What are their prospects? They can be nothing but the humblest of laborers, on account of their dark complexions; hence many of them lose their ambition, and become worthless. Look at our middle-aged men, clad in their rusty plaids and coats; in winter, every cent they earn goes to buy their wood and pay their rents; the poor wives also toil beyond their strength, to help support their families. Look at our aged sires, whose heads are whitened with the frosts of seventy winters, with their old wood-saws on their backs. Alas, what keeps us so? Prejudice, ignorance and poverty. But ah! methinks our oppression is soon to come to an end; yea, before the Majesty of heaven, our groans and cries have reached the ears of the Lord of Saboath [James 5:4]. As the prayers and tears of Christians will avail the finally impenitent nothing; neither will the prayers and tears of the friends of humanity avail us of anything, unless we possess a spirit of virtuous emulation within our breasts. Did the pilgrims, when they first landed on these shores, quietly compose themselves and say, "The Britons have all the money and all the power, and we must continue their servants forever?" Did they sluggishly sigh and say, "Our lot is hard, the Indians own the soil, and we cannot cultivate it?" No; they first made powerful efforts to raise themselves, and then God raised up those illustrious patriots, WASHINGTON and LAFAYETTE, to assist and defend them. And, my brethren, have you made a powerful effort? Have you prayed the legislature for mercy's sake to grant you all the rights and privileges of free citizens, that your daughters may rise to that degree of respectability which true merit deserves, and your sons above the servile situations which most of them fill?

Source: Marilyn Richardson (ed.), *Maria W. Stewart: America's First Black Woman Political Writer* (Bloomington: Indiana University Press, 1987), pp. 45–49.

7 Elizabeth Margaret Chandler, "On the Use of Free Produce," 1832

In 1829, poet Elizabeth Margaret Chandler (1807–1834) became the editor of the "Ladies' Repository" in Benjamin Lundy's anti-slavery newspaper the Genius of Universal Emancipation. *In this editorial, Chandler chided her female readers for continuing to buy the products of slavery, such as sugar and cotton, for their families. American women's boycott of British products during the Revolutionary War had inspired a successful British boycott of sugar in the 1790s. In 1824, an Englishwoman named Elizabeth Heyrick revived interest in "free" produce, attracting Chandler and other American women to the cause. Evoking middle-class women's role as moral guardians of their families, as well as their increasing prominence as consumers, Chandler urges wives and mothers to purify their hearts and their homes from the evil of slavery.*

This is a subject to which we have already frequently adverted, yet convinced as we are of the utility of that method of opposition to slavery, we believe we cannot err in again placing it before the attention of our readers. The use of Free Produce, though it has become much more general than formerly, is still far too limited. In very many sections of our country, none except the slave cultivated articles can be procured, though many persons in such places would undoubtedly give the preference to those of a contrary character, if they could be readily obtained. This is certainly to be regretted; yet there is sincerity and steadiness of purpose we believe that difficulties of this kind may be generally, at least in some measure, overcome. If in every neighborhood those families who are friendly to the rise of free produce would unite in requesting their storekeeper to procure for them the desired articles, we should suppose self-interest, if no better motive, would induce him to oblige them. Where this arrangement cannot be made, and no other method can be fallen upon, we would earnestly advise the friends of our cause, to provide themselves with no supplies in advance, and to carefully avoid the use of superfluous articles. But, again we repeat, a little exertion is often all that is necessary to obtain the wished for object.

To such of our sex as voluntarily give the preference to the products of slave labor, we would offer a word of serious expostulation on the inconsistency of their conduct. They would doubtlessly deny any wish to perpetuate the present condition of the slaves; nay, they will probably assert that their warmest wishes are engaged in behalf of abolition, and that the most active friends of that cause do not exceed themselves, in detestation of slavery. How ill do such protestations accord with their conduct. They abhor the system of oppression, and yet contribute their money to pay the slaveholder for maintaining it! They commiserate the slave, but instead of endeavoring to afford him relief, their whole assistance is given to those who retain him in bondage! They would probably advance many arguments in their justification, but unfortunately the slaveholder makes use of equally strong, and not unfrequently the very same, reasonings in favor of *his* conduct. And though we would not judge harshly, and are willing to make all due allowances for the effects of education and custom, we believe that both of them are actuated by the same principle of self-interest, though perhaps under different modifications. We entreat them to review more carefully the ground on which they are standing; to reflect on the strange impropriety of the course they are pursuing. How can they reconcile it to themselves that they, Christian mothers and wives and daughters, with all the kind and gentle sympathies of woman's nature playing about their hearts, should be accessories in supporting one of the most heinous systems of oppression ever known in the world. If an entire abstinence from the products of slave-labor is considered impracticable, certainly they ought to make use of them only when it is entirely out of their power to procure those of the other class. And surely this cannot be too much to ask any one, in support of such a cause as the overthrow of inhumanity and the relief of wretchedness.

Source: *Genius of Universal Emancipation*, January 1832.

8 Jarena Lee, "My Call to Preach the Gospel," 1836

Born in 1783, Jarena Lee was at the height of her career as a Methodist exhorter when she published this pamphlet. In 1804, after hearing a sermon by Richard Allen in Philadelphia, she converted to Methodism. As she describes in this excerpt, he initially discouraged her from preaching. In 1816, several years after this conversation occurred, Allen founded the African Methodist Episcopal (AME) Church, the first independent black denomination in the country. By the 1820s, Allen approved Lee's religious calling as an exhorter. She preached across the Northeast, traveling from the slave state of Maryland and into the western frontier of New York and Ohio. After delivering her sermons, Lee handed out copies of her narrative. By 1852, however, the well-established AME Church withdrew its support for Lee and other female preachers.

Between four and five years after my sanctification, on a certain time, an impressive silence fell upon me, and I stood as if some one was about to speak to me, yet I had no such thought in my heart. But to my utter surprise there seemed to sound a voice which I thought I distinctly heard, and most certainly understood, which said to me, "Go preach the Gospel!" I immediately replied aloud, "No one will believe me." Again I listened, and again the same voice seemed to say, "Preach the Gospel; I will put words in your mouth, and will turn your enemies to become your friends."

. . . Two days later, I went to see the preacher in charge of the African Society, who was the Rev. Richard Allen, the same before named in these pages, to tell him that I felt it my duty to preach the gospel. But as I drew near the street in which his house was, which was in the city of Philadelphia, my courage began to fail me; so terrible did the cross appear, it seemed that I should not be able to bear it. Previous to my setting out to go to see him, so agitated was my mind, that my appetite for my daily food failed me entirely. Several times on my way there, I turned back again but as often I felt my strength again renewed, and I soon found that the nearer I approached to the house of the minister, the less was the fear. Accordingly, as soon as I came to the door, my fears subsided, the cross was removed, all things appeared pleasant – I was tranquil.

I now told him, that the Lord had revealed it to me, that I must preach the gospel. He replied by asking, in what sphere I wished to move in? I said, among the Methodists. He then replied, that a Mrs. Cook, a Methodist lady, had also some time before requested the same privilege; who it was believed, had done much good in the way of exhortation, and holding prayer meetings; and who had been permitted to do so by some verbal license of the preacher in charge at the time. But as to women preaching, he said that our Discipline knew nothing at all about it – that it did not call for women preachers. This I was glad to hear, because it removed the fear of the cross – but not no sooner did this feeling cross my mind, than I found that a love of souls had in a measure departed from me; that holy energy which burned within me, as a fire, began to be smothered. This I soon perceived.

O how careful ought we to be, lest through our by-laws of church government and discipline, we bring into disrepute even the word of life. For as unseemly as it may appear now-a-days for a woman to preach, it should be remembered that nothing is impossible with God. And why should it be thought impossible, heterodox, or improper, for a woman to preach? seeing the Saviour died for the woman as well as the man.

If a man may preach, because the Saviour died for him, why not the woman? seeing as he died for her also. Is he not a whole Saviour, instead of a half one? As those who hold it wrong for a woman to preach, would seem to make it appear.

Did not Mary *first* preach the risen Saviour, and is not the doctrine of the resurrection the very climax of Christianity – hangs not all our hope on this, as argued by St. Paul? Then did not Mary, a woman, preach the gospel? for she preached the resurrection of the crucified Son of God.

But some will say, that Mary did not expound the Scripture, therefore, she did not preach, in the proper sense of the term. To this I reply, it may be that the term *preach*, in those primitive times, did not mean exactly what it is now *made* to mean; perhaps it was a great deal more simple then, than it is now: – if it were not, the unlearned fishermen could not have preached the gospel at all, as they had no learning.

To this it may be replied, by those who are determined not to believe that it is right for a woman to preach, that the disciples, though they were fishermen, and ignorant of letters too, were inspired so to do. To which I would reply, that though they were inspired, yet that inspiration did not save them from showing their ignorance of letters, and of man's wisdom; this the multitude soon found out, by listening to the remarks of the envious Jewish priests. If then, to preach the gospel, by the gift of heaven, comes by inspiration solely, is God straitened; must he take the man exclusively? May he not, did he not, and can he not inspire a female to preach the simple story of the birth, life, death, and resurrection of our Lord, and accompany it too, with power to the sinner's heart. As for me, I am fully persuaded that the Lord called me to labour according to what I have received, in his vineyard. If he has not, how could he consistently bear testimony in favour of my poor labours, in awakening and converting sinners?

In my wanderings up and down among men, preaching according to my ability, I have frequently found families who told me they had not for several years been to a meeting, and yet, while listening to hear what God would say by this poor coloured female instrument, have believed with trembling – tears rolling down their cheers, the signs of contrition and repentance towards God. I firmly believe that I have sown seed, in the name of the Lord, which shall appear with its increase at the great day of accounts, when Christ shall come to make up his jewels.

At a certain time, I was beset with the idea, that soon or late I should fall from grace, and lose my soul at last. I was frequently called to the throne of grace about this matter, but found no relief; the temptation pursued me still. Being more and more afflicted with it, till at a certain time when the spirit strongly impressed it on my mind the enter into my closet, and carry my case once more to the Lord; the Lord enabled me to draw nigh to him, and to his mercy seat, at this time, in an extraordinary manner; for while I wrestled with him for the victory over this disposition to doubt whether I should persevere, there appeared a form of fire, about the size of a man's hand, as I was on my knees; at the same moment, there appeared to the eye of faith a man robed in a white garment, from the shoulders down to the feet; from him a voice proceeded, saying: "Thou shalt never return from the cross." Since that time I have never doubted, but believe that god will keep me until the day of redemption. Now I could adopt the very language of St. Paul, and say that nothing could have separated my soul from the love of god, which is in Christ Jesus [Rom. 8:35–39]. From that time, 1807, until the present, 1833, I have not yet doubted the power and goodness of God to keep me from falling, through sanctification of the spirit and belief of the truth.

Source: Jarena Lee, *The Life and Religious Experience of Jarena Lee* (Philadelphia, 1836), in William L. Andrews (ed.), *Sisters of the Spirit: Three Black Women's Autobiographies of the Nineteenth Century* (Bloomington: Indiana University Press, 1986), pp. 35–38.

Suggested Questions for Discussion

1   What was the impact of education and/or religious revivalism on the expansion of women's activism in the early republic?
2   How did race shape women's experience of motherhood, work, and religious revivalism?
3   Catharine Beecher and Elizabeth Margaret Chandler tried to persuade white women to use their influence on behalf of suffering Indians and slaves. How were their strategies similar or different?

Chapter 6   Contested Spheres, 1835–1845

1 Lucy Larcom, Beginning to Work, 1889

Poet Lucy Larcom (1824–1893) worked in the Lowell, Massachusetts, textile mills from 1835 to 1845. In order to encourage young women and girls to leave their rural families, employers created an orderly community of factories, boarding houses, schools, and churches, and encouraged their employees to share their values and aspirations. With the financial support of mill owners, Larcom and other mill girls published their own newspaper, the Lowell Offering. *But they also launched some of the first labor actions among industrial workers. During the 1840s, as employers cut wages and increased the workload, Lowell employees petitioned the state legislature to mandate a 10-hour day. Larcom's account captures the period before these tensions prompted native New England women to leave the mill, to be replaced by immigrant labor.*

A CHILD does not easily comprehend even the plain fact of death. Though I had looked upon my father's still, pale face in his coffin, the impression it left upon me was of sleep; more peaceful and sacred than common slumber, yet only sleep. My dreams of him were for a long time so vivid that I would say to myself, "He was here yesterday; he will be here again to-morrow," with a feeling that amounted to expectation...

It was hardest of all for my mother, who had been accustomed to depend entirely upon him. Left with her eight children, the eldest a boy of eighteen years, and with no property except the roof that sheltered us and a small strip of land, her situation was full of perplexities which we little ones could

Women in American History to 1880: A Documentary Reader, by Carol Faulkner
© 2011 Blackwell Publishing Ltd.

not at all understand. To be fed like the ravens and clothed like the grass of the field seemed to me, for one, a perfectly natural thing, and I often wondered why my mother was so fretted and anxious ...

That it was a hard world for my mother and her children to live in at present I could not help seeing. The older members of the family found occupations by which the domestic burdens were lifted a little; but, with only the three youngest to clothe and to keep at school, there was still much more outgo than income, and my mother's discouragement every day increased ...

During my father's life, a few years before my birth, his thoughts had been turned towards the new manufacturing town growing up on the banks of the Merrimack. He had once taken a journey there, with the possibility in his mind of making the place his home, his limited income furnishing no adequate promise of a maintenance for his large family of daughters. From the beginning, Lowell had a high reputation for good order, morality, piety, and all that was dear to the old-fashioned New Englander's heart.

After his death, my mother's thoughts naturally followed the direction his had taken; and seeing no other opening for herself, she sold her small estate, and moved to Lowell, with the intention of taking a corporation-house for mill-girl boarders. Some of the family objected, for the Old World traditions about factory life were anything but attractive; and they were current in New England until the experiment at Lowell had shown that independent and intelligent workers invariably give their own character to their occupation. My mother had visited Lowell, and she was willing and glad, knowing all about the place, to make it our home.

The change involved a great deal of work – "Boarders" signified a large house, many beds, and an indefinite number of people. Such piles o sewing accumulated before us! A sewing-bee, volunteered by the neighbors, reduced the quantity a little, and our child-fingers had to take their part. But the seams of those sheets did look to me as if they were miles long! ...

Our house was quickly filled with a large feminine family. As a child, the gulf between little girlhood and young womanhood had always looked to me very wide. I supposed we should get across it by some sudden jump, by and by. But among these new companions of all ages, from fifteen to thirty years, we slipped into womanhood without knowing when or how.

Most of my mother's boarders were from New Hampshire and Vermont, and there was a fresh, breezy sociability about them which made them seem almost like a different race of beings from any we children had hitherto known.

We helped a little about the housework, before and after school, making beds, trimming lamps, and washing dishes. The heaviest work was done by a strong Irish girl, my mother always attending to the cooking herself. She was, however, a better caterer than the circumstances required or permitted.

She liked to make nice things for the table, and, having been accustomed to an abundant supply, could never learn to economize. At a dollar and a quarter a week for board, (the price allowed for mill-girls by the corporations) great care in expenditure was necessary. It was not in my mother's nature closely to calculate costs, and in this way there came to be a continually increasing lack in the family purse. The older members of the family did everything they could, but it was not enough. I heard it said one day, in a distressed tone, "The children will have to leave school and go into the mill."

There were many pros and cons between my mother and sisters before this was positively decided. The mill-agent did not want to take us two little girls, but consented on condition we should ensure to attend school the full number of months prescribed each year. I, the younger one, was then between eleven and twelve years old ...

I thought it would be a pleasure to feel that I was not a trouble or burden or expense to anybody. So I went to my first day's work in the mill with a light heart. The novelty of it made it seem easy, and it really was not hard, just to change the bobbins on the spinning-frames every three quarters of an hour or so, with half a dozen other little girls who were doing the same thing ...

And for a little while it was only a new amusement; I liked it better than going to school and "making believe" I was learning when I was not. And there was a great deal of play mixed with it. We were not occupied more than half the time. The intervals were spent frolicking among the spinning-frames, teasing and talking to the other girls, or entertaining ourselves with games and stories in a corner, or exploring, with the overseer's permission, the mysteries of the carding-room, the dressing-room, and the weaving-room.

I never cared much for machinery. The buzzing and hissing and whizzing of pulleys and rollers and spindles and flyers around me often grew tiresome. I could not see into their complications, or feel interested in them. But in a room below us we were sometimes allowed to peer in through a sort of blind door at the great waterwheel that carried the works of a whole mill ...

There were compensations for being shut in to daily toil so early. The mill itself had its lessons for us. But it was not, and could not be, the right sort of life for a child, and we were happy in the knowledge that, at the longest, our employment was only to be temporary.

When I took my next three months at the grammar school, everything there was changed. The teachers were kind, and thorough in their instruction ... I was prepared for the high school.

But alas! I could not go. The little money I could earn – one dollar a week, besides the price of my board – was needed in the family, and I must return to the mill. It was a severe disappointment to me, though I did not say so at home ...

... I think the resolution was then formed, inwardly, that I *would* go to school again, some time, whatever happened – I went back to my work, but now without enthusiasm. I had looked through an open door that I was not willing to see shut upon me.

I began to reflect upon life rather seriously for a girl of twelve or thirteen. What was I here for? What could I make of myself? Must I submit to be carried along with the current, and do just what everybody else did? No: I knew I should not do that, for there was a certain Myself who was always starting up with her own original plan or aspiration before me, and who was quite indifferent as to what people generally thought...

In the older times it was seldom said to little girls, as it always had been said to boys, that they ought to have some definite plan, while they were children, what to be and do when they were grown up. There was usually but one path open before them, to become good wives and housekeepers. And the ambition of most girls was to follow their mothers' footsteps in this direction; a natural and laudable ambition. But girls, as well as boys, must often have been conscious of their own peculiar capabilities, – must have desired to cultivate and make use of their individual powers. When I was growing up, they had already begun to be encouraged to do so...

... So the plan of preparing myself to be a teacher gradually and almost unconsciously shaped itself in my mind as the only practicable one. I could earn my living in that way, – an all-important consideration...

Source: Lucy Larcom, *A New England Girlhood: Outlined from Memory* (Boston: Northeastern University Press, 1985), pp. 137–161.

2 Angelina Grimké, "An Appeal to the Women of the Nominally Free States," 1837

Born into a slaveholding family in South Carolina, Angelina Grimké was the first female lecturer for the American Anti-Slavery Society. With the precedent of Beecher's anti-removal petition campaign, abolitionist women petitioned Congress to end the domestic slave trade and abolish slavery in the territories and Washington, DC. Their efforts were far more divisive, however, arousing the opposition of Beecher herself. By 1836, the flood of anti-slavery missives provoked the House of Representatives to pass a gag rule tabling these petitions. The following year, anti-slavery women held their first national convention, and endorsed Grimké's Appeal. In this publication, Grimke argued that northern women had a moral and political obligation to act against slavery and end racial prejudice.

BELOVED SISTERS:

... The women of the North have high and holy duties to perform in the work of emancipation – duties to themselves, to the suffering slave, to the slaveholder, to the church, to their country, and to the world at large, and, above all to their God. Duties, which if not performed now, may never be performed at all...

Every citizen should feel an intense interest in the political concerns of the country, because the honor, happiness, and well being of every class, are bound up in its politics, government and laws. Are we aliens because we are women? Are we bereft of citizenship because we are the *mothers, wives* and *daughters* of a mighty people? Have *women* no country – no interest stakes in public weal – no liabilities in common peril – no partnership in a nation's guilt and shame? – Has *woman* no home nor household altars, nor endearing ties of kindred, nor sway with man, nor power at a mercy seat, nor voice to cheer, nor hand to raise the drooping, and to bind the broken?...

What then is Slavery? It is that crime, which casts man down from the exaltation where God has placed him, "a little lower than the angels," and sinks him to a level with the beasts of the field. This intelligent and immortal being is confounded with the brutes that perish; he whose spirit was formed to rise in aspirations of gratitude and praise whilst here, and to spend an eternity with God in heaven, is herded with the beasts, whose spirits go downward with their bodies of clay, to the dust of which they were made. Slavery is that crime by which man is robbed of his inalienable right to liberty, and the pursuit of happiness, the diadem of glory, and honor, with which he was crowned, and that scepter of domination which was placed in his hand when he was ushered upon the theatre of creation...

It is gravely urged that as it is a *political subject, women* have no concernment with it; this doctrine of the North is a sycophantic response to the declaration of a Southern representative, that women have no right to send up petitions to Congress. We know, dear sisters, that the open and secret enemies of freedom in our country have dreaded our influence, and therefore have reprobated our interference, and in order to blind us to our responsibilities, have thrown dust into our eyes, well knowing that if the organ of vision is only clear, the whole body, the moving and acting faculties will become full of light, and will soon be thrown into powerful action. Some, who pretend to be very jealous for the honor of our sex, and are very anxious that *we* should scrupulously maintain the dignity and delicacy of female propriety, continually urge this objection to female effort. We grant that it is a political, as well as moral subject: does this exonerate women from their duties as subjects of the government, as members of the great human family? Have women never wisely and laudably exercised political responsibilities? ...

And, dear sisters, in a country where women are degraded and brutalized, and where their exposed persons bleed under the lash – where they are sold in the shambles of "negro brokers" – robbed of their hard earnings – torn from their husbands, and forcibly plundered of their virtue and their off-spring; surely, in *such* a country, it is very natural that *women* should wish to know "the reason *why*" – especially when these outrages of blood and nameless horror are practiced in violation of the principles of our national Bill of Rights and the Preamble of our Constitution. We do not, then, and cannot concede the position, that because this is a *political subject* women ought to fold their hands in idleness, and close their eyes and ears to the "horrible things" that are practiced in our land. The denial of our duty to act, is a bold denial of our right to act; and if we have no right to act, then may *we* well be termed "the white slaves of the North" – for, like our brethren in bonds, we must seal our lips in silence and despair... *All moral beings have essentially the same rights and the same duties, whether they are male or female* ...

Out of the millions of slaves who have been stolen from Africa, a very great number must have been women, who were torn from the arms of their fathers and husbands, brothers, and children, and subjected to all the horrors of the middle passage and the still greater sufferings of slavery in a foreign land... The great mass of female slaves in the southern states are the descendents of these hapless strangers: 1 000 000 of them now wear the iron yoke of slavery in the land of boasted liberty and law. They are our countrywomen – *they are our sisters*, and to us, as women, they have a right to look for sympathy with their sorrows, and effort and prayer for their rescue. Upon those of us especially, who have named the name of Christ, they have peculiar claims, and claims which *we must answer or we shall incur a heavy load of guilt.*

Women, too, have constituted by nature the peculiar guardians of children, and children are the victims of this horrible system. Helpless infancy is robbed of the tender care of the mother, and the protection of the father...

And now, dear sisters, let us not forget that *Northern* women are participators in the crime of Slavery – too many of *us* have surrendered our hearts and hands to the wealthy planters of the South, and gone down with them to live on the unrequited toil of the Slave. Too many of *us* have ourselves become slaveholders, our hearts have been hardened under the searing influence of the system, and we too, have learned to be tyrants in the school of despots...

But let it be so no longer. Let us henceforward resolve, that the women of the free states never again will barter their principles for the blood bought luxuries of the South – never again will regard with complacency, much less with the tender sentiments of love, any man "who buildeth his house by unrighteousness and his chambers by wrong, that useth his neighbor's service *without* wages, and giveth him *not* for his work."...

Multitudes of Northern women are daily making use of the products of slave labor. They are clothing themselves and their families in the cotton, and eating the rice and the sugar, which they well know has cost the slave his unrequited toil, his blood and his tears; and if the maxim in law be founded in justice and truth, that "the receiver is *as bad* as the theif," how much *greater* the condemnation of those, who, not merely receive the stolen products of the slave's labor, but *voluntarily* purchase them, and *continually appropriate them to their own use....*

In consequence of the odium which the degradation of slavery has attached to *color* even in the free states, our *colored sisters* are dreadfully oppressed here. Our seminaries of learning are closed to them, they are almost entirely banished from our lecture rooms, and even in the house of god they are separated from their white brethren and sisters as though we were afraid to come in contact with a colored skin...Yes, our sisters, little as we may be willing to admit it, yet it is assuredly true, that whenever we treat a colored brother and sister in a way different from that in which we would treat them, were they white, we do virtually *reproach our Maker* for having dyed their skins of a sable hue...

Much may be done, too, by sympathizing with our oppressed colored sisters, who are suffering in our very midst. Extend to them the right hand of fellowship on the broad principles of humanity and Christianity – treat them as *equals* – visit them as *equals* – invite them to cooperate with you in Anti-Slavery and Temperance, and Moral reform Societies – in maternal Associations, and Prayer meetings, and Reading Companies...Opportunities frequently occur in travelling, and in other public situations, when your countenance, your influence, and your hand, might shield a sister from contempt and insult, and procure for her comfortable accommodations...Multitudes of instances will continually occur in which you will have the opportunity of identifying yourselves with this injured class of our fellow-beings; embrace these opportunities at all times and in all places...In this way, and in this way alone, will you be enabled to subdue that deep-rooted prejudice which is doing the work of oppression in the Free States to a most dreadful extent.

Source: Kathryn Kish Sklar (ed.), *Women's Rights Emerges within the Antislavery Movement, 1830–1870* (New York: Bedford Books, 2000), pp. 100–103.

3 L.T.Y., "Just Treatment of Licentious Men," 1838

In the 1830s and 1840s, white middle-class women across the northeastern United States organized moral reform societies to fight sexual immorality. These women were particularly concerned about the prevalence of prostitution in cities like New York, but they also wanted to establish a standard of premarital chastity for young men and women. In addition to saving women from the fate of fictional characters like Charlotte Temple, whose loss of virtue meant death or a life of prostitution, they wanted to ensure that middle-class men controlled their sexual desires. In this article, published in the newspaper of the Boston Female Moral Reform Society, the author advises women to exclude promiscuous men from respectable society. Such private methods proved unsuccessful, however, and the moral reform movement began petitioning state legislatures to pass laws against seduction.

DEAR SISTERS: – As members with us of the body of the Lord Jesus Christ, we take the liberty of addressing you on a subject near our hearts, and of the deepest interest to our sex. We ask your serious attention, while we press upon your consciences the inquiry, "Is it right to admit to the society of virtuous females, those unprincipled and licentious men, whose conduct is fraught with so much evil to those who stand in the relation to us of sisters?" True, God designed that man should be our protector, the guardian of our peace, our happiness, and our honor; but how often has he proved himself a traitor to his trust, and the worst enemy of our sex? The deepest degradation to which many of our sex have been reduced, the deepest injuries they have suffered, have been in consequence of his perfidy. He has betrayed, and robbed, and forsaken his victim, and left her to endure alone the untold horrors of a life embittered by self-reproach, conscious ignominy, and exclusion from every virtuous circle. Is there a woman among us, whose heart has not been pained at the fall and fate of some one sister of her sex? Do you say the guilty deserve to suffer and must expect it? Granted. But why not let a part of this suffering fall on the destroyer? Why is he caressed and shielded from scorn by the countenance of the virtuous, and encouraged to commit other acts of perfidy and sin, while his victim, for one offence, is trampled upon, despised and banished from all virtuous society; The victim thus crushed, yields herself to despair, and becomes a practical illustration of the proverb that, "A bad woman is the worst of all God's creatures." Surely, if she is worse, after her fall, than man equally fallen, is there not reason to infer that in her nature there is something more chaste, more pure and refined, and exalted than in his? Is it then not worth while to do something to prevent her from becoming a prey to the perfidy and baseness of unprincipled man, and a disgrace to her sex? Do you ask, what can woman do, and reply as have some others, "We must leave this work for the men?" Can we expect the wolf, ravenous for his prey, to throw up a barrier to protect the defenceless sheep? As well might we expect this, as to expect that men as a body will take measures to redress the wrongs of woman.

Dear sisters, women have commenced this work, and women must see it carried through. Commenced by women? No it was commenced by one who is now, we trust, a sainted spirit in heaven, and who sacrificed his life in the cause. Yes, he fell a martyr in the conflict, but not till he had effectually roused the women of the nation to enlist in the cause he had commenced. Moral Reform is the first of causes to our sex. It involves principles, which if faithfully and perseveringly applied, will preserve the rights and elevate the standing of our sex in society. As times have been, the libertine has found as ready a passport to the society of the virtuous, as any one, and he has as easily obtained a good wife, as the more virtuous man. But a new era has commenced. Woman has erected a standard, and laid down the principle, that man shall not trample her rights, and on the honor of her sex with impunity. She has undertaken to banish licentious men from all virtuous society. And mothers, wives, sisters, and daughters will you lend your influence to this cause? Prompt action in the form of association will accomplish this work? Females in this manner must combine their strength and exert their influence. Will you not join one of these bands of the pious? The cause has need of your interest, your prayers, and your funds. Come then to our help, and let us pray and labor together.

Source: "Just Treatment of Licentious Men. Addressed to Christian Mothers, Wives, Sisters and Daughters," *Friend of Virtue*, January 1838, in Daniel S. Wright and Kathryn Kish Sklar, *What Was the Appeal of Moral Reform to Antebellum Northern Women, 1835–1841?* Available by subscription at http://asp6new.alexanderstreet.com/was2/was2.object.details.aspx?dorpid=1000678104

4 Petition Protesting the Gag Rule, 1838

In this anti-slavery petition, Angelina Grimké, her older sister Sarah, and women from Brookline, Massachusetts, protested the gag rule. Abolitionists designed this short form to circumvent the gag by enabling sympathetic congressmen to quickly read the document into the record. Following the first Anti-Slavery Convention of American Women, Sarah and Angelina began a controversial lecture tour of Massachusetts. Historians estimate that the sisters spoke to approximately 40 000 people between June and November 1837. The women of Brookline may have signed this petition after attending one of these lectures. Congress finally lifted the gag rule in 1844.

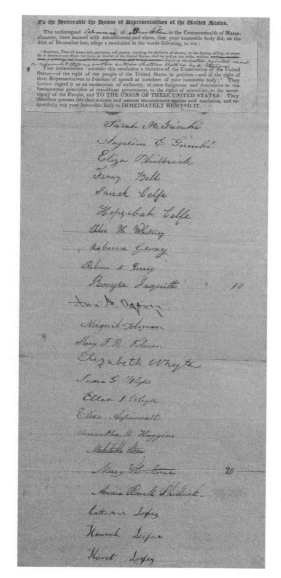

Figure 6.1 *Petition Protesting the Gag Rule, 1838, facsimile from "Our Mothers Before Us." Reproduced courtesy of the US National Archives and Records Administration.*

Source: Petitions and Memorials Which Were Tabled, HR25A-HI.7, 25th Congress, Records of the US House of Representatives, Record Group 233, National Archives and Records Administration, Washington DC.

5 S.E.C., "Mothers and Daughters," 1840

This article appeared in the Southern Ladies' Book, *a journal devoted to female education, published in Georgia and South Carolina between 1840 and 1843. As in northern women's magazines, the editors also instructed their readers on the qualities of good wives and mothers. This author, identified only by initials, emphasized the important role of mothers in discouraging frivolity and flirtatiousness among young women. Despite the author's reference to "mistresses," the concern with household economy suggests a middling rather than elite audience for this magazine. The article also reveals that young women may have viewed marriage as a weighty undertaking, and motherhood as a burden, to be delayed as long as possible.*

No relation in life is more interesting than that between the mother and daughter, and in none are the duties and obligations, on both sides, more intimate and important. How necessary is it, then, that the mother be qualified for the responsible station she occupies. The minds of her children and the ideas they have of right and wrong, will naturally run in the same channel as that from which they are derived; particularly is this the case with the daughter, who, being always under the watchful and vigilant eye of maternal love and care, the bias of her mind will naturally take the same direction as that of her fond parent.

But with the sons it is different; when they have arrived at that age in which boys consider themselves freed from the superintendence of their mother, when they prefer the crude and boisterous feats of those of their own age, to her private counsels and instructions, then she cannot follow them; but, like the hen who sees the ducklings she has reared, take to the water, she stands upon the brink and looks after them, astonished and frightened at their boldness; and all that a mother can then do for her boys, will be to pray that God may protect them, and that they may have strength of mind to resist temptation.

But it is when a young woman is about to enter the scenes of the world, to act a part on the great stage of existence, and to practise all those habits which she has formed in her earlier years, that the guiding and restraining influence of a mother's counsels are most needed and felt. If, then, it is a mother's office to superintend the morals and habits of her daughter, and give her such instruction as will fit her for the future scenes of existence, here and hereafter, she must have sufficient resolution to see that what she has taught is practised.

Too often is it the case that a mother, when she has spent a short time, now and then, in giving her daughter instruction; when she has gravely expatiated, in set phrases, on the necessity of good morals and virtuous conduct, considers that duty as completed, and proceeds to the more important one of decking the young lady for the ball-room, or the gay pleasure party; thus the good seed that was sown is choked by the weeds of pride and vanity, and all the good advice the daughter had received becomes obliterated from her memory, apparently with the sanction of her mother.

But more frequently is it the case that the wise counsels of a mother are totally disregarded by her thoughtless and careless daughter. The giddy girl, forgetful of the past, ignorant of the present, and thoughtless of the future, disdains the prudent advice of a mother, whose experience ought to entitle her to the implicit confidence of her daughter.

But, instead of making her mother her confidant, and communicating to her her secrets, she chooses to open her wise mouth to one or more of her wild companions, whom she designates by the name of "intimate friends." The grand question is, whether a certain gentleman is in love with her or not. After enumerating the few trivial circumstances which led her to form this supposition, she concludes with the unanimous consent of her companions, that he is actually smitten, although the attentions of the gentleman might have been nothing more than were instigated by politeness. Of course, the next time she meets him, she acts like a fool, and leaves him perfectly disgusted with her. So much for not consulting her mother, if she must talk at all upon these subjects.

Daughters are too apt to think that the cares and trials of a mother as mistress of the house, are evils to which she is necessarily subjected, and which no behavior of theirs could prevent or lighten. This is wrong; her many and severe duties may be greatly ameliorated by the affection and obedience of her child. When a mother sees her daughter profiting by the instruction which she receives, patient and persevering in overcoming difficulties, and industrious in the performance of her duties, she feels encouraged and repaid for all her cares, anxieties and expenses.

But it is not only necessary that the mother inculcate good morals and virtuous conduct; it is equally essential that she instruct her daughter in personal neatness and the different departments of housewifery. As she knows not in what situation of life she may be placed, it is best to look forward and prepare herself for the fulfillment of any duty that may devolve upon her. She may be situated in a part of the country where domestics cannot be obtained, or, if they can, must be considered as on an equality with herself. Here, then, she has her choice, either to do her work herself, or receive those who do it as in some measure her equals. If she chooses the former, she must not consider that she is degrading herself by these employments. No, there is as much difference in the manner of a lady's doing her work and her servants, as there is in their rank and station in life. Neither is her taste for intellectual pursuits and refined society diminished; on the contrary, after pursuing her daily avocations, and performing her duties faithfully, she sits down with her body strengthened and invigorated, and her mind healthy and clear, ready to peruse the deepest philosophical works, and the most refined literature of the day.

A young woman should not lay the foundation of her future happiness on riches; these may take to themselves wings and fly away. She is now young and thoughtless, and if she thinks of the future, it is only to expatiate on some happy dream in which she will be freed from the toilsome and vexatious cares of school; when she will figure in the ballroom, and command the admiration of the gay votaries of fashion and pleasure; and when she will be mistress of herself, her house and her servants. In a few years she is married; and then, as she understands nothing about the concerns of a family, she cannot be truly the mistress: the servants take upon themselves the management and direction of affairs.

If her husband chance to bring home an old acquaintance to dine with him, he is sure to meet with some mortifying proof of his wife's ignorance, and the mismanagement of the domestic concerns. Perhaps whilst he and his friend are regaling themselves with ill-done meats, vegetables half prepared, and sour bread, she will entertain them with a long account of the unfaithfulness of her servants, the difficulty of procuring good ones, and the trouble of keeping house. The materials her husband provides for the support of his family, are wasted by her culpable ignorance and indolence.

In the course of a few years he fails in his business, and care and trouble sinks him to a premature grave, leaving his wife destitute, with a family depending on her for support.

Where now are all her youthful dreams of happiness? Where are those pleasant hours which her imagination had destined to be spent in revelry and feasting? And where are those numerous friends who crowded around her in the days of her prosperity? Alas! they have vanished – her riches was the only magnet which drew them into her society. In vain she hears the cry of bread echoed around her ears by her half-famished children; she has neither strength nor energy sufficient to apply herself to a useful occupation by which she can support herself and them. In vain she now wishes that the many hours she had spent in pleasure, had been devoted to some useful employment, which would have prepared her for the performance of those duties that now devolve upon her.

But the most important of all a mother's duties is, that of instructing her child in religion. She must not merely direct their attention to the form, requiring them to repeat a few unmeaning words. She should make from her own warm heart appeals to theirs, and adapt her conversation to their understanding. She should strive to elevate the tone of their moral feeling, and lead them to consider their responsibility to their Maker, for the improvement of their time, talents and advantages. She should direct their young hearts to Jesus Christ as the pattern of their lives, as their only hope for a future existence; thus teaching them to aim at something higher than mere worldly applause and admiration.

S. E. C.

Source: "Mothers and Daughters," *Southern Ladies' Book*, Volume I, Issue 3 (1840), pp. 163–164. Available by subscription at http://www.everydaylife.amdigital.co.uk/Image.aspx?docref=SouthernLadiesBook&searchref=00000005&type=page&pageref=00000021

6 Oregon Missionary Narcissa Whitman, Letter to her Mother, May 2, 1840

Narcissa Prentiss was born in Steuben County, New York, in 1808. In 1819, during the Second Great Awakening, she experienced a profound religious conversion. After working as a school teacher, Narcissa applied to the American Board of Commissions for Foreign Missions in 1834. In 1836, she married Marcus Whitman and the two missionaries left immediately for Oregon territory. Narcissa's letter to her mother expresses her sense of calling as well as her loneliness. She also records her often negative impression of the Nez Percé and Cayuse Indians. In 1847, after a measles outbreak killed a number of Native American children, Cayuse Indians attacked the Whitman mission and killed Narcissa and her family.

My Dear Mother: – I cannot describe how much I have longed to see you of late. I have felt the want of your sympathy, your presence and counsel more than ever. One reason doubtless is it has been so long since I have received a single letter from any one of the dear friends at home. Could they know how I feel and how much good their letters do me, they would all of them write a great deal and write often, too, at least every month or two, and send to Boston and to Westport, to the care of Rev. Joseph McCoy; they would surely reach us. Our associates receive them in great numbers, which does not make us feel any better for ourselves. We are daily expecting the arrival of Mr. Lee's ship, laden with associates for that mission, and we have the encouragement from the board to expect four or five families for our own mission. By them we hope to receive letters in abundance. It is a consoling thought to us that we are permitted the prospect of having other fellow laborers to join us again so soon. We feel that we cannot do our work too fast to save the Indian – the hunted, despised and unprotected Indian – from entire extinction.

A tide of immigration appears to be moving this way rapidly. What a few years will bring forth we know not. A great change has taken place even since we first entered the country, and we have no reason to believe it will stop here. Instead of two lonely American females we now number four-teen, and soon may twenty or forty more, if reports are true. We are emphatically situated on the highway between the states and the Columbia river, and are a resting place for the weary travelers, consequently a greater burden rests upon us than upon any of our associates – to be always ready. And doubtless many of those who are coming to this mission their resting place will be with us until they seek and find homes of their own among the solitary wilds of Oregon. Could dear mother know how I have been situated the two winters past, especially winter before last, I know she would pity me. I often think how disagreeable it used to be to her feelings to do her cooking in the presence of men – sitting about the room. This I have had to bear ever since I have been here – at times it has seemed as if could not endure it any longer. It has been the more trying because our house has been so miserable and cold – small and inconvenient for us – many people as have lived in it. But the greatest trial to a woman's feelings is to have her cooking and eating room always filled with four or five more Indians – men – especially at meal time – but we hope this trial is nearly done, for when we get into our other house we have a room there we devote to them especially, and shall not permit them to go into the other part of the house at all. They are so filthy they make a great deal of cleaning wherever they go, and this wears out a woman very fast. We must clean after them, for we have come to elevate them and not to suffer ourselves to sink down to their standard. I hardly know how to describe my feelings at the prospect of a clean, comfortable house, and one large enough so that I can find a closet to pray in.

As a specimen I will relate a circumstance that occured this spring. When the people began to return from their winter quarters we told them it would be good for them to build a large house (which they often do by putting several lodges together) where it would be convenient for all to attend worship and not meet in the open air. They said they should not do it, but would worship in our new house, and asked us if there were not houses in heaven to worship in. We told them our house was to live in and we could not have them worship there for they would make it so dirty and fill it so full of fleas that we could not live in it. We said to them further, that they did not help us build it and that people in other places build their houses of worship and did not let one man do it all alone, and urged them to join together by and by and build one for themselves of adobe. But it was of no avail to them; they murmured still and said we must pay them for their land we lived on. Something of this kind is occurring almost all the time when certain individuals are here; such as complaining because we do not feed them more, or that we will not let them run all over the house, etc., etc.

They are an exceedingly proud, haughty and insolent people, and keep us constantly upon the stretch after patience and forbearance. We feed them far more than any of our associates do their people, yet they will not be satisfied. Notwithstanding all this there are many redeeming qualities in them, else we should have been discouraged long ago. We are more and more encouraged the longer we stay among them. They are becoming quite independent in cultivation and make all their ground look as clean and mellow as a garden. Great numbers of them cultivate, and with but a single horse will take any plow we have, however large, and do their own plough-ing. They have a great thirst for hogs, hens and cattle, and several of them have obtained them already.

Our greatest desire and anxiety is to see them becoming true Christians. For this we labor and pray, and trust in God for the blessing on our labors. But the labor is great and we are weak and feeble, and sometimes are ready to faint. We need the prayers of our Christian friends at home and I trust we have them. Could they know just how we are situated and all our discouragements I know they would pray more ardently for us and more importunately for us.

Dear father, I will relate one more anecdote and then must close. Te-lou-ki-ke said to my husband this morning: "Why do you take your wife with you to Mr. Walker's? Why do you not go alone? You see I am here without my wife; why do you always want to take your wife with you when you go from home? What do you make so much of her for?" He told him it was good for me to go with him; that we were one, and that wives were given as companions. He replied "that it was so with Adam because a rib was taken from him to make his wife, but it was not so now; it was different with us." This has often been brought up by them; the way I am treated, and con-trasted with themselves; they do not like to have it so; their consciences are troubled about it. May they be more and more so until a reformation is made among them ...

I do not know how many of my letters reach home or whether any of them. I write and send twice a year to some of them. I hope all who write will be careful to mention the reception of all our letters, so then we shall know what ones fail and what reach you.

Please give our love to all our friends who are interested in us, and accept much for dear father, mother and all the family.

Your affectionate daughter,
Narcissa Whitman.

Source: Available at www.nps.gov/whmi/historyculture/letter.htm (accessed August 18, 2010).

7 "Lives of the Nymphs: Amanda B. Thompson and her Attache," 1841

This article directed male readers to one of approximately 10 000 prostitutes among New York City's 312 000 residents. As young men and women streamed into the city in search of economic opportunity, so-called "flash" newspapers promoted an exciting urban male culture of gambling, sports, and commercial sex. Though most Americans viewed prostitutes as irredeemable, the flash press defended the sexual reputation and freedom of their favorite prostitutes. As in the case of Amanda Thompson, writers relied on romanticized tales of seduction to explain women's entry into prostitution, but money was women's primary motivation. Prostitution, especially in high-end brothels, offered women a rare measure of financial independence.

Our artist has engraved a most beautiful and exact likeness of this lady. Among the gay sisters of our city, this is without doubt the most remarkable and if respectability belongs to such a peculiar profession as that which she follows, she may be called respectable. Amanda is extremely beautiful with tresses black as get [jet], which she wears in the highest style of fashion, and eyes that might challenge comparison with the brightest beings of earth. A figure magnificent beyond description, a bust that defies the imitation of the sculptor, and a smile sweet beyond expression, are but a few among the many charms she possesses. She was born of parents in respectable circumstances and received the rudiments of a most excellent education. She was the belle of her native town and when at length the buds of youthful promise burst into womanhood, she did not want [lack] admirers who did her homage as their queen of beauty. But religion reigned supreme for a young clergyman walked over the course and imprinted his image on her too susceptible heart. At first a purely platonic affection, and then the warmer feeling of love, until

Figure 6.2   Amanda B. Thompson and Her Attache, *1841. Reproduced courtesy of the American Antiquarian Society.*

at length on a beautiful moonlight night after mutual confessions of constancy till death, they fled together. Hours and days, nay, months passed off, until one unlucky moment when a quarrel ensued

Alas how light a cause may move
Dissention between hearts that love
Hearts that the world in vain has tried
And sorrow but more closely tried
That stood the storm when waves were rough
Yet in a sunny hour fall off
Like ships that have gone down at sea
When Heaven was all tranquility

When young Buonapart visited this country, he became accidentally acquainted with Amanda and a second and sever affection sprang up which was not altogether of the Platonic order. Under his protection, and travelling with him, she was introduced to some of the first society in the country and wherever she went her beauty was the theme of boundless admiration. But, "hours will come to part," and once more she was left on her own resources. Other lovers followed scarcely less favored. Amanda now keeps a house in 474 Broome st where her arrangements are upon a gorgeous scale. – Scarcely any of the palaces of beauty set out in magnificence as the temples of licentiousness can bear a comparison with hers. She still retains all the beauty of her earlier years, and that fascination which once made her so distinguished.

Source: "Lives of the Nymphs: Amanda B. Thompson and her Attache," *True Flash*, 1841, in Patricia Cline Cohen, Timothy J. Gilfoyle, and Helen Lefkowitz Horowitz with the American Antiquarian Society, *The Flash Press: Sporting Male Weeklies in 1840s New York* (Chicago: University of Chicago Press, 2008), pp. 150–152.

8 Catharine Beecher, Excerpt from *A Treatise on Domestic Economy*, 1845

Following the initial publication of her popular book of domestic advice in 1841, Catharine Beecher became a national authority on American womanhood. Filled with practical guidance on cooking, cleaning, childrearing, physiology, and even plumbing, Beecher helped define women's influential status as mothers, wives, and homemakers. She portrayed the middle-class home as an essential democratic institution, accessible to all and fundamental to promoting American values. American women's exceptional domestic responsibility, Beecher believed, required them to be healthy and vigorous.

And when American women are called to the responsibilities of domestic life, the degree in which their minds and feelings are taxed, is altogether greater than it is in any other nation.

No women on earth have a higher sense of their moral and religious responsibilities, or better understand, not only what is demanded of them, as housekeepers, but all the claims that rest upon them as wives, mothers, and members of a social community. An American woman, who is the mistress of a family, feels her obligations, in reference to her influence over her husband, and a still greater responsibility in rearing and educating her children. She feels, too, the claims which the moral interests of her domestics have on her watchful care. In social life, she recognises the claims of hospitality, and the demands of friendly visiting. Her responsibility, in reference to the institutions of benevolence and religion, is deeply realized. The regular worship of the Lord's day, and all the various religious meetings and benevolent societies which place so much dependence on female influence and example, she feels obligated to sustain. Add to these multiplied responsibilities, the perplexities and evils which have been pointed out, resulting from the fluctuating state of society, and the deficiency of domestic service, and no one can deny that American women are exposed to a far greater amount of intellectual and moral excitement, than those of any other land. Of course, in order to escape the danger resulting from this, a greater amount of exercise in the fresh air, and all those methods which strengthen the constitution, are imperiously required.

But, instead of this, it will be found, that, owing to the climate and customs of this Nation, there are no women who secure so little of this healthful and protecting regimen, as ours. Walking and riding and gardening, in the open air, are practised by the women of other lands, to a far greater extent, than by American females. Most English women, in the wealthier classes, are able to walk six and eight miles, without oppressive fatigue; and when they visit this Country, always express their surprise at the inactive habits of American ladies. In England, regular exercise, in the open air, is very commonly required by the mother, as a part of daily duty, and is sought by young women, as an enjoyment. In consequence of a different physical training, English women, in those circles which enjoy competency, present an appearance which always strikes American gentlemen as a contrast to what they see at home. An English mother, at thirty, or thirty-five, is in the full bloom of perfected womanhood; as fresh and healthful as her daughters. But where are the American mothers, who can reach this period unfaded and unworn? In America, young ladies of the wealthier classes are sent to school from early childhood; and neither parents nor teachers make it a definite object to secure a proper amount of fresh air and exercise, to counterbalance this intellectual taxation. As soon as their school days are over, dressing, visiting, evening parties, and stimulating amusements, take the place of study, while the most unhealthful modes of dress add to the physical exposures. To make morning calls, or do a little shopping, is all that can be termed their exercise in the fresh air; and this, compared to what is needed, is absolutely nothing, and on some accounts is worse than nothing. In consequence of these, and other evils, which will be pointed out more at large in the following pages, the young women of America grow up with such a delicacy of constitution, that probably eight out of ten become subjects of disease, either before or as soon as they are called to the responsibilities of domestic life.

But there is one peculiarity of situation, in regard to American women, which makes this delicacy of constitution still more disastrous. It is the liability to the exposures and hardships of a newly-settled country ...

Such scenes, and such women, the writer has met, and few persons realize how many refined and lovely women are scattered over the broad prairies and deep forests of the West; and none, but the Father above, appreciates the extent of those sacrifices and sufferings, and the value of that firm faith and religious hope, which live, in perennial bloom, amid those vast solitudes. If the American women of the East merit the palm, for their skill and success as accomplished housekeepers, still more is due to the heroines of the West, who, with such unyielding fortitude and cheerful endurance, attempt similar duties, amid so many disadvantages and deprivations.

But, though American women have those elevated principles and feelings, which enable them to meet such trials in so exemplary a manner, their physical energies are not equal to the exertions demanded. Though the mind may be bright and firm, the casket is shivered; though the spirit may be willing, the flesh is weak. A woman of firm health, with the hope and elasticity of youth, may be envied rather than pitied, as she shares with her young husband the hopes and enterprises of pioneer life. But, when the body fails, then the eye of hope grows dim, the heart sickens, the courage dies; and, in solitude, weariness, and suffering, the wanderer pines for the dear voices and the tender sympathies of a far distant home. Then it is, that the darkest shade is presented, which marks the peculiar trials and liabilities of American women, and which exhibits still more forcibly the disastrous results of that delicacy of constitution which has been pointed out. For, though all American women, or even the greater part of them, are not called to encounter such trials, yet no mother, who rears a family of daughters, can say, that such a lot will not fall to one of her flock; nor can she know which will escape. The reverses of fortune, and the chances of matrimony, expose every woman in the Nation to such liabilities, for which she needs to be prepared.

Source: Catharine Beecher, *A Treatise on Domestic Economy For the Use of Young Ladies at Home and at School* (New York: Harper & Brothers, 1845). Available at www.gutenberg.org/etext/21829 (accessed August 13, 2010).

Suggested Questions for Discussion

1   Lucy Larcom recalls the possibilities and frustrations of life in the Lowell mills. How were other women's experiences of early industrialization similar or different?
2   Compare Angelina Grimké's *Appeal* to the documents by L.T.Y., S.E.C., Narcissa Whitman, or Catharine Beecher. Why might Americans view Grimké and other abolitionist women as dangerous?
3   In different ways, the articles from the *Friend of Virtue* and the *Southern Ladies' Book* expressed anxiety about young women's sexuality. What do these articles reveal about the relationship between sexual virtue and domesticity? How do the marriages anticipated in these articles compare to the portrait of prostitute Amanda Thompson?

Chapter 7   Partisans, 1845–1860

1 Susan Shelby Magoffin Describes Dona Gertrudis "La Tules" Barceló, 1846

Eighteen-year-old newlywed Susan Shelby Magoffin traveled with her businessman husband Samuel Magoffin down the Santa Fe Trail from Independence, Missouri, through Santa Fe, and into Mexico. Two weeks before their arrival in Santa Fe, the US army peacefully occupied the city. In her journal, Magoffin recorded her often critical views of Mexican women. She also described the famous Gertrudis Barceló, a businesswoman who grew wealthy by attracting American officers and businessmen to her dancehall and card rooms. Barceló served as a crucial mediator between the Spanish-Mexican residents and European-American occupiers.

Thursday 27th. Near San Miguel. We have passed through some two or three little settlements today similar to the Vegas, and I am glad to think that much is accomplished of my task. It is truly shocking to my modesty to pass such places with gentlemen.

The women slap about with their arms and necks bare, perhaps their bosoms exposed (and they are none of the prettiest or whitest) if they are about to cross the little creek that is near all the villages, regardless of those about them, they pull their dresses, which in the first place but little more than cover their calves – up above their knees and paddle through the water like ducks, sloshing and spattering every thing about them.

Women in American History to 1880: A Documentary Reader, by Carol Faulkner
© 2011 Blackwell Publishing Ltd.

Some of them wear leather shoes, from the States, but most have buckskin mockersins, Indian style.

And it is repulsive to see the children running about perfectly naked, or if they have a chimese it is in such ribbands it had better be off at once. I am constrained to keep my veil drawn closely over my face all the time to protect my blushes...

Friday 11th. What did I write of last yesterday? The managerie, well, now for a little critical view of it. I went in of course somewhat prepared to see; as I have often heard of such a show, I knew in a measure what to look for. First the ballroom, the walls of which were hung and fancifully decorated with the "stripes and stars," was opened to my view – there were before me numerous objects of the biped species, dressed in the seven rain-bow colours variously contrasted, and in fashions adapted to the reign of King Henry VIII, or of the great queen Elizabeth, *my memory* cannot exactly tell me which, they were entirely enveloped, on the first view in a cloud of smoke, and while some were circling in a mazy dance others were seated around the room next the wall enjoying the scene before them, and quietly puffing, both males and females their little cigarritas a delicate cigar made with a very little tobacco rolled in a corn shuck or bit of paper. I had not been seating more than fifteen minutes before Maj. Soards an officer, a man of quick perception, irony, sarcasm, and wit, came up to me in true Mexican style, and with a polite, "Madam will you have a cigarita," drew from one pocket a *handful of shucks and from an other a large horn of tobacco*, at once turning the whole thing to a burlesque.

Among the officers of the army I found some very agreeable, and all were very attentive to me. Liuts. Warner & Hammund, the principal managers of affairs did themselves credit in their interested and active movements to make the time pass agreeably to their visitors.

El Senor Vicario [the priest] was there to grace the gay halls with his priestly robes – he is a man rather short of statu[r]e, but that is made up in width, which not a little care for the stomach lends an assisting hand in completing the man. There was "Dona Tula" the principal *monte-bank keeper* in Sant Fé, a stately dame of a certain age, the possessor of a portion of that shrewd sense and fascinating manner necessary to allure the way-ward, inexperienced youth to the hall of final ruin...There, too, circling giddily through the dance, Cpt. M[oore] of [First] Dragoons; if necessary we can be sure of at least one person to testify to the "virtues or vices" of what has been graphically called "the ingredient." There in that corner sits a dark-eyed Senora with a human footstool; in other words with her servant under her feet – a custom I am told, when they attend a place of the kind to take a servant along and while sitting to use them as an article of furniture.

The music consisted of a gingling guitar, and violin with the occasional effort to chime in an almost unearthly voice. *Las Senoras y Senoritas* [the ladies and girls – young ladies] were dressed in silks, satins, ginghams & lawns, embroidered crape shawls, fine rabozos – and decked with various showy ornaments, such as hugh necklaces, countless rings, combs, bows of ribbands, red and other coloured handkerchiefs, and other fine *fancy* articles. This is a short sketch of a Mexican ball. Liuts Warner & Hammond called this evening to see how I *enjoyed* the dance (not that I joined [in] it myself).

Source: Stella M. Drumm (ed.), *Down the Santa Fe Trail and into Mexico: The Diary of Susan Shelby Magoffin, 1846–1857* (Lincoln: University of Nebraska Press, 1982), in Ernesto Chavez, *The U.S. War with Mexico* (New York: Bedford Books, 2008), pp. 91–93.

2 Lucretia Mott, Letter to Edmund Quincy, 1848

In this letter, published in the anti-slavery newspaper the Liberator, *Mott discusses her recent journey through Western New York. Her deep interest in the abolition of slavery took her to the Canadian Province of Ontario, where over 12 000 former American slaves had settled. As a member of a Quaker Indian Committee, she visited the Seneca on the Cattaraugus reservation. She also participated in two conventions devoted to women's rights, including the Seneca Falls Convention held July 19–20, 1848. Her letter reveals the multiple and sometimes conflicting reform interests of early women's rights activists.*

PHILADELPHIA, 8th mo., 24th, 1848.

MY DEAR FRIEND E.Q;

In the absence of our loved Wm. L. Garrison, I address a few lines to thee, to use or reject at discretion.

During the summer, my husband and self have had an interesting travel among the Cataragus [*sic*] Indians, of Western New York, and the self-emancipated slaves and other colored settlers of Canada West. J. Mott has given some account of these, their location, &c., in the Pennsylvania Freeman. It is worth a journey of many miles, to see "the colored man *a man*" – in the full exercise of his energies and ingenuity; fertile in expedient, laboring with all the industry and hopeful prospect of a settler in a new country. Many difficulties to contend with, of course, and these mighty to surmount, in view of those, who, wending their way thither from the enervating South, were ill-prepared to meet the giant-forests of their Canaan-land.

None, however, seem disposed to return to their worse than Egyptian bondage. They cheerfully toil on, and submit to their present privations, seeing "a good land and a large" before them.

The education of their children is claiming their attention, and a few years will shew a great change in the character of this people. Especially so, if their friends, the abolitionists, are unceasing in their efforts for the removal of the execrable system of slavery, and its ever-attendant prejudice, which have so sunk and degraded its victims. We had several interesting meetings and conferences with them, at Buffalo, Detroit, Chatham, Dawn, London, and Toronto. The kindness and hospitality extended to us, as well as to many others oft before, give evidence that they are not wanting in the delicacies and refinements of social life. The fugitive from the house of bondage can also speak of the generous aid, with limited means too, bestowed by those who had previously found a resting place there. These demands are happily so frequent, that assistance should be rendered from their friends in the States; guarded, however, against the unwise distribution, that has sometimes been made of money, articles of clothing, &c., sent them.

Few of the settlers are well-informed of the abolition movements, and the progress of the course of human freedom. The postage is so high, that not many of our papers are taken in Canada. But they will not long be dependent upon Anti-Slavery Periodicals, for their lessons of Liberty. The spirit of Freedom is arousing the world; and the press universal will echo the glad sound.

A word for the poor Indians. The few hundreds left of the Seneca Nation at the Cataraugus [sic] reservation, are improving in their mode of living, cultivating their land, and educating their children. They, too, are learning somewhat from the political agitations abroad; and, as man is wont, are imitating the movements of France and all Europe, in seeking larger liberty – more independence.

Their Chieftainship is therefore a subject of discussion in their councils, and important changes are demanded and expected, as to the election of their chiefs, many being prepared for a yearly appointment.

Two missionaries are settled among them, and some religious party strife is apparent. The pagans adhere, of course, to the sacred festivals of their fathers, and are not disposed to exchange them for the "bread and wine" &c., of the Christian party. We had an interesting conference with them, during which their differences were presented; but we declined to decide between them, as, if attempted, we might be found equally discountenancing each form, and recommending our Quaker non-conformity. But, as that was not our mission, we commended them to the "Great Spirit," believing that those who danced religiously, might be as nearly perfect, as were those who communed in some other chosen form – neither of these being the test of acceptance. We witnessed their strawberry dance, and grotesque though the figures were, fantastic their appearance, and rude their measured steps, and unharmonious their music, yet, in observing the profound veneration of the hundreds present, some twenty of whom were performers, and the respectful attention paid to the speeches of their chiefs, women as well as men, it was far from me to say, that our silent, voiceless worship was better adapted to their condition, or that even the Missionary Baptism, and Sabbath, and organ, are so much higher evidence of a civilized, spiritual and Christian state.

While in western New York, we attended two Conventions called to consider the relative position of woman in society – one held at Seneca Falls, the other at Rochester. The "proceedings" have been published in the North Star and several other papers.

The attendance and interest manifested, were greatly encouraging; and give hope that this long neglected subject will soon begin to receive the attention that its importance demands.

I have received some cheering letters upon the subject since our return home – one from Mass.: while, on the other hand, private and public testimony has been born against the movement. This must serve to impress the necessity of repeated meetings of similar character. All these subjects of reform are kindred in their nature; and giving to each its proper consideration, will tend to strengthen and nerve the mind for all – so that the abolitionist will not wax weaker in his advocacy of immediate emancipation. He will not love the slave less, in loving universal humanity more.
L. MOTT.

Source: *Liberator*, October 6, 1848, in Beverly Palmer, *Selected Letters of Lucretia Coffin Mott* (Chicago: University of Illinois Press, 2002), pp. 165–167.

3 Imogen Mercein Describes the Five Points Mission, 1852

In 1850, the Ladies' Home Missionary Society of the Methodist Episcopal Church founded the Five Points Mission in New York City in a neighborhood notorious for its poverty and prostitution. Though the female managers hired male missionaries (and their spouses) to live in the mission, they directed and administered all aspects of the mission's programs. They also visited the neighborhood to convert residents to Methodism. This report heralded the accomplishments of the mission and explained their conflict with their first missionary. Writing for the Ladies' Home Missionary Society, Imogen

Mercein defended their policy that conversion must come before the amelioration of physical wants. The following year, the Ladies' Home Missionary Society razed the Old Brewery and erected a new mission building.

The New York Ladies' Home Missionary Society of the M.E. Church have been requested to give a clear statement of their position, and relation to the mission at the Five Points. They are anxious to have their object clearly known to the public, who have so generously aided them during the last year, and who have been misinformed as to the object and hope of the mission in that heathen spot. They know that previous benevolent efforts had failed to a great degree, but as their object has always been, from their formation to have the Gospel preached in the most destitute parts of the city, they felt an especial call to make an effort there.

They formed their plans, chose their committee of gentlemen, and applied to Conference for a missionary, pledging themselves to raise one thousand dollars per annum for its support. In compliance with this request, Rev. Mr. Pease was sent to that mission; he found the society ready to cooperate, the committee of gentlemen waiting to accompany him to that locality; a band of teachers were chosen for the Sabbath school, and soon all was in active operation. Before the year had closed, the Society found, that whatever temporal good might be effected through Mr. Pease's energy, it would not rest on the moral basis, which alone would give it permanency and character, and, unwilling that police restraint should supersede the "law of love," which they felt should be the spirit of their mission, they unanimously concluded not to apply for him the second year.

The mooted question as to whether reformation should *precede* the preaching of the Gospel, or be its *result*, had, they thought, been decisively settled in the experiments of foreign missions. They hoped to lay a broad basis on a well-settled foundation, and while they laid hold on all temporary aid as an auxiliary never to be neglected, *renovation of character* by renewing of God's spirit, were the high mark to which all their efforts were directed. To this end a Temperance Society was immediately organized, preparations for a day school made, and a Sewing Society formed to aid in clothing the children. Appeals were written for different papers, and boxes of clothing from different States (and even far distant Wisconsin), were received for the benefit of this mission.

In compliance with the wishes of the ladies, Rev. Mr. Lucky, late Chaplain of the Sing sing State Prison, was appointed to succeed Mr. Pease, as missionary in that place; and we are happy to state that he and his wife have fully carried out the missionary designs contemplated, and by their visiting, their prayers, their daily efforts and their nightly toils, exerted a subduing and moral influence which is felt throughout the entire community; nor have they rested there.

They have distributed, throughout the last year alone, three thousand garments, without reference to color, sect, or country. Scores of men and women have, through their influence, been supplied with work; many children have been placed in the Home of the Friendless, or in respectable families; and neither time nor trouble have been spared to effect these objects. Want of room has prevented our carrying out our full designs, but with gratitude we announce that soon this difficulty will be remedied. The purchase money of the Old Brewery is raised, and very soon a new building will occupy that site ...

We invite our friends to visit us, and look at the Old Brewery, (ere it is demolished,) and see an infant class of eighty children – then to cross over to the mission room, and find a smaller number under faithful instruction – to tarry to the plain Gospel service, brought down to the comprehension of the most ignorant and degraded. We invite them, particularly, to aid Mr. Lucky on Sunday evenings, when the wretched adults, who shrink from daylight exposure, creep in to seek aid to break the fearful chains of intemperance which so strongly bind them – or on Tuesday evening, to the prayer meeting – or, on Wednesday evening, to the children's singing school, when the ragged, dirty little urchins crowd into the Brewery by the scores, and make the Five Points ring with their sweet childish melody...

Thus we define our mission – to feed the hungry, to clothe the naked, to educate the ignorant, to aid all willing to work, to obtain suitable employment, to promote the cause of temperance to the utmost, to preach the gospel to the poor, and thus try to throw every moral and religious influence around this hitherto neglected community...

By order of the board.   Imogen Mercein, Cor. Sec.

Donations will be thankfully received by Rev. Mr. Lucky, at his office, No. 59 Cross-street, in the Old Brewery.

Source: Imogen Mercein, "Five Points Mission," *New York Times*, November 10, 1852.

4 Excerpt on Complex Marriage from *Bible Communism*, 1853

This document offers a brief history of the utopian Oneida Community as well as religious justification for their social arrangements. Founder John Humphrey Noyes criticized the oppressiveness of the institution of marriage, but, unlike early feminists, he did not propose to reform the law to give women more rights. Instead, the Oneida Community instituted a system called "complex marriage," in which all members of the community were married to each other. To prevent possessiveness in intimacy as well as property, Noyes and the community guarded against exclusive sexual relationships. Noyes solved the threat of unwanted pregnancy in this "free love" community with male continence, or withholding orgasm. The Oneida Community lasted until 1879.

PRELIMINARIES.

This Report would not be complete without a frank and full exhibition of the theory of the Association in regard to the relation of the sexes. An argument therefore, on this subject, prepared by J. H. NOYES early in the spring of 1848, and adopted by the Association from the beginning, as a declaration of its principles, will here be presented, after a few introductory remarks.

1. The radical principles developed in this argument, were early deduced from the religious system evolved at New Haven in 1834, were avowed in print by J. H. NOYES in 1837, and were discussed from time to time in the publications of the Putney press during nine years.
2. The complete elaboration of these principles was a progressive work, carried on in connection with the long continued growth and education of the Putney Association.
3. These principles, though avowed (as before stated) in 1837, were not carried into action in any way by any of the members of the Putney Association till 1846.
4. It is not immodest, in the present exigency, to affirm that the leading members of the Putney Association belonged to the most respectable families in Vermont, had been educated in the best schools of New England morality and refinement, and were by the ordinary standards irreproachable in their conduct, so far as sexual matters are concerned, till they deliberately commenced, in 1846, the experiment of a new state of society, on principles which they had been long maturing and were prepared to defend before the world.
5. It may also be affirmed without fear of contradiction, that the main body of those who have joined the Association at Oneida, are sober, substantial men and women, of good previous character, and position in society.
6. The principles in question, have never been carried into full practical embodiment, either at Putney or Oneida, but have been held by the

Association, as the principles of an *ultimate state*, toward which society among them is advancing, slowly and carefully, with all due deference to sentiments and relations established by the old order of things.

7. The Association abstains from all proselyting, aggressive operations, publishing its sexual theory (at this time, as heretofore) only in self-defence, and at the command of public sentiment.

8. The Association, in respect to practical innovations limits itself to its own family circle, not invading society around it, and no just or even legal complaint of such invasions can be found at Putney or Oneida.

9. The Association may fairly demand toleration of its theory and experiment of society, on the ground that liberty of conscience is guarantied by the Constitution of the United States and of the several states, and on the ground that Quakers, Shakers, and other religion-ists, are tolerated in conscientious deviations from the general order of society.

10. The principles to be presented are not more revolutionary and offen-sive to popular sentiment, than the speculations of Fourier on the same subject; and are simply parallel in their scope (not in their nature) with the theory of marriage and propagation which Robert Dale Owen and Frances Wright propounded some years ago, in the public halls of New York, with great eclat. If infidels may think and speak freely on these "delicate" subjects, why may not lovers of Christ and the Bible take the same liberty, and be heard without irritation?

11. The ensuing argument professes to be nothing more than an *outline* or *programme* of fundamental principles, and the original intention of the author was to have expanded it largely before publishing it. The proper limits of this Report, however, rather require that it should be condensed. It is especially deficient in the development of the prudential and transitory principles which govern the Associ-ation in practice.

12. The argument cannot be perused with the fullest advantage by any but those who are familiar with the religious theory, of which it is the sequel...

CHAPTER II

Showing that Marriage is not an institution of the Kingdom of Heaven, and must give place to Communism...

PROPOSITION VI.- In the kingdom of heaven, the intimate union of life and interests, which in the world is limited to pairs, extends through the whole body of believers; i.e. *complex* marriage takes the place of simple.

John 17: 21. Christ prayed that *all* believers might be one, *even as* he and the Father are one. His unity with the Father is defined in the words, "*All mine are thine, and all thine are mine.*" Ver. 10. This perfect community of interests, then, will be the condition of all, when his prayer is answered. The universal unity of the members of Christ, is described in the same terms that are used to describe marriage-unity. Compare 1 Cor. 12: 12–27, with Gen. 2: 24. See also 1 Cor. 6: 15–17, and Eph. 5: 30–32.

Note.- Love between the children of God is excited and developed by a motive similar to that which produces ordinary family *affection*: "Every one that loveth him that begat, loveth also him that is begotten of him." 1 John 5: 1. The exciting cause is not sexuality, or any other external quality, but the fact that the parties have one Father, and of course, one life. The sons and daughters of God, must have even a stronger sense of their blood-relationship than ordinary brothers and sisters; because the Spirit of the Father, by which they are begotten, is their abiding Comforter, always renewing their consciousness of unity with him and with each other. Marriage in the world, requires a man to "*leave father and mother and cleave unto his wife.*" But the sons and daughters of God can never leave their Father and mother. Of course, the paramount sexual affection, required by the law of marriage, can have no place among them. They live as children with their Father forever, and the paramount affection of the household is not sexual, but *brotherly* love, an affection that grows directly out of the common relationship to the Father and of course is as universal as that relationship, and as appropriate between male and male, as between male and female. This affection as it exists between the different sexes, is necessarily unlimited as to number. A brother may love ten sisters, or a sister ten brothers, according to the customs of the world. The exclusiveness of marriage does not enter the family circle. But heaven is a family circle; and when we say that brotherly love is the *paramount* affection of that circle, we mean that it takes the place of supremacy which the matrimonial affection occupies in this world; it is that by which the members of God's family are brought into the closest possible union; that which controls and directs the sexual, as well as every other subordinate affection. For this reason there is neither marrying nor giving in marriage in the resurrection. Marriage makes of "*twain one flesh,*" but the brotherly love of heaven, makes of *all one spirit.* The unity of *all* God's family is described in Christ's prayer, John 17: 21–23, as far more complete, than any that earthly imaginations conceive of as existing in the conjugal relation ...

PROPOSITION IX.- The abolishment of sexual exclusiveness is involved in the love-relation required between all believers by the express injunction of

Christ and the apostles, and by the whole tenor of the New Testament. The new commandment is, that we "love one another," and that, not by pairs, as in the world, but *en* masse. We are required to love one another *fervently*, (I Peter I: 22,) or, as the original might be rendered, *burningly*. The fashion of the world forbids a man and woman who are otherwise appropriated, to love one another burningly – to flow into each other's hearts. But if they obey Christ they must do this; and whoever would allow them to do this, and yet would forbid them (on any other ground than that of present expediency) to express their unity of hearts by bodily unity, would "strain at a gnat and swallow a camel;" for unity of hearts is as much more important than the bodily expression of it, as a camel is bigger than a gnat.

Note.- The tendency of religious unity to flow into the channel of amativeness, manifests itself in revivals and in all the higher forms of spiritualism. Marriages or illegitimate amours usually follow religious excitements. Almost every spiritual sect has been troubled by amative tendencies. These facts are not to be treated as unaccountable irregularities, but as expressions of a law of human nature. Amativeness is in fact (as will be seen more fully hereafter) the first and most natural channel of religious love. This law must not be despised and ignored, but must be investigated and provided for. This is the object of the present treatise.

PROPOSITION XIII.- The law of marriage "worketh wrath." I. It provokes to secret adultery, actual or of the heart.- 2. It ties together unmatched natures. 3. It sunders matched natures. 4. It gives to sexual appetite only a scanty and monotonous allowance, and so produces the natural vices of poverty, contraction of taste, and stinginess or jealousy. 5. It makes no provision for the sexual appetite at the very time when that appetite is the strongest. By the custom of the world, marriage, in the average of cases, takes place at about the age of twenty-four: whereas puberty commences at the age of fourteen. For ten years, therefore, and that in the very flush of life, the sexual appetite is starved. This law of society bears hardest on females, because they have less opportunity of choosing their time of marriage than men. This discrepancy between the marriage system and nature, is one of the principal sources of the peculiar diseases of women, of prostitution, masturbation, and licentiousness in general.

Note.- The only hopeful scheme of Moral Reform, is one which will bring the sexes together according to the demands of nature. The desire of the sexes is a stream ever running. If it is dammed up, it will break out irregularly and destructively. The only way to make it safe and useful, is to give it a free natural channel or to vary the illustration, the attractions of male and female are like positive and negative electricities. In equilibrium, they are quiet. Separate them, and they become turbulent. Prostitution, masturbation, and obscenity in general, are injuirious eruptions, incident to unnatural separations of the male and female elements. Reform, in order to be effectual must base itself on the principle of restoring and preserving equilibrium by free intercourse Even in the world it is known that the mingling of the sexes to a certain extent, is favorable to purity; and that sexual isolation, as in colleges, monasteries, &c., breeds salacity and obscenity. A system of complex-marriage, which shall match the demands of nature, both as to time and variety, will open the prison doors to the victims both of marriage and celibacy: to those in married life who are starved, and those who are oppressed by lust; to those who are tied to uncongenial natures, and those who are separated from their natural mates; – to those in the unmarried state who are withered by neglect, diseased by unnatural abstinence, or plunged into prostitution and self-pollution, by desires which find no lawful channel.

Source: *Bible communism: a compilation from the annual reports and other publications of the Oneida Association and its branches; presenting, in connection with their history, a summary view of their religious and social* theories (Brooklyn, 1853), Oneida Community Collection, Department of Special Collections, Syracuse University Library. Available at http://library.syr.edu/digital/collections/b/Bible-Communism/ (accessed August 13, 2010).

5 Women of the Oneida Community, undated

This image offers a glimpse of the distinctive femininity embraced by Noyes and his followers. Similar to the bloomer or "Turkish" costume of women's rights advocates, women at the Oneida Community wore short dresses with pantelettes. Unlike most American women, they also cut their hair to fall around their shoulders. Intended to liberate women from the bonds of fashion, Noyes and his followers also believed the short dress and hair were more modest than the latest styles. Indeed, Noyes deliberately described the style of Oneida Community women as similar to children's dress. While women's rights advocates responded to public ridicule and abandoned the bloomer costume by the mid-1850s, Oneida Community women persisted in wearing the short dress through the 1860s and 1870s.

Figure 7.1   Women of Oneida Community, undated (H. Mallory, Ellen Miller, Fidelia Burt, Helen Miller, Louisa Waters). Reproduced courtesy of Oneida Community Mansion House.

Source: #231 View of Community Women (stereograph), from *William A. Hinds Album* (1906,) held by the Oneida Community Mansion House, Inc. Syracuse University Library, Department of Special Collections, Oneida Community Collection, Oneida Community Photographs: A Finding Aid to Selected Images, Digital Edition. Available at http://library.syr.edu/digital/images/o/OneidaCommunityPhotos/ and   http://library.syr.edu/digital/images/o/OneidaCommunityPhotos/231.jpg   (both accessed August 13, 2010).

6 Julia Gardiner Tyler, "To the Duchess of Sutherland and Ladies of England," 1853

Julia Gardiner Tyler (1820–1889) was the wife of former President John Tyler. Approximately 70 slaves lived on their Virginia plantation, Sherwood Forest. In this essay, Tyler responds to the enormous success of Harriet Beecher Stowe's anti-slavery novel Uncle Tom's Cabin *in England. She begins by distinguishing American women, especially southern women, for their attention to the private sphere of family. After explaining her individual foray into the political sphere, Tyler praises American self-government and condemns British aristocracy. She rejects the interference of British noblewomen as inappropriate and hypocritical. Tyler also defends slavery using familiar arguments, pointing to the happiness and piety of American slaves.*

Your address to your sisters, the women of the United States. on the subject of Domestic Slavery, as it exists among us, which has appeared in our public journals, should be acknowledged by some one of the vast number of those to whom it is addressed, without awaiting the publication of the more former communication. There are some of the concerns of life in which conventionalities are properly to be disregarded, and this is one of them. A reply to your address must necessarily be the work of some one individual among us, or must go altogether unperformed. Woman, in the United States, with but few exceptions, confines herself within that sphere for which the God who created her seems to have designed her. Her circle is, literally and emphatically, that of her family; and such she is content that it shall be ... No; the vestments they wear are those of meekness and charity, their diamonds are gems of the heart, and their splendor the neatness, and order, and contentment, which everywhere greets the eye; and that neatness, that order, and that contentment, is in nothing more observable than in the well clothed and happy domestics who welcome your arrival, and heap upon you every comfort during your sojourn under the roofs of their masters. You will see then how utterly impossible it would be to expect the women of the United States to assemble in convention, either in person or by proxy, in order to frame an answer to your address. Nay, I must, moreover, in all frankness, declare to you, that the women of the South, especially, have not received your address in the kindest spirit. They regard it as entirely incompatible with all confidence in or consideration for them, to invoke the interposition of the women of what are called the Free States, in a matter with which they have no more to do than have yourselves, and whose interference in the question can produce no other effect than to excite disturbance, and agitation, and ill-will, and possibly, in the end, a total annihilation of kind feeling between geographical sections. It is the province of the women of the Southern States to preside over the domestic economy of the estates and plantations of their husbands . . . and it is felt to be but a poor compliment to the women of the South to suppose it necessary to introduce other superintendence than their own over the condition of their dependents and servants . . . They also see, or fancy that they see, in your movement, the fingers of your greatest statesmen. The Countess of DERBY the Viscountess PALMERSTON, the Countess of CARLISLE, Lady JOHN RUSSELL, not to mention others of distinction and notoriety, would scarcely be complimented by a supposition that they had signed or openly approved such an address without the concurrence of their husbands. The women of the Southern States are, for the most part, well educated; indeed, they yield not in this respect to any females on earth, and have peculiar opportunities of acquiring knowledge in regard to the public concerns of the world. Politics is almost universally the theme of conversation among the men . . . and the women would be stupid indeed, if they did not gather much information from this abundant source. Hence they are not ignorant of the rapid growth of their beloved country, or of the promises of its early future . . . Believe me that its magnitude now, and its importance in the future, is as fully known to the women of the United States, as it is to your husbands, and editors, and statesmen. Our census tables show a duplication of our population in every cycle of twenty-three years; so that by the time the infant now in the cradle shall have attained to the age of manhood, that population will have increased to 50 000 000; and by the time that same infant attains to middle age, it will have swollen into 100 000 000. We need go no further in the estimate, in order to unveil that immense future which lies before us – a future, unrivaled in point of power by any thing the world has heretofore seen – a future which already fixes upon it the intense and steadfast gaze of the statesmen of other countries – a future to be regarded with rapture by the lover of man, and which may cause privilege to shiver and tremble with fear in all its fibers and arteries. I allude not to any power of the sword. No, I allude to a power more resistless, and more certain in its results – the power of example – the example of a free, prosperous, and great people, among whom all artificial distinctions of society are unknown; where preferment is equally open to all, and man's capacity for self-government is recognized and conclusively established. The women of the United States foresee all this, and they also thoroughly comprehend the fact that all confederacies have heretofore, in the history of the world, been broken up and destroyed by the machinations of foreign governments...

Nor is this suspicion in any degree removed by the fact on which you predicate your address, viz: the fact that your country inflicted on her then colonies the "curse" of Slavery in opposition to their frequent and solemn protests. In the historical fact you are certainly correct. The colony of Virginia, and, I believe, most of the other colonies, were constant in their earnest remonstrances... Thus, then, England not only permitted, but encouraged the slave trade, for the period of a century and a half, as a means of swelling her coffers; and the infamous traffic could only be expelled from this country by the force and power of the sword. Your Kings and Queens, sustained by your Parliament and people, entered into treaties, and formed contracts, for the purpose of reaping a rich harvest of profit from the trade; and the voice of the slave dealer on the shores of Africa was perfect music in their ears... The colonies remonstrated, and remonstrated in vain, until driven to desperation by her perseverance, they severed the bonds that bound them to England, and established their independence, and abolished the slave trade by their only resource – the power of the sword. The great slave market, in which England had enjoyed a monopoly, was thus lost to her; and from that moment she began to discover that there was something rather immoral in the traffic ... Would England, with a continuance of a monopoly of the trade over our broad acres up to the present day, have clothed herself in sackcloth and ashes, as she now has done? Where was her humanity and Christian philanthropy for the long period of 150 years?... It will be a very, very difficult matter, to furnish us with satisfactory reasons for this great and sudden conversion of a whole people, after losing the American market, on the subject of the slave trade, and we, women of the United States, must ever receive with suspicion all interference with our domestic affairs on the part of the noble ladies of England, or any portion of her inhabitants. Such interference implies either a want of proper and becoming conduct on our part in the management of our negroes, or it seeks to enlist the sympathies of the world against us. Your own address, (I have the charity to suppose that it was written in ignorance of the fact, as it is,) represents the Southern States as denying to their slaves all religious instruction – a calumny more false was never uttered. So far from it, no Sabbath goes by that the places of worship are not numerously attended by the black population – edifying the discourses are delivered to them, and often by colored pastors, and large numbers of them are in communion with the churches. And yet your tears are made to flow freely over the sad and melancholy privations of the children of Africa, to whom the bread of life is represented as denied. Your assertion could only have been derived from some dealer in, and retailer of fiction. It is known how readily woman's heart responds to real or imaginary distress, and when woman joins in the concerns of the busy world, how readily her sympathies become excited by an artificial, as well as a real, picture of human suffering. This sympathy, makes her the gem of creation, rather disqualifies her as a legislator, and subjects her to be made the instrument of the designing. One fact is incontrovertible, and I recommend it to the consideration of the DUCHESS OF SUTHERLAND, and her compeers of high and low degree – that England, when she had the power to prevent the introduction of slavery into the United States, most obstinately refused to do it; but now that she is deprived of her authority, either to advise or dictate, she sighs and sheds tears, and complains over the injustice and the wrong. The crocodile, good sisters of England, is said to cry most piteously; but woe to the unhappy traveler who is beguiled by its tears! ...

[handwritten margin note: England's fault that slave was not stopped]

Source: Julia Gardiner Tyler, "To the Duchess of Sutherland and Ladies of England," *New York Times*, February 5, 1853.

7 Horace Greeley *et al.*, "Woman and Work," 1854

The mostly middle-class men and women of the antebellum women's rights movement were deeply interested in women's economic inequality.
They lobbied for legal protection of married women's property and wages; they also sought equal pay and greater opportunities in the labor force.
This statement, authored in part by New York Tribune *editor Horace Greeley and Syracuse feminist Matilda Joslyn Gage, connects women's economic and political subordination. Though they focus on the poor working conditions of domestic servants, the document also exposes women's rights activists' class and ethnic biases.*

Whether women should or should not be permitted to vote, to hold office, to serve on juries, and to officiate as lawyers, doctors, or divines, are questions about which a diversity of opinions is likely long to exist. But that the current rates of remuneration for woman's work are entirely, unjustly inadequate, is a proposition which needs only to be considered to insure its hearty acceptance by every intelligent, justice-loving human being. Consider a few facts:

Every able-bodied man inured to labor, though of the rudest sort, who steps on shore in America from Europe, is worth a dollar per day, and can readily command it. Though he only knows how to wield such rude, clumsy implements as the pick and spade, there are dozens of places where his services are in request at a dollar per day the year through, and he can even be transported hence to the place where his services are wanted, on the strength of his contract to work and the credit of his future earnings. We do not say this is the case every day in the year, for it may not be at this most inclement and forbidding season; but it is the general fact, as every one knows. And any careful, intelligent, resolute male laborer is morally certain to rise out of the condition of a mere shoveler, into a position where the work is lighter and the pay better after a year or two of faithful service.

But the sister of this same faithful worker, equally careful, intelligent, and willing to do anything honest and reputable for a living, finds no such chances proffered her. No agent meets her on the dock to persuade her to accept a passage to Illinois or Upper Canada, there to be employed on fair work at a dollar per day and expectations. On the contrary, she may think herself fortunate if a week's search opens to her a place where by the devotion of all her waking hours she can earn five to six dollars per month, with a chance of its increase, after several years' faithful service, to seven or eight dollars at most.

The brother is in many respects the equal of his employer; may sit down beside him at the hotel where they both stop for dinner; their votes may balance each other at any election; the laborer lives with those whose company suits him, and needs no character from his last place to secure him employment or a new job when he gets tired of the old one. But the sister never passes out of the atmosphere of caste – of conscious and galling inferiority to those with whom her days must be spent. There is no election day in *her* year, and but the ghost of a Fourth of July. She must live not with those she likes, but with those who want her; she is not always safe from libertine insult in what serves her for a home; she knows no ten-hour rule, and would not dare to claim its protection if one were enacted. Though not a slave by law, she is too often as near it in practice as one legally free can be.

Now this disparity between the rewards of man's and woman's labor at the base of the social edifice, is carried up to its very pinnacle. Of a brother and sister equally qualified and effective as teachers, the brother will receive twice as much compensation as the sister. The mistress who conducts the rural district school in summer, usually receives less than half the monthly stipend that her brother does for teaching that same school in winter, when time and work are far less valuable; and here there can be no pretence of a disparity in capacity justifying that in wages. Between male and female workers in the factories and mills, the same difference is enforced.

Who does not feel that this is intrinsically wrong? that the sister ought to have equal (not necessarily identical) opportunities with the brother – should be as well taught, industrially as well as intellectually, and her compensation made to correspond with her capacity, upon a clear understanding of the fact that, though her muscular power is less than his, yet her dexterity and celerity of manipulation are greater?

Where does the wrong originate? Suppose that, by some inexorable law in the spirit of Hindoo caste, it were settled that negroes, regardless of personal capacity, could do nothing for a living but black boots, and that red-haired men were allowed to engage in no avocation except horse-currying; who does not perceive that, though boot-blacking and horse-currying might be well and cheaply done, black-skinned and also red-haired men would have but a sorry chance for making a living? Who does not see that their wages, social standing, and means of securing independence, would be far inferior to those they now enjoy?

The one great cause, therefore, of the inadequate compensation and inferior position of woman, is the unjust apportionment of avocation. Man has taken the lion's share to himself, and allotted the residue to woman, telling her to take that and be content with it, if she don't want to be regarded as a forward, indelicate, presuming, unwomanly creature, who is evidently no better than she should be. And woman has come for the most part to accept the lot thus assigned her, with thankfulness, or, rather, without thought, just as the Mussulman's wife rejoices in her sense of propriety which will not permit her to show her face in the street, and the Brahmin widow immolates herself on the funeral pyre of her husband.

What is the appropriate remedy?

Primarily and mainly, a more rational and healthful public sentiment with regard to woman's work; a sentiment which shall welcome her to every employment wherein she may be useful and efficient without necessarily compromising her purity or overtasking her strength. Let her be encouraged to open a store, to work a garden, plant and tend an orchard, to learn any of the lighter mechanical trades, to study for a profession, whenever her circumstances and her tastes shall render any of these desirable. Let woman, and the advocates of justice to women, encourage and patronize her in whatever laudable pursuits she may thus undertake; let them give a preference to dry-goods stores wherein the clerks are mainly women; and so as to hotels where they wait at table, mechanics' shops in which they are extensively employed and fairly paid. Let the ablest of the sex be called to the lecture-room, to the temperance rostrum, etc.; and whenever a post-office falls vacant and a deserving woman is competent to fill and willing to take it, let her be appointed, as a very few have already been. There will always be some widow of a poor clergyman, doctor, lawyer, or other citizens prematurely cut off, who will be found qualified for and glad to accept such a post if others will suggest her name and procure her appointment. Thus abstracting more and more of the competent and energetic from the restricted sphere wherein they now struggle with their sister for a meager and precarious subsistence, the greater mass of self-subsisting women will find the demand for their labor gradually increasing and its recompense proportionally enhancing. With a larger field and more decided usefulness will come a truer and deeper respect; and woman, no longer constrained to marry for a position, may always wait to marry worthily and in obedience to the dictates of sincere affection. Hence constancy, purity, mutual respect, a just independence and a little of happiness, may be reasonably anticipated.

HORACE GREELEY, MARY VAUGHAN, ABRAHAM PRYNE, SARAH PELLET, MATILDA JOSLYN GAGE. ALBANY CONVENTION. FEBRUARY 14 AND 15, 1854.

Source: Elizabeth Cady Stanton, Susan B. Anthony, and Matilda Joslyn Gage, *History of Woman Suffrage*, Vol. 1: *1848–1861* (New York: Fowler and Wells, Publishers, 1881), pp. 589–591.

8 Clarina Howard Nichols, "To the Women of the State of New York," c.1856

In 1854, the Kansas–Nebraska Act introduced the doctrine of popular sovereignty to Kansas territory. The law, which stipulated that the territory's citizens determine the legality of slavery, prompted a flood of anti-slavery settlers from New England and pro-slavery settlers from Missouri. Both pro- and anti-slavery settlers resorted to violence to ensure their dominance in the state. In May 1856, pro-slavery settlers invaded the anti-slavery town of Lawrence. In retaliation, abolitionist John Brown killed five pro-slavery settlers. Clarina Howard Nichols, a native of Vermont, moved to Kansas to participate in this political and violent struggle. In this document, she appeals to New York women to support the anti-slavery settlers.

Sisters:–

Your hearts have been stirred by tales of Kansas outraged, wronged; the Constitutional rights of her people struck down; "the enjoyment of life, liberty and the pursuit of happiness" made treasonable; and all the God-given means of subsistence and general prosperity perverted from the dwellers in that beautiful land, by the iron heart and strong hand of *tyrant power!*

Government heeds not, hears not, the cry of the afflicted. Good men *may* struggle in vain to rescue the victims by the speedy election of righteous rulers, and the wealth, locked in the treasuries of Free States and rich men's coffers, may be too tardy or insufficient to save the suffering, starving inhabitants of Kansas from death upon her soil, or the necessity of returning to the Free States to be fed. Supported they must be, either in Kansas or out of it; for they have expended, or been robbed, of their all in the struggle for free homes. The question, in a pecuniary point of view, then, is, *where* shall they be fed? Humanity – struggling for freedom *to be* in the image of its Maker – cries, in *Kansas*, where, to hold free homes, is to ensure the cause of Freedom and stay the waves of oppression.

Are you mothers? Let me speak to you for the mothers of Kansas. *I* am one of them. My sons are among the sufferers and the defenders of that ill-fated Territory; their blood has baptized the soil which they yet live to weep over, to love, and to defend. I ask of you, mothers of New York, but a tithe of the sacrifices and devotion of the mothers of Kansas. *Their* "jewels," more precious than silver, or gold, or houses and lands, are already laid a sacrifice upon the altar. Can *you* withhold from them the bread that shall win to you the blessing of those ready to perish?

Look upon your sons, secure in the pursuit of all that is ennobling – look upon your fair daughters, safe from the outrages of a degraded and ruffian soldiery – look upon your infants, smiling in the sweet security and sunshine of homes running over with comfort and happiness and plenty, and from your stores give to those who have none of all these but the mother-love, which, in the absence of every means to succor and save, is crushing the over-taxed heart into the blackness of despair!

Are you wives? Brave, loving men have tracked the prairie paths to bring bread, and never returned; have turned to the fields of their labor, and, with the last fond kiss yet warm upon their lips, been felled by the stealthy foe. Brave, loving men are now tracking the prairies with unshod feet and bleeding hearts. Brave, loving women weep, and pray, and toil to wipe away their tears and smile a welcome to the husbands that come sad and empty-handed back! Wives of New York, will you fill the empty hands and win the speechless gratitude of those suffering ones?

Are you sisters? Fond, noble brothers appeal to dear sisters in the East for help in their need. Your sympathy cannot comfort them, even, in their distress. The appeal of such a one lies before me now. "Nothing to eat; no money; nothing but *'sympathy!'* Oh, don't ever mention the word again if you love me. Don't ever tell me 'your eastern friends sympathize with you in your noble struggle for liberty.' Such friends, if one were hanging to a rope for dear life, would look over from the ship's side and cry, 'my *sympathies are with you, hang on till you drown!'* " Sisters of New York, will you send out the life-boat to save these sinking, struggling victims of foul oppression?

Words are too poor to give expression to my deep sense of peril, the suffering, the need, which is weighing upon the hearts and shutting out sunshine and health from the homes of the people of Kansas.

I leave my appeal with you, women of New York, confident in a generous response and an earnest cooperation.

To many of you I may speak as personal friends and former co-workers in the cause of Humanity. I know your zeal. I know your labors. I count upon your utmost efforts in this the crisis hour of the accumulated oppressions of the past – in this the grey dawning of a resurrection day for Humanity, such as the world has never seen, which the past has promised without comprehending, and groped after without the strong faith that alone can win it. C.I.H. NICHOLS.

Source: Available at http://www.territorialkansasonline.org/imlskto/cgi-bin/index. php?SCREEN=view_image&document_id=100147&file_name=h000416 (accessed August 13, 2010).

9 Illustration of Women's Procession, Lynn, Mass., Shoemakers' Strike, 1860

This illustration documents the participation of women in the failed shoemakers' strike in Lynn, Massachusetts, in February and March 1860. The shoemaking industry employed young single women in factories as stitchers; bosses also hired married women who worked from home as binders. Responding to the mechanization of shoemaking in the 1850s, the strikers sought to raise wages, but male and female workers disagreed over the necessity of increasing women's pay. While female stitchers wanted to raise the pay of female factory and home workers, male shoemakers focused on their own wages, which, they argued, supported entire families. Female home workers ultimately united with male shoemakers around the family wage, but the unmarried women pictured here continued to demand fair pay. In the banner, they refer to themselves as "ladies," a strategy that both unmarried and married women used to gain sympathy for the strike. The banner's message also relied on slavery as a metaphor, a common tactic in the antebellum labor movement.

Figure 7.2   *Illustration of Women's Procession, Lynn, Mass., Shoemaker's Strike,* Frank Leslie's Illustrated Magazine, *March, 17, 1860. Reproduced courtesy of the Library of Congress.*

Source: *Frank Leslie's Illustrated Magazine,* March 17, 1860, Library of Congress, Illus. in AP2.L52 1860. Available at www.loc.gov/pictures/item/2007677064/ (accessed August 18, 2010).

10 Ernestine Rose on Divorce, 1860

Born in Poland to Jewish parents, Ernestine Rose (1810–1892) migrated to the United States in the 1830s. A dynamic and popular speaker, Rose advocated racial and sexual equality. Yet as an ethnic Jew and an avowed atheist, she faced anti-Semitism and discrimination from her fellow activists. During the 1850s,

women's rights advocates defended themselves from accusations of "free love."
At the Tenth National Women's Rights Convention, Elizabeth Cady Stanton
defied these critics by introducing the controversial topic of divorce. Horace
Greeley and Antoinette Brown Blackwell, the first woman ordained as a
minister in the United States, opposed the resolution as scandalous and
detrimental to women's rights. Rose spoke in favor of Stanton's resolution,
arguing that liberal divorce laws were essential to egalitarian marriages.

ERNESTINE L. ROSE said: – Mrs. President – The question of a Divorce law seems to me one of the greatest importance to all parties, but I presume that the very advocacy of divorce will be called "Free Love." For my part (and I wish distinctly to define my position), I do not know what others understand by that term; to me, in its truest significance, love must be free, or it ceases to be love. In its low and degrading sense, it is not love at all, and I have as little to do with its name as its reality.

The Rev. Mrs. Blackwell gave us quite a sermon on what woman ought to be, what she ought to do, and what marriage ought to be; an excellent sermon in its proper place, but not when the important question of a Divorce law is under consideration. She treats woman as some ethereal being. It is very well to be ethereal to some extent, but I tell you, my friends, it is quite requisite to be a little material, also. At all events, we are so, and, being so, it proves a law of our nature. (Applause).

It were indeed well if woman could be what she ought to be, man what he ought to be, and marriage what it ought to be; and it is to be hoped that through the Woman's Rights movement – the equalizing of the laws, making them more just, and making woman more independent – we will hasten the coming of the millennium, when marriage shall indeed be a bond of union and affection. But, alas! it is not yet; and I fear that sermons, however well meant, will not produce that desirable end; and as long as the evil is here, we must look it in the face without shrinking, grapple with it manfully, and the more complicated it is, the more courageously must it be analyzed, combated, and destroyed. (Applause).

Mrs. Blackwell told us that, marriage being based on the perfect equality of husband and wife, it can not be destroyed. But is it so? Where? Where and when have the sexes yet been equal in physical or mental education, in position, or in law? When and where have they yet been recognized by society, or by themselves, as equals? "Equal in rights," says Mrs. B. But are they equal in rights? If they were, we would need no conventions to claim our rights. "She can assert her equality." Yes, she can assert it, but does that assertion constitute a true marriage? And when the husband holds the iron heel of legal oppression on the subjugated neck of the wife until every spark of womanhood is crushed out, will it heal the wounded heart, the lacerated spirit, the destroyed hope, to assert her equality? And shall she still continue the wife? Is that a marriage which must not be dissolved? (Applause).

According to Mr. Greeley's definition, viz., that there is no marriage unless the ceremony is performed by a minister and in a church, the tens of thousands married according to the laws of this and most of the other States, by a lawyer or justice of the peace, a mayor or an alderman, are not married at all. According to the definition of our reverend sister, no one has ever yet been married, as woman has never yet been perfectly equal with man. I say to both, take your position, and abide by the consequences. If the few only, or no one, is really married, why do you object to a law that shall acknowledge the fact? You certainly ought not to force people to live together who are not married. (Applause).

Mr. Greeley tells us, that, marriage being a Divine institution, nothing but death should ever separate the parties; but when he was asked, "Would you have a being who, innocent and inexperienced, in the youth and ardor of affection, in the fond hope that the sentiment was reciprocated, united herself to one she loved and cherished, and then found (no matter from what cause) that his profession was false, his heart hollow, his acts cruel, that she was degraded by his vice, despised for his crimes, cursed by his very presence, and treated with every conceivable ignominy – would you have her drag out a miserable existence as his wife?" "No, no," says he; "in that case, they ought to separate." Separate? But what becomes of the union divinely instituted, which death only should part? (Applause)...

But what is marriage? A human institution, called out by the needs of social, affectional human nature, for human purposes, its objects are, first, the happiness of the parties immediately concerned, and, secondly, the welfare of society. Define it as you please, these are only its objects; and therefore if, from well-ascertained facts, it is demonstrated that the real objects are frustrated, that instead of union and happiness, there are only discord and misery to themselves, and vice and crime to society, I ask, in the name of individual, happiness and social morality and well-being, why such a marriage should be binding for life? – why one human being should be chained for life to the dead body of another? "But they may separate and still remain married." What a perversion of the very term! Is that the union which "death only should part"? It may be according to the definition of the Rev. Mrs. Blackwell's theology and Mr. Greeley's dictionary, but it certainly is not according to common-sense or the dictates of morality. No, no! "It is not well for man to be alone," before nor after marriage. (Applause).

I therefore ask for a Divorce law. Divorce is now granted for some crimes; I ask it for others also. It is granted for a State's prison offense. I ask that personal cruelty to a wife, whom he swore to "love, cherish, and protect," may be made a heinous crime – a perjury and a State's prison offense, for which divorce shall be granted. Willful desertion for one year should be a sufficient cause for divorce, for the willful deserter forfeits the sacred title of husband or wife. Habitual intemperance, or any other vice which makes the husband or wife intolerable and abhorrent to the other, ought to be sufficient cause for divorce. I ask for a law of Divorce, so as to secure the real objects and blessings of married life, to prevent the crimes and immoralities now practiced, to prevent "Free Love," in its most hideous form, such as is now carried on but too often under the very name of marriage, where hypocrisy is added to the crime of legalized prostitution. "Free Love," in its degraded sense, asks for no Divorce law. It acknowledges no marriage, and therefore requires no divorce. I believe in true marriages, and therefore I ask for a law to free men and women from false ones. (Applause) ...

Finally, educate woman, to enable her to promote her independence, and she will not be obliged to marry for a home and a subsistence. Give the wife an equal right with the husband in the property acquired after marriage, and it will be a bond of union between them. Diamond cement, applied on both sides of a fractured vase, re-unites the parts, and prevents them from falling asunder. A gold band is more efficacious than an iron law. Until now, the gold has all been on one side, and the iron law on the other. Remove it; place the golden band of justice and mutual interest around both husband and wife, and it will hide the little fractures which may have occurred, even from their own perception, and allow them effectually to re-unite. A union of interest helps to preserve a union of hearts. (Loud applause).

Source: Elizabeth Cady Stanton, Susan B. Anthony, and Matilda Joslyn Gage, *History of Woman Suffrage*, Vol. 1: *1848–1861* (New York: Fowler and Wells, Publishers, 1881), pp. 729–732. Available by subscription at http://asp6new.alexanderstreet.com/was2/was2.object.details.aspx?dorpid=1000675460

Suggested Questions for Discussion

1   In what ways did women participate in the growing sectional conflict over slavery? How did pro- and anti-slavery arguments depend on differing views of womanhood?
2   What were early women's rights activists' criticisms of the economic, political, and legal status of women?
3   What was the connection between women's rights and other reforms? How did other forms of activism – abolition, Indian reform, urban missions, communitarian experiments, labor reform – address women's status?

Chapter 8   Civil Wars

1 Louisa May Alcott Treats the Wounded after the Battle of Fredericksburg, 1863

Published in 1863, Louisa May Alcott's Hospital Sketches, *an autobiographical account of her experiences as a nurse at the Union Hotel Hospital in Washington, DC, was a bestseller. Like many other northern women, Alcott and her character Tribulation Periwinkle wanted to aid the Union cause. Women's contributions as nurses, fundraisers, patriots, civil servants, and writers expanded their presence in the public realm. Periwinkle's hesitation in bathing wounded soldiers captures the novelty of Civil War nursing, which also required women to be in close physical contact with strange men. Dorothea Dix, the head of Union Army nurses, wanted to avoid any possibility of sexual scandal, so she recruited only spinsters – or women beyond marriageable age – as nurses.*

"They've come! they've come! hurry up, ladies – you're wanted."

"Who have come? the rebels?"

This sudden summons in the gray dawn was somewhat startling to a three days' nurse like myself, and, as the thundering knock came at our door, I sprang up in my bed, prepared

> "To gird my woman's form,
> And on the ramparts die,"

Women in American History to 1880: A Documentary Reader, by Carol Faulkner
© 2011 Blackwell Publishing Ltd.

If necessary, but my room-mate took it more coolly, and, as she began a rapid toilet, answered my bewildered question, –

"Bless you, no child; it's the wounded from Fredericksburg; forty ambulances are at the door, and we shall have our hands full in fifteen minutes."

"What shall we have to do?"

"Wash, dress, feed, warm and nurse them for the next three months, I dare say. Eighty beds are ready, and we were getting impatient for the men to come. Now you will begin to see hospital life in earnest, for you won't probably find time to sit down all day, and may think yourself fortunate if you get to bed by midnight. Come to me in the ball-room when you are ready, the worst cases are always carried there, and I shall need your help."

So saying, the energetic little woman twirled her hair into a button at the back of her head, in a "cleared for action" sort of style, and vanished, wresting her way into a feminine kind of pea-jacket as she went...

The sight of several stretchers, each with its legless, armless, or desperately wounded occupant, entering my ward, admonished me that I was there to work, not to wonder or weep; so I corked up my feelings, and returned to the path of duty, which was rather "a hard road to travel" just then. The house had been a hotel before hospitals were needed, and many of the doors still bore their old names; some not so inappropriate as might be imagined, for my ward was in truth a *ball-room*, if gun-shot wounds could christen it. Forty beds were prepared, many already tenanted by tired men who fell down anywhere, and drowsed until the smell of food roused them. Round the great stove was gathered the dreariest group I ever saw – ragged, gaunt and pale, mud to the knees, with blood bandages untouched since put on days before; many bundled up in blankets, coats being lost, or useless; and all wearing that disheartened look which proclaimed defeat, more plainly than any telegram of the Burnside blunder. I pitied them so much, I dared not speak to them, though, remembering all they had been through since the route at Fredericksburg, I yearned to serve the dreariest of them all. Presently, Miss Blank tore me from my refuge behind piles of one-sleeved shirts, odd socks, bandages and lint; put basin, sponge, towels, and a block of brown soap into my hands, with these appalling directions:

"Come, my dear, begin to wash as fast as you can. Tell them to take off socks, coats and shirts; scrub them well, put on clean shirts, and the attendants will finish them off, and lay them in bed."

If she had requested me to shave them all, or dance a hornpipe on the stove funnel, I should have been less staggered; but to scrub some dozen lords of creation at a moments notice, was really – really –. However, there was no time for nonsense, and, having resolved when I came to do everything I was bid, I drowned my scruples in my washbowl, clutched my soap manfully, and, assuming a business-like air, made a dab at the first dirty specimen I saw, bent on performing my task *vi et armis* if necessary. I chanced to light on a withered old Irishman, wounded in the head, which caused that portion of his frame to be tastefully laid out like a garden, the bandages being the walks, his hair the shrubbery. He was so overpowered by the honor of having a lady wash him, as he expressed it, that he did nothing but roll up his eyes, and bless me, in an irresistible style which was too much for my sense of the ludicrous; so we laughed together, and when I knelt down to take off his shoes, he "flopped" also and wouldn't hear of my touching "them dirty craters. May your bed above be aisly darlin', for the day's work ye be doon! – Woosh! There ye are, and bedad, it's hard tellin' which is the dirtiest, the fut or the shoe." It was; and if he hadn't been to the fore, I should have gone on pulling, under the impression that the "fut" was a boot, for trousers, socks, shoes and legs were a mass of mud. This comical tableau produced a general grin, at which propitious beginning I took heart and scrubbed away like any tidy parent on a Saturday night. Some of them took the performance like sleepy children, leaning their tired heads against me as I worked, others looked grimly scandalized, and several of the roughest colored like bashful girls.

Source: Alice Fahs, ed., *Hospital Sketches* (New York: Bedford Books, 2004), pp. 68–72.

2 Advertisement for the Great Western Sanitary Fair, 1863

After the beginning of the Civil War, northern women formed soldiers'
aid societies to help supply the initially ill-provisioned Union Army.
The goal of the US Sanitary Commission, led by prominent men such as
Henry Bellows and Frederick Law Olmstead, was to direct the labor of
these women. Women in local soldiers' aid societies and branches of the
Sanitary Commission defied male direction, however, and wielded
influence through their organizational ability and successful fundraising.
By the end of the war, sanitary fairs had raised approximately $4.4 million.
In addition to sewing uniforms and raising money, female members of the
Sanitary Commission served as nurses, managed hospital boats, and
staffed kitchens in army camps.

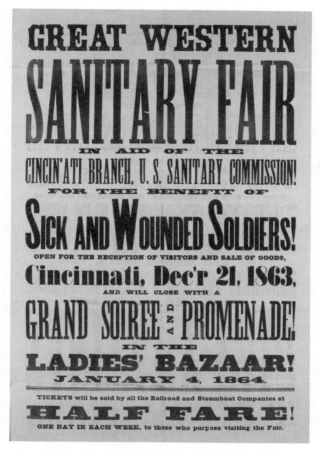

Figure 8.1   Advertisement for the Great Western Sanitary Fair, December 21, 1863 to January 4, 1864. Reproduced courtesy of Ohio Historical Society.

Source: Ohio Historical Society. Available at http://ohsweb.ohiohistory.org/ohiopix/Image.cfm?ID=5757 (accessed August 16, 2010).

3 John Burnside and Abisha Scofield, Affidavits on the Removal of Black Soldiers' Families from Camp Nelson, Kentucky, 1864

From the first battles of the Civil War, enslaved men and women fled to Union lines seeking freedom and employment. While some officers viewed former slaves as a logistical and financial burden, many employed freedmen and women. In Union camps, freedwomen worked as laundresses, cooks, and sometimes nurses. By 1863, the Emancipation Proclamation authorized the enlistment of black troops. In these documents, soldier John Burnside and missionary Abisha Scofield testify about the expulsion of black families from an army camp. These affidavits reveal that black soldiers and their families faced threats from former owners as well as mistreatment by the Union Army.

Camp Nelson KY. Dec. [15] 1864.

Personally appeared before me. E. B. W. Restieaux Capt and A[sistant]. Q[uarter]. M[aster]. John Burnside – a man of color who being sworn upon oath says – I am a solider in Company K. 124 Regt. U.S.C.T. I am a married man. My wife and children belonged to William Royster of Garrard County Ky. Royster had a son John who was with [Confederate General John H.] Morgan during his raid into Kentucky in June 1863. He got separated from Morgan's command and went home. The Provost Marshal instituted a search for him at two different times. He was not found. My family were charged with giving the information which led to the measures of the Provost Marshal. William Royster told me that my wife had been trying to ruin him for the last two years and if he found out that this – meaning the information went out through the black family – meaning my family – he would scatter them to the four winds of heaven. This was said about the last of September 1864. In consequence of this threat my family were in constant dread, and desired to find protection and employment from the Government. At that time I had been employed at Camp Nelson and was not enlisted. A few days afterward I was sick at my mothers. I sent my sister to see Col. Sedgwick and inquire if my family might come to Camp, and if they might, would they be protected: She returned the same night and informed me that Col. Sedgwick said tell him (me) to bring them in and I, Col. Sedgwick, will protect them. Before, I was unwilling that they should come but on receiving the promised protection of Col. Sedgwick. I told them to come. While my wife and family were in Camp they never received any money or provision from the government but earned their living with hard work

On Friday afternoon Nov. 28 [25] 1864 the Provost guard ordered my wife and family out of Camp. The guard had a wagon into which my wife and family were forced to go and were then driven out the lines

They were driven to a wood belonging to Mr. Simpson about seven miles from Camp and there thrown out without any protection or any home. While they were in the wood it rained hard and my family were exposed to

the storm. My eldest daughter had been sick for some time and was then slowly recovering. and further this deponent saith not.
John Burnside

Camp Nelson Ky Dec. 16th 1864
    Personally appeared before me E B W Restieaux Capt and A.Q.M. Abisha Scofield who being duly sworn upon oath says. I am a clergyman of the congregational denomination and have been laboring among the Freedmen at Camp Nelson Ky. under the auspices of the American Missionary association since the 20th of Sept 1864. The families of the colored solders who were in Camp lived in cabins and huts erected by the colored solders or at the expense of the women. During my labors among them I have witnessed about fifty of these huts and cabins erected and the material of which they were constructed was unserviceable to the Government. I have had extensive dealing with these people and from my observation I believe that they supported themselves by washing cooking and &c.
    Until the 22nd of last November I never heard any objection made by the military authorities of the Post to the women and children of colored soldiers residing within the limits of the camp. On Tuesday the 22nd of November last the huts and cabins in which the families of the colored soldiers lived were torn down and the inhabitants were placed in Government wagons and driven outside the lines. The weather at the time was the coldest of the season. The wind was blowing quite sharp and the women and children were thinly clad and mostly without shoes. They were not all driven out on one day but their expulsion occupied about three days.
    When they were driven out I did not know where they were to be taken and on the following Sabbath Nov 27th I went in search of the exiles. I found them in Nicholasville about six miles from Camp scattered in various places. Some were in the old Store house, some were straying along and lying down in the highway and all appeared to be suffering from exposure to the weather. I gave them some food. I received the provisions from Capt. T.E. Hall A.Q.M.
    The food was absolutely needed. On Monday Nov. 28 I saw and conversed with about sixteen women and children who had walked from Nicholasville in the hopes of getting into Camp. The guard refused them admittance. I told the guard that the order by which the women and children were expelled had been countermanded. The guard told me that he had strict orders not to admit them They were not admitted. Among the number was a young woman who was quite sick and while I was conversing with the guard she lay on the ground. A day or two after this they were allowed to return to Camp. They were then very destitute most all

complaining of being unwell. Children trembling with cold and wearied with fatigue. Since that time they have been crowded in a school room in Camp and their condition has been most abject and miserable, whereas they were pretty comfortable before they were driven out. While out of Camp they incurred disease and are now suffering from the effects of this exposure As a clergyman I have no hesitation in pronouncing the treatment to which these poor people have been subjected as exceedingly demoralizing in its effects in addition to the physical suffering it entailed. And further this deponent saith not
Abisha Scofield

Source: Ira Berlin *et al.*, *Free At Last: A Documentary History of Slavery, Freedom and the Civil War* (New York: The New Press, 1992), pp. 384–397.

4 Thomas Nast, *Emancipation*, 1865

Before the Civil War, Harriet Beecher Stowe and other anti-slavery writers contrasted the middle-class ideal of domesticity with the realities of slavery, including the separation of families, particularly mothers and children, and the brutal and sexualized violence directed at enslaved women. This wood engraving depicts the promise of emancipation for African American families. At the center of the illustration is an idealized African American family. The scenes to the right of the central image show children going to school, and families seeking aid from a Freedmen's Bureau agent.

Figure 8.2   *Thomas Nast, Emancipation, 1865. Reproduced courtesy of the Library of Congress.*

Source: Library of Congress, PGA – King & Baird – Emancipation. Available at www.loc.gov/pictures/item/2004665360/ (accessed August 20, 2010).

5 Jane Kamper, Milly Johnson, and Rebecca Parsons, Testimony on the Apprenticeship of Their Children, 1864–1867

As a slaveholding Union state, Maryland abolished slavery in 1864. Jane Kamper's dispute with her former master over her children predicted similar struggles across the postwar south. Freed people's principal goal after the Civil War was the reunification of their families, but they confronted tremendous geographic and legal obstacles. As these documents show, former slave owners apprenticed children in order to retain their labor and to exert continued power over the mother. Freedwomen turned to the Freedmen's Bureau for help in fighting the apprenticeship of their children.

Baltimore (Md.) Nov 14″/64
Statement of Jane Kamper
Slave of Wm Townsend of Talbot County Md.

I was the slave of Wm Townsend of Talbot county & told Mr. Townsend of my having become free & desired my master to give my children & my bedclothes he told me that I was free but that my Children Should be bound to me [him]. He locked my Children up so that I could not find them I afterwards got my children by stealth & brought them to Baltimore. I desire to regain possession of my bed clothes & furniture.

My Master pursued me to the Boat to get possession of my children but I hid them on the boat
Her
Jane X Kamper (f[ree] n [egro])
Mark

Chapel Hill, N.C. March, 26th 1867
Sir:–...

It is my purpose, to advertise for my children,

When I last knew them they were 2 of them in Esics county Va a girl and Boy, Living with their former owners. The Boy Belonged to Hugh Billaps The Girl Belonged to Dr Richards. The Boys name was Musco Johnson – The Girl Letty Johnson This accounts for 2 –

There is another two a Girl and Boy. They were sold to speculators at Richmond Va Where they were carried I do not Know. the girl's name was Henrietta Johnson The Boy William Quals Johnson. There is still another Anna Johnson who is Living in Hertford Co., N.C. with Mr. Albert Elliot my former owner and since the [Confederate] surrender he took her from me I protested against but of no avail I have tried several times since to get her. I wrote to him Last year and he would make no reply to my letters. he said when he took my child that she belonged to him, and I herd that his wife said that she intended to Keep her till she was 21 years of age. all this was done against my will. Now Sir I want her. If I cannot hear from the others she can be gotten I presume

Now Sir:

You will do me a lasting favor to attend to this matter for me as promptly as possible I convey the Matter into your hands, – hopeing that there can some information be gained from my children

Intrusting the matter with you sir I am Very Resptfully Sir:–
Milly Johnson

Georgia Washington County 28th April 1867

Before me came Rebecca Parsons – a freedwoman of this County who being duly sworn deposeth & saith, that she was when freed by the Government a Slave of T A Parsons of Johnson County– That she has four children now in possession of said Parsons – That when she was freed she informed said Parsons that she was going to her kindred who lived in Elbert County Ga – He told her that she might go but her children belonged to Him & she should not have them – That she was thus compelled to remain with Him – That in September last because she had hired one of the children to work with a neighbor and refused to take her and place her with Him said Parsons cruelly beat her deponent and drove her from his place thus separating her from her children

That she found a home in Washington County & in February last she went to Parsons & demanded her children– That Parsons told her "they were bound to him and that she should not have them unless she paid Him four thousand dollars" That she was thus compelled to return without them – And she left them crying to go with Her

Her
Rebecca X Parsons
Mark

Source: Ira Berlin and Leslie S. Rowland (eds.), *Families and Freedom: A Documentary History of African-American Kinship in the Civil War Era* (New York: New Press, 1997), pp. 214–218.

6 Testimony of Rhoda Ann Childs, 1866

After the end of the Civil War, the Freedmen's Bureau supervised the transition from slavery to a "free" labor system in the South. Former slaves and slave owners signed labor contracts determining the nature and length of work

as well as the pay. But, as Childs testifies, many whites wanted to maintain their control over former slaves. Eight men targeted Childs and her family because of her husband's service in the Union Army and, perhaps, the family's modest financial independence. To reassert their racial prerogatives over the bodies of black women, these white men raped and assaulted Childs and her daughters.

[Griffin, Ga.] Sept. 25,

Rhoda Ann Childs came into this office and made the following statement:

"Myself and husband were under contract with Mrs. Amelia Childs of Henry County, and worked from Jan. 1, 1866, until the crops were laid by, or in other words until the main work of the year was done, without difficulty. Then, (the fashion being prevalent among the planters) we were called upon one night, and my husband was demanded; I Said he was not there. They then asked where he was. I Said he was gone to the water mellon patch. They then Seized me and took me Some distance from the house, where they 'bucked' me down across a log, Stripped my clothes over my head, one of the men Standing astride my neck, and beat me across my posterior, two men holding my legs. In this manner I was beaten until they were tired. Then they turned me parallel with the log, laying my neck on a limb which projected from the log, and one man placing his foot upon my neck, beat me again on my hip and thigh. Then I was thrown upon the ground on my back, one of the men Stood upon my breast, while two others took hold of my feet and stretched My limbs as far apart as they could, while the man Standing upon my breast applied the Strap to my private parts until fatigued into stopping, and I was more dead than alive. Then a man, Supposed to be an ex-confederate Soldier, as he was on crutches, fell upon me and ravished me. During the whipping one of the men ran his pistol into me, and Said he had a hell of a mind to pull the trigger, and Swore they ought to Shoot me, as my husband had been in the 'God damned Yankee Army,' and Swore they meant to kill every black Son-of-a-bitch they could find that had ever fought against them. They then went back to the house, Seized my two daughters and beat them, demanding their father's pistol, and upon failure to get that, they entered the house and took Such articles of clothing as Suited their fancy, and decamped. There were concerned in this affair eight men, none of which could be recognized for certain.

Her

Rhoda Ann X Childs

Mark

Source: Ira Berlin *et al.*, *Free At Last* (New York: New York Press, 1992), pp. 537–538.

7 Historical Sketch of the Ladies' Memorial Society of New Bern, North Carolina, 1885

Immediately after the Civil War, Ladies' Memorial Associations (LMAs) appeared throughout the South with the shared goal of tending to and memorializing the remains of the Confederate dead. But their work also served larger ideological and political purposes. Southern white women were among the first to commemorate the Lost Cause, an idealized view of slavery, patriarchy, and chivalry in the antebellum South. Women in LMAs relied on their gender to hide the subversive intent of their actions: continued loyalty to the former Confederacy. In the 1880s, as southern states began to strip African Americans of their newfound civil and political rights, the LMAs enlisted a new generation of white southerners, who openly celebrated the memory of the Confederacy.

DURING the late sad war New Bern was long occupied by the Federal troops. At its close, the old citizens, long exiles from their homes, returned, broken in fortune, poor in worldly goods, but rich in patriotic fervor. The large-hearted women of New Bern determined, in some way, to commemorate the devotion of the dead Confederate soldiers of this section of the old North State. No means were available except what continuous effort could realize.

On November 17, 1866, the Board of City Councilmen, by a vote of four to two, passed the following ordinance:

"It is ordained by the Mayor and Council of the city of New Bern, that the plat of ground in Cedar Grove Cemetery, known as the Circle, and the four adjoining triangles, be, and the same are hereby given, set apart, and appropriated to the New Bern Memorial Association, for the legitimate purposes for which said Association was formed.

"Be it further ordained, that the Mayor and Council of said city shall, and will convey by deed to said Association said plat of ground, so soon as said Association shall be prepared legally to receive the same."

"The Ladies' Memorial Association of New Bern" was organized in January, 1867, with the following officers: President, Mrs. E. B. Daves; Vice-Presidents, Mrs. J. A. Guion, Mrs. W. P. Moore and Mrs. M. McK. Nash; Secretary, Miss H. Lane; Treasurer, Mrs. Julius Lewis. For the past eighteen years they have labored with commendable perseverance to accomplish their worthy aims. Money has been gathered from annual dues, festivals, concerts, mite chests, donations, and a final handsome and successful effort through the columns of the New Bern Daily Journal, by its editor, Mr. H. S. Nunn. Altogether they have received about $3,700.

On May 2d, 1867, was laid the corner-stone of the mausoleum or vault beneath centre plat. It was completed at a cost of about $2,000. Herein have been deposited sixty-seven bodies of Confederates, who died or were killed in or near the city during the war. Their names are preserved by the Society. Three other interments have been made since; and any Confederate soldier, remaining true to the "Lost Cause," may be buried here, if his family so desire.

Above this mausoleum, on the summit of the mound, stands the Association's crowning work – the beautiful monument reproduced in the frontispiece. It rises from a bottom base, four feet square, to a total height of eighteen feet. The bottom and subbase, die and shaft, are of fine Rutland blue marble. The life-size statue on top was cut, after a design expressly for this monument, by the best workman in Carrara, Italy. It represents a Confederate soldier in uniform and overcoat, on picket, with every sense awake as he keenly watches for the slightest hostile movement. Calm, faithful, brave, he will never be surprised. A noble face and figure, a typical hero from the ranks! In procuring and setting in place this statue, Mr. J. K. Willis, the skilled marble worker of New Bern, kindly assisted the ladies without charge for his personal care and superintendence.

Just as this statue was put in position, the first and only president of the Association, Mrs. Daves, passed from her service here to her reward. Her last moments were cheered by the announcement of the happy completion of this work, so dear to her noble heart.

The monument was finished in time for the annual May celebration, 1885. So Monday, May 11th, a most charming and auspicious day, was appropriated to the Inauguration Ceremonies.

Steamer and railroad poured in their contributions from river and inland, from Morehead, Kingston and Smithfield, until a dense throng gathered around the tastefully decorated speaker's stand, under the pleasant shade of the Academy's beautiful grove of elms. Prominent in front were the old shot-rent and battle-inscribed flag of the Forty-eighth North Carolina Regiment, and the bright banner of the Sixty-seventh North Carolina Regiment, borne by a one-armed ex-Confederate. Old veterans of these commands honored their remembered ensigns of trying days.

After music by the choir and a prayer by Rev. V. W. Shields, Mr. Clement Manly introduced the orator of the day, Captain Hamilton C. Graham, of Dallas county, Ala., but a native of Halifax county, N.C., and formerly a captain in the Seventh North Carolina Regiment, who then, in response to the invitation of the Memorial Association, delivered the handsome address which follows, on the Life and Services of General James Johnston Pettigrew.

Source: *Confederate Memorial Addresses* (1885). Available at Eastern North Carolina Digital Library, http://digital.lib.ecu.edu/historyfiction/item.aspx?id=lac (accessed August 16, 2010).

Suggested Questions for Discussion

1 Thomas Nast's image depicts the potential for emancipation to reunite black families. How did the experiences of African American women compare to his idealized portrayal?
2 How did northern and southern women participate in the Civil War? Did their experiences differ?

Chapter 9   Redefining Citizenship, 1865–1880

1 Jeannette Gilder and Senator Cattell, Correspondence Regarding Job in the US Mint, 1867–1868

In this exchange, Jeannette Gilder (1849–1916) writes her US Senator from New Jersey, Alexander Cattell, seeking a job in the US Mint in Philadelphia. Her father's death in 1864 forced Gilder into the ranks of working women. In 1850, the US Mint began hiring female clerks, and civil service positions for women expanded during the Civil War. As Cattell's mention of Henry Richard Linderman (the Mint's director from 1866 to 1869) reveals, these jobs often depended on political connections. Gilder later became a well-known journalist. In 1894, she published a pamphlet explaining her opposition to women's suffrage.

Bordentown, N.J.

Sept. 67

To
The Hon. Alex. G. Cattell

Dear Sir:
   I have been made aware of your kindness through our mutual friend His Excellency Geo. Ward, and take this one ans of thanking you for the trouble you have taken in my behalf. It is more of a kindness on your part than it

Women in American History to 1880: A Documentary Reader, by Carol Faulkner
© 2011 Blackwell Publishing Ltd.

would be on that of most men, as you must necessarily have a great deal to attend to, and I do assure you the attention is fully appreciated.

Since my father's death it has become necessary for me to add something towards the support of family and I do consider myself most fortunate in getting such a pleasant situation, which without your influence should have been unable to have attained, and for which I beg you to accept my grateful acknowledgements.

Will you be kind enough to tell me at about what time my services will be required at the mint.

Yours with great respect.

Jeane L. Gilder

Will you please tell me of getting in the mint by your influence it will be necessary for me to have security, and, about what time my services will be required.

United States Senate Chamber
Washington. April 11th 1868

My Dear Miss:

I am in receipt of your letter of the 9th Instant and delighted to learn that you have at last received the appointment at the mint. You must be charitable to Dr. Linderman for to my personal knowledge the work at the mint has so much fallen off that he has been compelled to reduce considerably his force. Under these circumstances it was difficult for him to fulfill the promise which he made me in regard to your service. I did not mean however to fail altogether in the matter and it is a source of great satisfaction to me to know that you are now regularly installed. Hoping that you will find the situation pleasant and with my best wishes for your health and happiness

Yours truly,

Alexr G. Cattell

Source: Jeannette L. Gilder Papers, 1865–1917. A-141, folder 10, Schlesinger Library, Radcliffe Institute, Harvard University, Cambridge, MA. Available at http://pds.lib.harvard.edu/pds/view/2582662 (accessed August 20, 2010).

2 Susan B. Anthony, Remarks to the American Equal Rights Association, 1869

On May 12, 1869 Susan B. Anthony spoke before the last meeting of the short-lived American Equal Rights Association, as abolitionists and feminists debated the Fifteenth Amendment, which stated, "The right of

citizens of the United States to vote shall not be denied or abridged by the United States or by any State on account of race, color, or previous condition of servitude." As Anthony points out, members disagreed vehemently on the issue of precedence, or, as Frederick Douglass put it, the "urgency" of placing the ballot in the hands of black men. These divisions had a lasting impact on the women's movement. Shortly after this speech, Susan B. Anthony and Elizabeth Cady Stanton formed the first organization devoted to women's rights, the National Woman Suffrage Association. Later that year, activists who supported the Fifteenth Amendment formed the American Woman Suffrage Association, but neither organization offered a platform for the civil and political rights of African American men and women.

Miss Susan B Anthony said: The question of precedence has no place on an equal rights platform. The only reason why it ever found a place here was that there were some who insisted that a woman must stand back & wait until another class should be enfranchised. In answer to that, my friend Mrs. Stanton & others of us have said, If you will not give the whole loaf of justice to the entire people, if you are determined to give it, piece by piece, then give it first to women, to the most intelligent & capable portion of the women at least, because in the present state of government it is intelligence, it is morality which is needed. We have never brought the question upon the platform, whether women should be enfranchised first or last. I remember having a long discussion with Tilton, Powell, & Phillips on this very question, when we were about to carry up our petitions to the Constitutional Convention. We took the name of an Equal Rights association, & were thinking of making another person president. I remember then that Mr Tilton said to me that we should urge the amendment to our Constitution to strike out the word "white" as the thing to be accomplished by that Convention, & he added, "The question of striking out the word 'male' we shall of course, as an Equal Rights association, urge as an intellectual theory, but we cannot demand it as a practical thing to be accomplished at this Convention." Mr Phillips acceded to that, & I think all the *men* acceded to that, all over the State. But there was one woman there who did not. My friend Mrs Stanton kept very good natured in the discussion; but I was boiling over with wrath; so much so that my friend Tilton noticed it & said, "What ails Susan? I never saw her behave so badly before." I will tell you what ailed Susan. It was the downright insolence of those two men, when I had canvassed the entire State from one end to the other, county by county, with petitions in my hand asking for woman suffrage, – if those two men, among the most advanced & glorious men of the nation, that they should dare to look me in the face & speak of this great earnest purpose of man as an "intellectual theory" but not to be practised, or for us to hope to attain. (Applause)

If Mr. Douglass had noticed who clapped him when he said "black men first, & white women afterwards," he would have seen that they were all men. The women did not clap him. The fact is that the men cannot understand us women. They think of us as some of the slaveholders used to think of their slaves, all love & compassion, with no malice in their hearts, but they thought "The negro is a poor lovable creature, kind, docile, unable to take care of himself, & dependent on our compassion to keep them"; & so they consented to do it for the good of the slaves. Men feel the same today. Douglass, Tilton, & Phillips, think that women are perfectly contented to let men earn the money & dole it out to us. We feel with Alexander Hamilton, "Give a man power over my substance, & he has power over my whole being." There is not a woman born, whose bread is earned by another, it does not matter whether that other is husband, brother, father, or friend, not one who consents to eat the bread earned by other hands, but her whole mortal being is in the power of that person. (Applause)

When Mr. Douglass tells us today that the case of the black man is so perilous, I tell him that wronged & outraged as they are by this hateful & mean prejudice against color, he would not today exchange his sex & color, wronged as he is, with Elizabeth Cady Stanton.

Mr Douglass. Will you allow me a question?

Miss Anthony. Yes; anything for a fight today.

Mr Douglass. I want to inquire whether granting to woman the right of suffrage will change anything in respect to the nature of our sexes.

Miss Anthony. It will change the nature of one thing very much, & that is the pecuniary position of woman. It will place her in a position in which she can earn her own bread, so that she can go out into the world an equal competitor in the struggle for life; so that she shall not be compelled to take such positions as men choose to accord to her & then take such pay as men choose to give her. In our working women's meetings it was proposed that the question of the decrease of marriages in this country should be taken into consideration, & Mr Crowly (of the "world," said, "I should like to know what you working women are up to; what has the increase or decrease of marriages to do with working women?" I replied, Send your reporters next Wednesday evening & we will show you. Men say that all women are to be married & supported by men, & the laws & customs & public sentiment are all based on that assumption. Wherever there is a woman loose – for we have sometimes women loose, as they had negroes loose, in slavery, & we have fugitive wives as they had fugitive slaves – whenever there is a woman loose or a fugitive wife, thrown out upon the world for support, she is an interloper, & she is paid but one half or one third the price that men receive. When a woman therefore is thrown upon her own resources, she has to choose one of two things, marriage or prostitution. Then it is getting to be a common saying among men all over the country, "Marriage is too expensive a luxury; men cannot afford it." There is the explanation. What we demand is that woman shall have the ballot, for she will never get her other rights until she demands them with the ballot in her hand. IT is not a question of precedence between women & black men. Neither has a claim to precedence upon an Equal Rights platform. But the business of this association is to demand for every man black or white, & for every woman, black or white, that they shall be this instant enfranchised & admitted into the body politic with equal rights & privileges.

Source: Ann D. Gordon (ed.), *The Selected Papers of Elizabeth Cady Stanton & Susan B. Anthony*, Vol. II: *Against an Aristocracy of Sex, 1866–1873* (New Brunswick, NJ: Rutgers University Press, 2000), pp. 238–241.

3 Elizabeth Cady Stanton, Speech on the Acquittal of Daniel McFarland, 1870

In 1868, actress Abby Sage McFarland moved to Indianapolis, Indiana, in order to secure a divorce from her husband Daniel McFarland. One year later, soon after her divorce was finalized, she became engaged to Albert Richardson, a New York Tribune journalist. Outraged, Daniel McFarland shot Richardson, who died several days later. In a deathbed ceremony performed by the Rev. Henry Ward Beecher, Abby Sage married Richardson. Elizabeth Stanton saw McFarland's acquittal as an example of women's abject status in marriage and the need for liberal divorce laws. Though she anticipates and deflects accusations of free love, Stanton invites controversy with the claim that the McFarland marriage was legalized prostitution.

<Ladies, I have sometimes been accused of free-love proclivities. My answer to that accusation is that I've lived thirty years with one man, and expect to live with him to the end, and I'll let my life speak for me.>

The deep interest of the entire nation in the McFarland trial, for the last month, is due not to any particular regard for the man, or abhorrence of the legal punishment for such crime, but to the fact that the trial indirectly involves the solution of the momentous questions of marriage and divorce – questions that underlie our whole social, religious, and political life.

As I have never seen the faces of either Daniel McFarland or Abby S. Richardson, I have no personal prejudices or preferences to bias my judgment in this matter. I will not admit now what I confess I did feel in earlier life, a prejudice always in favor of my own sex, for with sons and daughters alike growing up, my mother's heart has taught me to balance all questions with equal reference to both sexes. Nevertheless, I have felt during the past month, as Boston Abolitionists felt when Anthony Burns, the black man, the runaway slave, was condemned in their courts and marched through their streets, the sad, helpless victim of a false American public sentiment, who, having just tasted the sweets of liberty, was remanded by Massachusetts law to Southern slavery.

As I sat alone late one night and read the simple, truthful story of Abby S. Richardson, the fugitive wife, I tried to weigh the mountain of sorrow that had rolled over that poor woman's soul through these long years of hopeless agony; though the fiery ordeal of a public trial in our unjust decision, setting a madman free, to keep that poor brokenhearted woman in fear for her life as long as he lives. As I pondered all these things in the midnight hour, and recalled the hideous insults through the person of Abby S. Richardson on the entire womanhood of the nation, I resolved that, as I had devoted my life heretofore to the enfranchisement of woman, my future work should be to teach woman her duties to herself in the home...

To begin then with the present ugly fact and go back step by step to the foundation question, how comes it that a man who by our courts has been declared so insane that he may commit murder without being morally responsible to the State, is let loose on society to repeat such depredations, while the helpless victim of his hate and lust still lives and is liable at any moment to be sacrificed by his hand...

For the entire lack of chivalry shown in the late trial – alike by the court and the press – for the noble women innocently involved in the proceedings, we have but one remedy, and that is to have judges, jurors, advocates, reporters, editors of our own sex, that by the united action of man and woman the refined sentiments and manners of polite society may be carried into our public life.

But all these questions are secondary to the fundamental falsehood on which the opinions of the press, the decision of the court, the defence of the prisoner and his bloody deed are based, namely, "the husband's right of property in the wife." The old common law of the barbarous ages reflected in our statutes controls the public sentiment of the nineteenth century – though the real character and position of woman has entirely changed from the thoughtless, ignorant toy or drudge of the past to the enlightened, dignified, moral being of to-day. These one-sided, degrading statutes on marriage and divorce, which at this hour our sons are reading in their law schools, are daily educating them into low, gross ideas of their mothers, sisters, future wives, preparing them to contemplate with stolid indifference the hideous features of our present marriage institution, and to call that sacred that every pure woman feels to be unnatural and infamous...

While the stricken, heart-broken woman, to-day a target for the nation's scorn, has through struggle and humiliation given us a glowing but painful picture of the depths of degradation a wife may be called to endure, and thus touched a new chord of sympathy for the multitudes she represents, others of us, not crushed or perplexed with domestic discord and tyranny, or cumbered with the thoughts of our daily bread, have been solving the problem of woman's wrongs, and revising for her benefit the statute laws of many of the States...

Mrs. McFarland's married life from her own confession of loathing and abhorrence, was nothing more nor less than legalized prostitution, as Richter said, "no better than a work of adultery," and every pure woman must feel that when she sundered that tie she took the first step toward virtue and self-respect. As some criticism has been made on her subsequent action, though to my mind, beset as she was with poverty, innumerable difficulties, and temptations, some blunders are pardonable; yet I must say I should have liked her mode of accomplishing what she did better, had she openly demanded a divorce and obtained it in the State of New York, for when, by a little delay and painstaking, we can do a grand work for others as well as ourselves, the easy, hasty way – always prompted by selfishness – may prove a grave mistake even to ourselves. As every divorce helps to educate other wives similarly situated into higher ideas of purity, virtue, self-respect, the more publically given to the success of each case the better. As the highest happiness of society and the individual always lie in the same direction, a woman with a ready pen and tongue should not fear criticism, opposition, or persecution, nor accept personal freedom except through a fair debate of the higher position she intends to take, that thus she may help to mould public sentiment in harmony with her opinions and enable society to sanction her action. Another good effect of trying to take the world with us is that we shall move with greater deliber- ation. This is my idea of true reform, not to coquette with unjust law, thrust it one side, or try to get beyond its reach, but to fight it where it is, and fight it to the death. Let the women of this State rise in mass and say they will no longer tolerate statutes that hold pure, virtuous women indissolubly bound to gross, vicious men, whom they loath and abhor, and we shall soon have a complete codification of our laws...

From my standpoint the first step I see to be taken, is to set woman absolutely free, to make her in all things man's equal before the law, that we may have her thought and voice in this great social institution. The wide difference in the nature and offices of men and women makes it impossible for man alone to legislate wisely on a social arrangement in which the joys and sorrows are shared alike by both parties. It was impos- sible for black men and white to live together in peace so long as by the laws and religion of the country their relation was master and slave. It is just as impossible for men and women to live together in that relation. However the hardship and degradation of that condition are modified or annulled by the personal excellence of the man in any given individual case, our laws on this question decide the status of all married women to be slaves. Hence I ask that all marriage and divorce laws shall be made to bear equally on both man and woman...

When women are independent, self-supporting, fewer will enter the marriage relation with the present grim conceptions of its rights and duties. The true element of pure, refined women will find outlets in art, science, philosophy, giving us that glorious period when "old maids" will be honored and revered. The world has always had its Marys as well as its Marthas, women who preferred to sit at the feet of wisdom, to learn science and philosophy, rather than to be busy housewives; mothers of ideas, of music, poetry, painting, rather than of men> the world has always had its Mary Carpenters, Florence Nightingales, Charlotte Brontes, Catharine Beechers, Rosa Bonheurs, Charlotte Cushmans, Rachels, Maria Mitchels, Harriet Hosmers, Susan B. Anthonys, and Anna Dickinsons, its long line of saints and philanthropists, who have devoted themselves to religion and benevolence; and it is as absurd to educate all women for wives as it would be to educate all men for husbands. With the scientific education of woman we shall have her idea of this relation. Hitherto marriage in a large majority of cases has been a mere physical union, in which men have not sought companionship in the higher departments of thought or the practical affairs of the outside world; and women have been dwarfed and crippled into mere machines, where in neglect, discord, disease, they have been robbed of health, happiness, freedom and ill-starred children have gathered round the hearthstones where the fires of love had all gone out...

...When marriages result from true unions of intellect and spirit between healthy, happy men and women, and when mothers and fathers give to these holy offices the same preparation of soul and body that a true artist gives to the conception of his poem, statue, or landscape, then will maternity acquire a new sacredness and dignity, and a nobler type of manhood and womanhood will glorify the earth.

Source: Ann D. Gordon (ed.), *The Selected Papers of Elizabeth Cady Stanton & Susan B. Anthony*, Vol. II: *Against an Aristocracy of Sex, 1866–1873* (New Brunswick, NJ: Rutgers University Press, 2000), pp. 336–353.

4 Our Goddess of Liberty, 1870

This offensive image illustrates the racist and nativist views of many European Americans after the Civil War. A "white" female allegory of liberty appears at the center of the image. She is surrounded by alternative symbols of the nation. Moving clockwise from the top left, liberty appears as an Irish American, African American, Asian American, and Native American woman. The caption suggests that one of these racialized symbols might be the future of the United States. Five years after the cartoon appeared, Congress passed the Page Act, which prohibited the immigration of Asian prostitutes, and effectively limited the immigration of all Asian women by association. The Page Act was the first federal effort to restrict immigration. Well into the twentieth century, politicians voiced fears that "native born" Americans could be overwhelmed by the reproductive capabilities of immigrant women and women of color.

Figure 9.1   Our Goddess of Liberty, *1870. Reproduced courtesy of the Library of Congress.*

Source: "Our Goddess of Liberty – what is she to be? To what complexion are we to come at last?" Composite caricature of 5 female heads, different racial versions of Liberty, *Frank Leslie's Illustrated Newspaper*, Vol. 30 (1870 July 16), p. 288. Library of Congress, Prints and Photographs. Available at www.loc.gov/pictures/item/2001696533/ (accessed August 16, 2010).

5 Mother [Eliza Daniel] Stewart, Excerpt from *Memories of the Crusade*, 1873

In the midst of an economic depression and a bitter winter, evangelical women organized to protest the liberalization of state liquor laws, launching a new phase in the temperance movement and in women's political activism. Historians estimate that over 60 000 women in Ohio and Michigan succeeded in closing approximately 1000 bars. In this excerpt, Mrs. Virginia Holmes describes the women's temperance crusade in Clark County, Ohio. Following the successful campaign, temperance women formed the Women's Christian Temperance Union (WCTU), which eventually adopted the motto "Do Everything." Annie Wittenmyer, the organization's first president, was active in soldiers' aid and sanitary work during the Civil War. Under the leadership of the second president, Frances Willard, the WCTU, the largest organization of women in the country, endorsed women's right to vote.

The women of to-day have, through a baptism of suffering, developed a new phase in the history of their sex. Men for ages have been worshiping, not God, but a hideous serpent, whose mammoth proportions have enabled it to swallow relentlessly myriads of [*sic*] votaries, who have offered themselves living sacrifices to its insatiable demands.

The mother or wife readily recognizes in this creature Strong Drink, and in its victims, father, husband, sons. In the fear of the Lord, and praying for his guidance and protection, taking the sword of the Spirit, and the shield of faith, with the helmet of salvation, and the banner of our Savior's love over us, we marched straight into the presence of our enemy. He raised his head, shot out his forked tongue and thought to frighten us.

But we said in the name of the Lord Jesus and suffering humanity we come. And as the mouths of the lions of old were stopped, so was the power of this beast to harm restrained, and the semblance of death fell upon him for about the space of four months. But, alas, even in this seeming death he deceived the too confident, who were thereby thrown off their watch-tower. Nevertheless the nation has been aroused as never before, and though we did not succeed in entirely conquering our enemy, we did awaken the public sentiment, and the work goes on and will till we do gain the victory.

Fancy the strangeness of the work; we, who had never in all our lives entered one of the dens, where the beast made his lair, were brought face to face with him day and night, till his hated visage became familiar. We did also make the discovery that some rum-sellers at least were susceptible of better impulses than their business engendered or fostered. Though we watched their bars incessantly to prevent the traffic, they treated us with uniform courtesy with but few exceptions. One instance I think of on a bitter cold morning, when our patrols were almost perishing with cold, two ladies entered one of the most dreaded saloons. The keeper professed great solicitude for their comfort, and proceeded to close all ventilation, and with bar-room stove at whiteheat, and about a dozen stalwart tobacco-chewers spitting all over it, the situation was fearful. They came near fainting, but they did not yield their post till, fortunately, a couple of their sisters hearing of their situation, came and called them away to another point. The wife of this man assisted him in the sale of liquor, and vindicated the female character even in wickedness, for while the men were usually polite she was abusive.

But the charity that endureth all things, hopeth all things, sustained this consecrated band of women through all trials, whether of patience, faith or physical endurance.

Our Crusade lasted eight weeks, in the months of February and March, in the midst of the most inclement weather. Day after day we marched the streets, watching inside and out of saloons, never allowing a moment in which an unobserved sale could be made. We met alternately at the two churches for prayer and business meetings in the morning, and again in the afternoon, in order to form our line of march to the saloons, at each of which we formed our positions into two lines, one on each side of the pavement. Then we sang those precious hymns that will always be remembered as the rallying cry of the army that expect yet to take the citadel of this archenemy of mankind. And then such petitions would ascend as have seldom touched the great heart of the Father, because they were carried straight to the throne on the strong pinions of faith in His beloved Son, and direct answers came as a benediction to all hearts.

We were armed with the various pledges for saloonkeepers, property-holders, druggists and drinkers, and constantly presented them through committees appointed for the purpose. We sought in all our intercourse with those engaged in the business to have our hearts controlled by the charity that suffereth long and is kind, that is not easily provoked. And we relied firmly upon our Savior's promise, "My grace is sufficient for you," and we were not confounded. Our male citizens did all they could under the circumstances for our comfort and the advancement of our cause. In one instance they achieved almost a miracle. We held two mass-meetings each week in the renown Hall, which were the largest and most enthusiastic meetings ever held in our place. It was at one of these, after the work had been progressing some time, and the weather bitterly inclement, that a large-hearted gentleman proposed to raise funds for the building of a church right in the enemy's stronghold, there being a vacant lot just suited for the purpose. This occurred on Friday night. The money was raised, and all the carpenters and men gave an herculean lift to the wheel, and the next day – Saturday – at 2 o'clock, our church was regularly dedicated to the service of God, and stood there before us a monument of faith and works, with floor, roof, windows, seats and glowing stove, all complete.

How thankful we felt for this special providence in our favor. Our Church overlooked the whole rum traffic in our place. From it the saloon-keepers could hear the voices of prayer and supplication ascending in their behalf, and in its erection they saw a determination of purpose that thoroughly awed them. It was not long till they began signing our pledge, one at a time, tin every saloon was emptied, swept and garnished-scrubbed out, I should say, and groceries put in.

Never shall I forget the night on which we received the intelligence of our first very important surrender. Our meeting was unusually crowded that night, and near the close a messenger brought us the glad tidings, when instantly all were on their feet; and accompanied by our brass band, we poured forth like the sound of many waters,

"Praise God from whom all blessings flow."

We then formed a triumphal procession, and men and women and children marched to the saloon. The band serenaded them while those most interested shook hands with and congratulated them as they stood in their door. Who will blame us for feeling unspeakably happy, for we saw the light gleaming over the hill tops.

At each surrender we had all the church and school-bells ring out their loudest peals. All our ladies who could, went into the work, for this was no partisan movement; all distinction of church, politics and cast was ignored, and the sound of thanksgiving went up as that of one voice. Religiously speaking, we had a short millennium. Oh, how glorious it was!

But this sin-cursed world of ours is not well adapted to a millennial condition. The arch enemy has not yet been chained, or entirely shorn of his power to hurt, or work evil...

Source: Mother Eliza Daniel Stewart, *Memories of the Crusade, a Thrilling Account of the Great Uprising of the Women of Ohio in 1873, Against the Liquor Crime* (Columbus: Wm. G. Hubbard & Co.). Available at http://prohibition.osu. edu/content/clark-co.cfm (accessed August 16, 2010).

6   Frances Ellen Watkins Harper, Speech at the Centennial of the Pennsylvania Abolition Society, 1875

Frances Ellen Watkins Harper (1825–1911) was an anti-slavery poet and activist. In this speech at the 100th anniversary celebration of the Pennsylvania Abolition Society, Harper criticizes the violent repression of black political equality and the national reluctance to intervene. Her plea for Christian aid to the weak and feeble echoes an earlier speech to white women's rights activists, but in this speech she calls on African American men and women to "upbuild" their race. Harper's warning that African American women might meet "coolness" reflected her disappointment in the postwar women's rights and temperance movements.

It may not seem to be a gracious thing to mingle complaint in a season of general rejoicing. It may appear like the ancient Egyptians seating a corpse at their festal board to avenge the Americans for their short-comings when so much has been accomplished. And yet with all the victories and triumphs which freedom and justice have won in this country, I do not believe there is another civilized nation under Heaven where there are half so many people who have been brutally and shamefully murdered, with or without impunity, as in this republic within the last ten years. And who cares? Where is the public opinion that has scorched with red-hot indignation the cowardly murderers of Vicksburg and Louisiana? Sheridan lifts up the vail from the Southern society, and behind it is the smell of blood, and our bones scattered at the grave's mouth; murdered people; a White League with its "covenant of death and agreement with hell." And who cares? What city pauses one hour to drop a pitying tear over these mangled corpses, or has forged against the perpetrator one thunderbolt of furious protest? But let there be a supposed or real invasion on Southern rights by our soldiers, and our great commercial emporium will rally its forces from the old man in his classic shades, to clasp hands with "Dead Rabbits" and "Plug-uglies" in protesting against military interference. What we need to-day in the onward march of humanity is a public sentiment in favor of common justice and simple mercy. We have a civilization which has produced grand and magnificent results, diffused knowledge, overthrown slavery, made constant conquests over nature, and built up a wonderful material prosperity. But two things are wanting in American civilization – a keener and deeper, broader and tenderer sense of justice – a sense of humanity, which shall crystallize into the life of a nation the sentiment that justice, simple justice, is the right, not simply of the strong

and powerful, but of the weakest and feeblest of all God's children; a deeper
and broader humanity, which will teach men to look upon their feeble breth
[r]en not as vermin to be crushed out, or beasts of burden to be bridled and
bitted, but as the children of the living God, of that God whom we may
earnestly hope is in perfect wisdom and in perfect love working for the best
good of all. Ethnologists may differ about the origin of the human race.
Huxley may search for it in his protoplasms and Darwin send for the missing
links, but there is one thing of which we may rest assured – that we all come
from the living God and that He is the common Father. The nation that has
not reverence for man is also lacking in reverence for God and needs to be
instructed. As fellow-citizens, leaving out all humanitarian views – as a
matter of political economy it is better to have the colored race a living
force animated and strengthened by self-reliance and self-respect, than a
stagnant mass, degraded and self-condemned. Instead of the North relaxing
its efforts to diffuse education in the South, it behooves us for our national
life, to throw into the South all the healthful reconstructing influences we can
command. Our work in this country is grandly constructive. Some races have
come into this world and overthrown and destroyed. But if it is glory to
destroy, it is happiness to save; and Oh! what a noble work there is before our
nation! Where is there a young man who would consent to lead an aimless life
when there are such glorious opportunities before him? Before young men is
another battle – not a battle of flashing swords and clashing steel – but a
moral warfare, a battle against ignorance, poverty, and low social condition.
In physical warfare the keenest swords may be blunted and the loudest
batteries hushed; but in that great conflict [f]or moral and spiritual progress
your weapons shall be brighter for their service and better for their use. In
fighting truly and nobly for others you win the victory for yourselves.

Give power and significance to your own life, and in the great work of
upbuilding there is room for woman's work and woman's heart. Oh, that our
hearts were alive and our vision quickened, to see the grandeur of that work
that lies before. We have some culture among us, but I think our culture lacks
enthusiasm. We need a deep earnestness and a lofty unselfishness to round
out our lives. It is the inner life that develops the outer, and if we are in earnest
the precious things lie all around our feet, and we need not waste our strength
in striving after the dim and unattainable. Woman in your golden youth;
mother, binding around your heart all the precious ties of life – let no
magnificence of culture, or amplitude of fortune, or refinement of sensibil-
ities, repel you from helping the weaker and less favored. If you have ampler
gifts, hold them as larger opportunities with which you can benefit others.
Oh, it is better to fell that the weaker and feebler our race the closer we will
cling to them than it is to isolate ourselves form them in selfish, or careless

unconcern, saying there is a lion without. Inviting you to this work I do not promise you fair sailing and unclouded skies. You may meet with coolness where you expect sympathy; disappointment where you feel sure of success; isolation and loneliness instead of heart-support and cooperation. But if your lives are based and built upon these divine certitudes, which are the only enduring strength of humanity, then whatever defeat and discomfiture may overshadow your plans or frustrate your schemes, for a life that is in harmony with God and sympathy for man there is not such word as fail. And in conclusion, permit me to say, let no misfortunes crush you; no hostility of enemies or failure of friends discourage you. Apparent failure may hold in its rough shell the germs of a success that will blossom in time, and bear fruit throughout eternity. What seemed to be a failure around the Cross of Calvary and in the garden, has been the grandest recorded success.

Source: Alice Moore Dunbar (ed.), *Masterpieces of Negro Eloquence* (New York: Bookery, 1914) pp. 101–106.

7 Florence Kelley, Letter to William D. Kelley, 1878

Florence Kelley (1859–1932) wrote this letter as an undergraduate at Cornell University. Her father was a prominent Republican Congressman from Philadelphia. Though she expresses the familiar homesickness of a college student, her letter is also striking for their shared interest in politics, revealed in her reference to Denis Kearney, founder of the California Workingmen's Party and anti-Chinese activist. Florence Kelley was in the first generation of women to have wider access to a college education, made possible in part by the Morrill Act of 1862, which granted land to states to build co-educational colleges. She refers to the future "editors statesmen and lawyers" among her female classmates. After her graduation in 1882, Florence Kelley had a notable career as a Progressive reformer, head factory inspector for the State of Illinois, and the General Secretary of the National Consumers' League.

Ithaca
Dec. 2nd 1878
My Dear Father, –

I should have written more promptly to acknowledge your letter and its enclosure, – but for the fact that every moment has been crowded to the utmost.

I thought of you all, on Thanksgiving day, wondering how you were spending it, and, when I received first will's letter, then yours, then one from Grandma, all mentioning the dear boy's success, – I was seized with such a longing to go home and express my feelings that I could hardly bear seeing Charles and Archer depart without me. However, a fortnight more will bring us all together again. I never looked forward so eagerly to a vacation.

You can hardly conceive of a life so uneventful as mine, – there is absolutely nothing in it of the excitement which penetrates even life in sleepy Philadelphia.

Perhaps you may be interested, however, in knowing that we students have formed a Social Science club which avows its intention of discussing "all live questions social, moral, and political." I have the honor to be secretary thereof and there are three or four professors who come very regularly, and, once in a while, take part in the debate. Last time we had a very heated argument over Kearneyism in general and Kearney in particular; and you would have been very much pleased, I think, with the rational tone of the whole performance.

I am heartily interested in my work this term. I have, as regular university work, eight lessons of an hour each with a Greek professor every week and to that I give my most careful study. Besides this I have wonderfully fine lectures on Modern European History from President White who speaks admirably just as long as he confines himself to History which is properly his "last" and does not fly off into discussions of monetary questions. He keeps very close to the line of his work which is the "Development of Rationalism in Europe."

Then, distributed through the week, there are lectures on Literature and lessons in Italian. On Monday evenings, Prof. Corson reads us Shakespeare; – and, on Saturday, four of us, – Misses Clements, Hicks, Mills, and Kelley – meet him in his library and he reads us Robert Browning's "Ring and the Book." Then too, every fortnight we write an essay on English History. That is the most satisfactory work of my college course. The subjects for this term have been (1.) "The Political Institutions of the Saxons in Germany" (2.) The Effect of the Norman Conquest on Anglo Saxon Institutions" 3. "Magna Charta; Its Origin and Results". 4 "Growth of Parliament down to Henry VII" and "Suspension of Parliament under the Tudors." Next term we shall [write] seven more essays concerning American Constitutional History down to 1860. Isn't that good work for future editors statesmen and lawyers? In reading for them we get a knowledge of the style and methods of all the best historians English and American.

I owe you an apology for boring you with all this account of myself and my avocations, – but it is hard to remember that what interests me is not necessarily of exciting import to those I love ...

I am ever as simply
FMK

Source: Kathryn Kish Sklar and Beverly Wilson Palmer, *The Selected Letters of Florence Kelley, 1869–1931* (Urbana: University of Illinois Press, 2009), pp. 12–13.

8 Pretty Shield Describes the Disappearance of the Buffalo, 1932

Medicine woman Pretty Shield (1856–1944) was the younger sister of Plenty Coups, the last chief of the Crow Indians. Montana writer and Indian advocate Frank Linderman published these recollections of Pretty Shield in 1932. Pretty Shield did not speak English, so Linderman communicated with her using Native sign language and an interpreter. Linderman also noted how unusual it was for a Native American woman to tell her story; he described them as "diffident" and "self-effacing" strangers. Pretty Shield's account communicated the material and spiritual connection between the fate of the buffalo and the future of the Crow.

I wondered if I could get Pretty-shield to talk of the days when her people were readjusting themselves to present conditions. Plenty-coups, the aged Chief, had refused to speak of the days that immediately followed the passing of the buffalo, saying: "When the buffalo went away the hearts of my people fell to the ground, and they could not lift them up again. After this nothing happened. There was little singing anywhere. Besides, you know that part of my life as well as I do. You saw what happened to us when the buffalo went away."

Now I asked Pretty-shield, "How old were you when the buffalo disappeared?"

She hesitated. "Tst, tst, tst! I haven't seen a buffalo in more than forty years," she said slowly, as though she believed herself to be dreaming.

"The happiest days of my life were spent following the buffalo herds over our beautiful country. My mother and father and Goes-ahead, my man, were all kind, and we were so happy. Then, when my children came I believed I had everything that was good on this world. There were always so many, many buffalo, plenty of good fat meat for everybody.

"Since my man, Goes-ahead, went away twelve snows ago my heart has been falling down. I am old now, and alone, with so many grandchildren to watch," she interposed, and fell silent.

"I do not hate *anybody,* not even the white man, she said, as though she had been accused by her conscience. "I have never let myself hate the white man, because I know that this would only make things worse for me. But he changed everything for us, did many bad deeds before we got used to him.

"Sign-talker," she said, leaning toward me, "white cowboys met a deaf and dumb Crow boy on the plains, and because he could not answer their questions, could not even hear what they said, they roped him and dragged him to death."

"Tell me what happened when the buffalo went away," I urged.

"Sickness came, strange sickness that nobody knew about, when there was no meat," she said, covering her face with both hands as though to shut out the sight of suffering. "My daughter stepped into a horse's track that was deep in the dried clay, and hurt her ankle. I could not heal her; nobody could. The white doctor told me that the same sickness that makes people cough themselves to death was in my daughter's ankle. I did not believe it, and yet she died, leaving six little children. Then my other daughter died, and left hers. These things would not have happened if the Crows had been living as we were intended to live. But how could we live in the old way when everything was gone?

"Ahh, my heart fell down when I began to see dead buffalo scattered all over our beautiful country, killed and skinned, and left to rot by white men, many, many hundreds of buffalo. The first I saw of this was in the Judith basin. The whole country there smelled of rotting meat. Even the flowers could not put down the bad smell. Our hearts were like stones. And yet nobody believed, even then, that the white man could kill *all* the buffalo. Since the beginning of things there had always been so many! Even the Lacota, bad as their hearts were for us, would not do such a thing as this; nor the Cheyenne, nor the Arapahoe, nor the Pecunnie; and yet the white man did this, even when he did not want the meat.

"We believed for a long time that the buffalo would again come to us; but they did not. We grew hungry and sick and afraid, all in one. Not believing their own eyes our hunters rode very far looking for buffalo, so far away that even if they had found a herd we could not have reached it in half a moon. 'Nothing; we found nothing,' they told us; and then, hungry, they stared at the empty plains, as though dreaming. After this their hearts were no good any more. If the Great White Chief in Washington had not given us food we should have been wiped out without even a chance to fight for ourselves.

"And then white men began to fence the plains so that we could not travel; and anyhow there was now little good in traveling, nothing to travel for. We began to stay in one place, and to grow lazy and sicker all the time. Our men had fought hard against our enemies, holding them back from our beautiful country by their bravery; but now, with everything else going wrong, we began to be whipped by weak foolishness. Our men, our leaders, began to drink the white man's whisky, letting it do their thinking. Because we were used to listening to our chiefs in the buffalo days, the days of war and excitement, we listened to them now; and we got whipped. Our wise-ones became fools, and drank the white man's whisky. But what else was there for use to do? We knew no other way than to listen to our chiefs and head men. Our old men used to be different; even our children were different, when the buffalo were here.

"Tst, tst, tst! We were given a reservation, a fine one, long ago. We had many, many horses, and even cattle that the Government had given us. We might have managed to get along if the White Chief in Washington had not leased our lands to white stockmen. These men, some of them, shot down our horses on our own lands, because they wanted all the grass for themselves.

"Yes," she went on, her eyes snapping, "these white men shot down our horses so that their cows and sheep might have grass. They even paid three dollars for each pair of horse's ears, to get our horses killed. It was as though our horses, on our own lands, were wolves that killed the white men's sheep."

She quickly curbed the anger that these thoughts had aroused. "I have not long to stay here," she said, solemnly. "I shall soon be going away from this world; but my grandchildren will have to stay here for a long time yet. I wonder how they will make out. I wonder if the lease-money that is paid to the Government in Washington by the white stockmen will be given to my grandchildren when it is paid in, or if they will have to wear out their moccasins going to the Agency office to ask for it, as I do.

"But then," she added quickly, the light of fun leaping to her eyes, "I suppose they will be wearing the white man's shoes, because shoes last longer than moccasins."

Source: Frank B. Linderman, *Pretty-Shield: Medicine Woman of the Crows* (Lincoln: University of Nebraska Press, 1932), pp. 248–253.

Suggested Questions for Discussion

1 How did the Civil War and Reconstruction expand educational, employment, and political opportunities for women? What were the limits of women's citizenship?

2 Elizabeth Cady Stanton argued that "the momentous questions of marriage and divorce" informed American "social, religious, and political life." Why did she see the issue of marriage and divorce as so important? What was the relationship between marriage and politics after the Civil War?

3 What were the different visions for the future of the nation offered by white, black, and Indian women?

Further Reading

1 Seekers, 1540–1680

Brown, Kathleen. *Good Wives, Nasty Wenches, and Anxious Patriarchs: Gender, Race, and Power in Colonial Virginia*. Chapel Hill: University of North Carolina Press, 1996.

Demos, John. *The Unredeemed Captive: A Family Story from Early America*. New York: Vintage Books, 1995.

Godbeer, Richard. *Sexual Revolution in Early America*. Baltimore: Johns Hopkins University Press, 2002.

Gutiérrez, Ramón A. *When Jesus Came, the Corn Mothers Went Away: Marriage, Sexuality, and Power in New Mexico 1500–1846*. Palo Alto: Stanford University Press, 1991.

Townsend, Camilla. *Pocahontas and the Powhatan Dilemma*. New York: Hill and Wang, 2005.

2 Colonists and Colonized, 1660–1730

Brooks, James F. *Captives and Cousins: Slavery, Kinship, and Community in the Southwest Borderlands*. Chapel Hill: University of North Carolina Press, 2001.

Clark, Emily. *Masterless Mistresses: The New Orleans Ursulines and the Development of a New World Society, 1727–1834*. Chapel Hill: University of North Carolina Press, 2007.

Morgan, Jennifer L. *Laboring Women: Gender and Reproduction in New World Slavery*. Philadelphia: University of Pennsylvania Press, 2004.

Women in American History to 1880: A Documentary Reader, by Carol Faulkner © 2011 Blackwell Publishing Ltd.

Norton, Mary Beth. *In the Devil's Snare: The Salem Witchcraft Crisis of 1692*. New York: Vintage, 2003.

Reis, Elizabeth. *Damned Women: Sinners and Witches in Puritan New England*. Ithaca: Cornell University Press, 1999.

Wulf, Karin. *Not All Wives: Women of Colonial Philadelphia*. Philadelphia: University of Pennsylvania Press, 2005.

3 Conceptions of Liberty, 1730–1780

Brekus, Catherine A. *Strangers and Pilgrims: Female Preaching in America, 1740–1845*. Chapel Hill: University of North Carolina Press, 1998.

Gates, Henry Louis Jr. *The Trials of Phyllis Wheatley: America's First Black Poet and Encounters with the Founding Fathers*. New York: Basic Civitas Books, 2003.

Norling, Lisa. *Captain Ahab Had a Wife: New England Women and the Whalefishery, 1720–1870*. Chapel Hill: University of North Carolina Press, 2000.

Norton, Mary Beth. *Founding Mothers and Fathers: Gendered Power and the Forming of American Society*. New York: Vintage, 1997.

Pybus, Cassandra. *Epic Journeys of Freedom: Runaway Slaves of the American Revolution and Their Global Quest for Liberty*. Boston: Beacon Press, 2007.

4 Revolution, 1780–1810

Branson, Susan. *These Fiery Frenchified Dames: Women and Political Culture in Early National Philadelphia*. Philadelphia: University of Pennsylvania Press, 2001.

Foster, Thomas A., ed. *Long Before Stonewall: Histories of Same-Sex Sexuality in Early America*. New York: New York University Press, 2007.

Norton, Mary Beth. *Liberty's Daughters: The Revolutionary Experience of American Women, 1750–1800*. New York: HarperCollins, 1980.

Ulrich, Laurel Thatcher. *A Midwife's Tale: The Life of Martha Ballard, based on her diary, 1785–1812*. New York: Vintage, 1990.

Young, Alfred. *Masquerade: The Life and Times of Deborah Sampson, Continental Soldier*. New York: Vintage, 2005.

Zagarri, Rosemarie. *Revolutionary Backlash: Women and Politics in the Early American Republic*. Philadelphia: University of Pennsylvania Press, 2007.

5 Awakenings, 1810–1835

Boylan, Anne M. *The Origins of Women's Activism: New York and Boston, 1797–1840*. Chapel Hill: University of North Carolina Press, 2002.

Hewitt, Nancy A. *Women's Activism and Social Change: Rochester, New York, 1822–1872*. Ithaca: Cornell University Press, 1984.

Horton, James Oliver and Lois Horton. *Black Bostonians: Family Life and Community Struggle in the Antebellum North*. Teaneck, NJ: Holmes & Meier, 2000.

Perdue, Theda. *Cherokee Women: Gender and Culture Change, 1700–1835*. Lincoln: Bison Books, 1999.

White, Deborah Gray. *Ar'n't I A Woman: Female Slaves in the Plantation South*. New York: W. W. Norton, revised edition, 1999.

Yellin, Jean Fagan and John C. Van Horne, eds. *The Abolitionist Sisterhood: Women's Political Culture in Antebellum America*. Ithaca: Cornell University Press, 1994.

6 Contested Spheres, 1835–1845

Cohen, Patricia Cline. *The Murder of Helen Jewett: The Life and Death of a Prostitute in Nineteenth-Century New York*. New York: Vintage Books, 1998.

Dublin, Thomas. *Women at Work: The Transformation of Work and Community in Lowell, Massachusetts, 1826–1860*. Ithaca: Cornell University Press, 1981.

Jabour, Anya. *Scarlett's Sisters: Young Women in the Old South*. Chapel Hill: University of North Carolina Press, 2007.

Portnoy, Alisse. *Their Right to Speak: Women in the Indian and Slave Debates*. Cambridge, MA: Harvard University Press, 2005.

Wright, Daniel S. *"The First of Causes to Our Sex": The Female Moral Reform Movement in the Antebellum Northeast, 1834–1848*. New York: Routledge, 2006.

Zaeske, Susan. *Signatures of Citizenship: Petitioning, Antislavery, and Women's Political Identity*. Chapel Hill: University of North Carolina Press, 2003.

7 Partisans, 1845–1860

Blewett, Mary H. *Men, Women, and Work: Work, Gender, and Protest in the New England Shoe Industry, 1780–1910*. Urbana: University of Illinois Press, 1988.

Gonzalez, Deena J. *Refusing the Favor: The Spanish-Mexican Women of Santa Fe, 1820–1880*. New York: Oxford University Press, 1999.

Isenberg, Nancy. *Sex and Citizenship in Antebellum America*. Chapel Hill: University of North Carolina Press, 1998.

Oertel, Kristen Tegtmeier. *Bleeding Borders: Race, Gender, and Violence in Pre-Civil War Kansas*. Baton Rouge: Louisiana State University Press, 2009.

Pierson, Michael D. *Free Hearts and Free Homes: Gender and American Antislavery Politics*. Chapel Hill: University of North Carolina Press, 2003.

Sklar, Kathryn Kish. *Catharine Beecher: A Study in American Domesticity*. New York: W. W. Norton, 1973.

Varon, Elizabeth. *We Mean to Be Counted: White Women and Politics in Antebellum Virginia*. Chapel Hill: University of North Carolina Press, 1998.

Wellman, Judith. *The Road to Seneca Falls: Elizabeth Cady Stanton and the First Women's Rights Convention*. Chicago: University of Illinois Press, 2005.

8 Civil Wars

Faust, Drew Gilpin. *Mothers of Invention: Women of the Slaveholding South in the American Civil War*. Chapel Hill: University of North Carolina Press, 1996.

Frankel, Noralee. *Freedom's Women: Black Women and Families in Civil War Era Mississippi*. Bloomington: Indiana University Press, 1999.

Janney, Caroline E. *Burying the Dead but Not the Past: Ladies' Memorial Associations and the Lost Cause*. Chapel Hill: University of North Carolina Press, 2007.

Leonard, Elizabeth D. *Yankee Women: Gender Battles in the Civil War*. New York: W. W. Norton, 1994.

Schultz, Jane E. *Women at the Front: Hospital Workers in Civil War America*. Chapel Hill: University of North Carolina Press, 2007.

Schwalm, Leslie A. *A Hard Fight for We: Women's Transition from Slavery to Freedom in South Carolina*. Chicago: University of Illinois Press, 1997.

9 Redefining Citizenship, 1865–1880

Aron, Cindy Sondik. *Ladies and Gentleman of the Civil Service: Middle-Class Workers in Victorian America*. New York: Oxford University Press, 1987.

Bordin, Ruth. *Woman and Temperance: The Quest for Power and Liberty, 1873–1900*. New Brunswick: Rutgers University Press, 1990.

DuBois, Ellen Carol. *Feminism and Suffrage: The Emergence of an Independent Women's Movement in America, 1848–1869*. Ithaca: Cornell University Press, 1978.

Gordon, Ann D., Bettye Collier-Thomas, John H. Bracey, Arlene V. Avakian, and Joyce A. Berkman. *African-American Women and the Vote, 1837–1965*. Amherst: University of Massachusetts Press, 1997.

Hartog, Hendrik. *Man and Wife in America: A History*. Cambridge, MA: Harvard University Press, 2002.

Pascoe, Peggy. *Relations of Rescue: The Search for Female Moral Authority in the American West, 1874–1939*. New York: Oxford University Press, 1993.

Sklar, Kathryn Kish. *Florence Kelley and the Nation's Work: The Rise of Women's Political Culture, 1830–1900*. New Haven: Yale University Press, 1997.

Index